VATICAN II:
THE UNFINISHED AGENDA

A Look to the Future

Edited by
Lucien Richard, O.M.I.
with
Daniel T. Harrington, S.J.
and
John W. O'Malley, S.J.

PAULIST PRESS
New York/Mahwah

Library of Congress Cataloging-in-Publication Data

Vatican II.

    1. Catholic Church—Doctrines. 2. Vatican Council
(2nd : 1962–1965) 3. Rahner, Karl, 1904–
I. Weston School of Theology.
BX1755.V247   1987   282′.09′048   87-7294
ISBN 0-8091-2927-2 (pbk.)

Published by Paulist Press
997 Macarthur Boulevard
Mahwah, New Jersey 07430

Printed and bound in the
United States of America

CONTENTS

Lucien Richard, O.M.I.
INTRODUCTION

Speaking at the Weston School of Theology in 1979, Karl Rahner affirmed that at Vatican II the Church emerged for the first time as a world Church. This book, the result of a course given by the faculty of Weston School of Theology, is dedicated to Karl Rahner. Twenty-five years after Vatican II it is apparent that faithfulness to the inheritance of Vatican II is a fundamental question for the Church. Fidelity is not to be interpreted as a static traditionalism. According to Rahner, Vatican II can be viewed as "the beginning of a beginning." It stands as a challenge to theologians to continue the never-ending task of "aggiornamento."

The various essays presented in this book deal with the context, the reception, and the contemporary and future challenges of some of the more fundamental ideas of Vatican II. Each author presents themes related to his/her particular area of expertise and interest and for which he/she is responsible.

As editor of this collection, I wish to thank the contributors for their generous cooperation.

1

Leo J. O'Donovan, S.J.

FOR CHURCH AND WORLD:
A MESSENGER OF FAITH AND HOPE

On April 8, 1979, just over a month after Karl Rahner's seventy-fifth birthday, Weston School of Theology was privileged to honor him at an academic convocation and to award him an honorary degree. Rahner had been traveling through the United States to receive awards at universities such as Marquette and John Carroll and also to be delighted by citations such as the one which named him "Honorary Captain of the Belle of Louisville." At Weston, before a gathering of faculty and students from the Boston Theological Institute, he offered an English version of the essay we are pleased to reprint in this volume. It serves here to indicate Weston's indebtedness to Father Rahner as well as his legacy to our whole Church in its continuing effort to live out the aggiornamento of Vatican II.

Ecclesiological themes figured prominently in Karl Rahner's writings, even though he never taught a formal treatise on the subject.[1] In his earlier work, between *Hearers of the Word* and his major essay on membership in the Church, he staked out the ground for an organic conception of human solidarity graced by God's abiding presence. Gradually he developed liberating insights on God's fidelity to a sinful Church and also on the Holy Spirit's continuing bestowal of unforeseeable charisms. The incarnational emphasis of his early Christological essays was reflected in the ecclesiology of living grace that informed his decisive study on *The Church and the Sacraments*. Nevertheless, the paschal and eschatological dimension of his thought as a whole was also present from the beginning, with moving lucidity in some of the earlier spiritual writings and with increasing systematic emphasis developing toward essays such as "The Church and the Parousia of Christ."[2]

There were phases, of course, in Rahner's thinking, marked perhaps most clearly by the historical circumstances of war, restored peace and construction, conciliar engagement, and efforts toward a full appropriation of the Council.[3] However, reading his later writings has led me to interpret his entire corpus in a more dialectical sense than I previously recognized. Looking back over his career, I think we can see a deepening and increasingly explicit concern for God's entry into human history with all its vicissitudes and uncertainties, its aspirations and tragedies.[4] More and more, I believe, Rahner sought a radically temporal and historical conception of God and the people of God.

From the start, he had seen the human spirit as existing only in an historical world and seeking God's word precisely through the course of its history. In agreement with Aquinas, he had argued that we understand only by *conversio ad phantasma,* by grounding responsible intelligence in the imaginative expression of historical experience. Apologetically, he had wanted to show how revelation can emerge in the world, its history, ourselves. Systematically, he had reconceived human history as the addressee of the absolutely free God's loving revelation and gift of self.

But in his later years we read a further phase of Rahner's journey into history. Nature and humanity are conceived as dialectically united in a single world-historical process. The incarnation is firmly related to our hope for universal redemption. The paschal mystery of Christ becomes the central dynamic in enacting the full material meaning of time. These were, if you will, Rahner's final efforts at temporalizing the imagination, proposing a conversion to imagination through time. To a rising tide of relativism and skepticism he offered the Gospel of a traditional faith newly conceived. The cross discovered through the course of history reveals and promises the incomprehensible God's power to gather time into the communion of eternal life.

From this perspective Rahner's anthropological focus on freedom acquires new historical and social dimension. Freedom is not only the graced capacity to become finally oneself before God. It is, more comprehensively, the shared human capacity to forge a common future. "For the present is always the fulfillment of a task, risking the future, carrying out the testament of the past exactly through what is new and not already in an evolutionary way hidden in the old."[5] Rahner conceived this task most fundamentally as a dialogue or conversation, the "unrepeatable history of the freedom of God and of humanity in an unrepeatable dialogue."[6] The dialogue is conclusive inasmuch as it has entered a stage in which the assurance of grace of irreversible. But it is decidedly inconclusive inasmuch as we cannot know, apart from Jesus, Mary, and the most obvious saints, who wins the victory of life, where, or when.

Although historians today refuse to speak of history as a unity, Christian faith does assert a unity for its origin, course, and goal. In the course of his life's work Rahner realized with increasing acuity that such a unity may indeed have been initiated but that it remains more invoked than realized. It is the unity of a human creative possibility prepared and projected but still decidedly at issue for the multiple subjects of freedom. It may be possible to sketch a theological periodization for the course of history. It may be true that all theological statements about the world's origin dialectically include an understanding of its ultimate destiny, and vice versa. But the material outcome of the world's history remains radically shrouded for us in the mystery of our human freedom as well as in God's.

Dialectic was Rahner's way to conceive identity in history, acknowledging both continuity and discontinuity through the passage of time and emphasizing that finite reality must change in order to remain itself. Among the themes that most concerned him in the last decade of his life, his essays on history and society embody a dialectic of fragmentary wholeness in time. His ecclesiological writings employ a dialectic of sacramental reality, centering on Vatican II's interpretation of the Church as "universal sacrament of salvation." This sacramental dialectic has ultimate theological foundation in the conviction that grace works everywhere in the world, leading to the possibility of recognizing its finally personal and universally available presence in Jesus of Nazareth as God's own Word for the world. Throughout, Rahner showed himself a preeminently dialectical religious thinker who came more and more to recognize theology's mediating role in a culturally pluralistic world.

He wrote creatively still on the origin of the Church and its universal salvific role, on the enduring place of office (with special attention to the papacy and to priesthood), and on the new importance of a vigorous ecumenism and a genuine dialogue with world religions. But his reflections on the world Church may have offered his most striking and influential new insight. Several lectures he gave in the late 1970s proposed that the most fundamental significance of Vatican II lay in its being, at least in an initial way, the first historical manifestation of a genuinely world Church, acting through the mutual influence of its various parts. Previously the Church had been characteristically Western both in its style at home and in its missionary effort. But in an epoch-making way the Council intimated a basically new experience of Church. Its bishops came for the first time from their own countries in every part of the world. The Constitution on the Liturgy enabled the vernacular to replace Latin liturgically. The doctrinal decrees show an effort to speak in a more generally understandable, less rigidly neo-Scholastic language. *Gaudium et spes* acknowledges the entire Church's responsibility for the coming future of humanity. A much more positive evaluation was made of other world religions, and repeated references to the universal salvific will of God laid foundations for genuine dialogue with them.

Rahner even compared this event to the transition from a purely Jewish Christianity to one that included the mission to the Gentiles. We are moving, he insisted, from a time of the Church centered culturally in Europe and North America to a period in which its life unfolds in the world as a whole. This will require as profound a reassessment as accompanied the early Church's realization that the Gospel was meant not only for Israel but for all peoples. While most consequences of the development may be as yet unforeseen, Rahner thought it had major implications for the manner and conceptuality of evangelization, for variation in liturgical forms, and for real pluralism in Church law and practice. One may ask whether "world Church" is the best term for what he intuited. He did recognize the great question posed by China, with a quarter of the world's population relatively impervious to Christianity—not to mention the general systematic problem of translating a religious heritage from one cultural context into another. But the issue and the force with which he put it seem among his most significant ecclesiological contributions.

Expressing his thanks to Marquette University for the Père Marquette Discovery Medal on March 28, 1979, Rahner spoke of the thrust of Catholic theology since World War II. He was, naturally, considering "an orthodox Catholic theology." A theology which would not be obedient and docile under the word of God as it is proclaimed in the Church would not be Catholic theology. "But I am envisaging," he continued, "a Catholic theology that is courageous and does not shun relative and restricted conflicts with Church authorities. I am thinking of a theology which can no longer be uniform in a neo-Scholastic approach . . . a theology which is in dialogue with its time and lives courageously with it and in it."

Rahner thought that such a theology could be attempted because it is typical of our time "to be at a critical distance from itself, something *God makes possible*. It is a special grace to this age to be able now to have a critical distance from ourselves given us from the Cross of Christ. In this more critical distance," he continued, "I envisage a theology which in the Church at large must be the theology of a worldwide Church. That means a theology which does not only recite its own medieval history, but one that can listen to the wisdom of the East, to the longing for freedom in Latin America, and also to the sound of African drums." In the stirring conclusion to his remarks he assured the audience that "my purpose is not to degrade the old theology, whose grateful children we are and remain. It has been rather to hint from afar that our time calls also us theologians sleeping under the broom tree of orthodoxy like Elijah in old days: *Surge, grandis tibi restat via*—Arise, a long journey lies ahead of you."[7]

Two weeks later, after hearing his now classic "Towards a Fundamental Theological Interpretation of Vatican II," Weston School of Theology was able to applaud the journey Karl Rahner himself had made. The degree citation read:

> From your earliest reflection on the human spirit in the world to your latest efforts at exploring the foundations of faith, your theological investigations have come to constitute an encyclopedia for theology and the Church. Asking us how we believe in God, you have led us more deeply into the mystery which reigns in all our lives. Helping us to express our faith in Jesus Christ, you have taught us to find the unity of the love of God and of our neighbor in the man from Nazareth who is God's word made flesh and our own humanity made divine. You have never tired of urging us not to extinguish the Spirit; you have opened for us again and again the challenge of Christian commitment and the possibility of belief today; you seem always to have gone before us in being a Christian in the world. In your own life you have so richly exemplified the dynamic element in the Church that you have led us to new love for the Church and the sacraments and to new hope for the shape of the Church to come. But it is also our everyday faith, our efforts at prayer, and our encounters with silence for which you have provided the spiritual exercises we needed. You have indeed shown us, Father Rahner, and marvelously taught us to understand how hearers of the word may become servants of the Lord.
>
> With a view, then, to our common humanity, the Church's task in the world today, and the praise of God, Weston School of Theology is joyfully grateful to acknowledge now the indebtedness it shares with so many other men and women of good will and to declare you

THE REVEREND KARL RAHNER,
OF THE SOCIETY OF JESUS,
Doctor of Humane Letters, honoris causa.

And now also a revered father of our faith and hope in the kingdom of God to come.

NOTES

1. Cf. L. J. O'Donovan, ed., "A Changing Ecclesiology in a Changing Church: A Symposium on Development in the Ecclesiology of Karl Rahner," *Theological Studies* 38 (1977) 736–62.
2. Cf. L. J. O'Donovan, "The Word of the Cross," *Chicago Studies* 25 (April 1986) 95–110.
3. Cf. Karl Lehmann, "Karl Rahner. Ein Porträt," in K. Lehmann and A. Raffelt, *Rechenschaft des Glaubens. Karl Rahner—Lesebuch* (Freiburg: Herder, 1979) 13*–53*, at 39*–40*.
4. Cf. my two articles: "A Journey into Time: The Legacy of Karl Rahner's Last Years," *Theological Studies* 46 (1985) 621–646, and "A Final Harvest: Karl Rahner's Last Theological Writings," *Religious Studies Review* 11 (1985) 357–361.
5. *Schriften zur Theologie 15: Wissenschaft und christlicher Glaube* (Zurich: Benziger, 1983) 183.
6. Ibid., 191.
7. Rahner's Marquette remarks are found in the "Foreword," in William J. Kelly, ed., *Theology and Discovery: Essays in Honor of Karl Rahner, S.J.* (Milwaukee: Marquette University Press, 1980).

Karl Rahner, S.J.

TOWARDS A FUNDAMENTAL
THEOLOGICAL INTERPRETATION
OF VATICAN II

If I am going to discuss here a fundamental theological interpretation of the Second Vatican Council, it will be helpful to make some preparatory remarks before turning to the theme itself. In speaking of a fundamental interpretation, I will mean one that is not imposed on the Council from outside but is rather suggested by the Council itself, so that fundamental nature and fundamental interpretation in this case will mean the same thing. The presupposition for this fundamental interpretation is, of course, the conviction that despite all the historical contingencies which also accrue to such an event, the Council was not simply an arbitrary accumulation of individual events and decisions. No, there was an inner, essential connection among its individual occurrences; they were not interrelated simply by the formally juridical character of a council. In this respect, it is ultimately unimportant how clearly and thoroughly this fundamental conception of the Council was present or not in the explicit consciousness of its organizers. The meaning and nature of events that have genuinely existential significance in the life of any human being always include more than the person objectifies and strives for in explicit consciousness. And this holds true, above all, for significant events in the history of the Church, which are directed in a special and singular way by the Spirit of the Church. If we look at the explicit intentions of John XXIII with re-

Editor's Note.—This is the final English text of an address delivered by Karl Rahner on April 8, 1979, at an academic convocation in Cambridge, Mass., at which the Weston School of Theology awarded him the honorary degree of Doctor of Humane Letters. The translation was made by Leo J. O'Donovan, S.J., professor of systematic theology at Weston. The article first appeared in *Theological Studies* 40 (1979) 716–27.

spect to the Council, we cannot say much more than this: even after Vatican I with its "papalism," the Pope thought a council would be meaningful and opportune, and he wanted a "pastoral" council. But this by no means rules out the possibility of a fundamental theological conception that is deeper and more comprehensive.

I am seeking a fundamental theological interpretation, because, although I cannot discuss in any detail how theology and Church history are related, it is my opinion that Church history differs specifically from secular history: its precise goal is to describe the *history* of the Church's *essence*. In a relation of reciprocal interdependence, the Church's essence both supplies the hermeneutical principle for its history and, since it is essence in history, reveals itself through that history.

Difficult though it be and perhaps only partially successful, still let me try to formulate in advance the basic idea with which our question is concerned, so that we do not lose sight of the connection among the individual observations and considerations that follow. I say: the Second Vatican Council is, in a rudimentary form still groping for identity, the Church's first official self-actualization *as* a world Church. This thesis may seem exaggerated; surely it needs further precision and clarification to sound acceptable. It is, of course, already open to misunderstanding, inasmuch as the Church was always a world Church "in potency" and that potency could only be actualized in the course of an extensive historical process whose origins go back to the beginning of European colonialism and the modern world-mission of the Church in the sixteenth century. Even today that actualization is not yet at its term. But one can consider the official activity of the Church in a macroscopic way and see clearly that despite the implied contradiction to its essence, the actual concrete activity of the Church in its relation to the world outside of Europe was in fact (if you will pardon the expression) the activity of an export firm which exported a European religion as a commodity it did not really want to change but sent throughout the world together with the rest of the culture and civilization it considered superior. In this light it does appear meaningful and justified to consider Vatican II as the first major official event in which the Church actualized itself precisely as a *world Church*. Of course, the event had antecedents such as the ordination of indigenous bishops (although this occurred extensively only in our century) or the withdrawal of European mission practices which had been cemented by Rome in the Rites Controversy in the East. Such antecedents should not be glossed over, nor their importance minimalized, but one must notice that they did not really have any such consequences for the European and North American Church as we begin to recognize at Vatican II. And for that reason they were really only antecedents of what we observe in Vatican II, even if only in an initial and tentative way, often overlaid by the earlier style of the European Church: a world Church as such begins to act through the reciprocal influence exercised by all its components.

This most general thesis on the fundamental understanding of Vatican II, as I have said, does not deny that the actualization of the essence of the Church as a world Church at this Council made its appearance only initially and diffidently. The existence of contrary tendencies should not be concealed. In the next few years, for example, will the new Code of Canon Law being prepared in Rome avoid the danger of being once again a Western Code that is imposed on the world Church in Latin America, Asia, and Africa? Do not the Roman Congregations still have the mentality of a centralized bureaucracy which thinks it knows best what serves the kingdom of God and the salvation of souls throughout the world, and in such decisions takes the mentality of Rome or Italy in a frighteningly naive way as a self-evident standard? Admittedly, such questions about the de-Europeanizing of the Church raise theoretical problems which are anything but clear. Must the marital morality of the Masais in East Africa simply reproduce the morality of Western Christianity, or could a chieftain there, even if he is a Christian, live in the style of the patriarch Abraham? Must the Eucharist even in Alaska be celebrated with grape wine? Theoretical questions like these imply, more often than not, theoretical hindrances to the actualization of the world Church as such. Along with many other reasons, they help us to understand that the full official actualization of the world Church began to appear at Vatican II in a relatively initial and diffident way. At Mass before the individual sessions, when the different rites of the Church were presented, one still could not see any African dances.

Finally, while the Church must be inculturated throughout the world if it is to be a world Church, nevertheless we cannot overlook the fact that the individual cultures themselves are today involved in a process of change to a degree and at a rate previously unknown. As a result, it is not easy to say what content bearing importantly on the future the individual cultures can offer for a Church that is meant to become a world Church in the full sense. Whatever we may say about these and many other questions, it is incontestable that at Vatican II the Church appeared for the first time as a world Church in a fully official way. In what follows let me first offer a broad demonstration of this thesis, then apply it to the question of epochs in

Church history, and finally consider some of its more concrete implications.

BROAD DEMONSTRATION OF THE THESIS

First, the Council was for the first time formally a Council precisely of the world Church. One need only compare it with Vatican I to see that this Council was a new event in a formally juridical way. Of course, there were representatives of Asian or African episcopal sees at Vatican I. But they were missionary bishops of European or North American origin. At that time there was not yet an indigenous episcopate throughout the world. But this is what appeared at Vatican II. Perhaps not at all in proportion to the representation of the Western episcopate. But it *was* there. These bishops did not come to Rome as individual, modest visitors who had accounts to render and alms to bring home. At Vatican II we have for the first time a gathering of the world episcopate not as an advisory body for the pope but rather with him and under him the final teaching and decision-making body in the Church. For the first time a world-wide Council with a world-wide episcopate came into existence and functioned independently. In point of fact, the importance of the non-western part of the total episcopate may still have been relatively modest. The repercussions of the conciliar process on the extraconciliar life of the Church may still be very limited, as the subsequent synods of bishops in Rome show. But this does not alter the fact that at the Council a Church appeared and became active that was no longer the Church of the West with its American spheres of influence and its export to Asia and Africa. Under the appearance of an obvious and gradual development, something like a qualitative leap took place here, even though this world Church's new essence is masked to a considerable extent not only potentially but actually by characteristics of the old Western Church.

The leap to a world Church can be further clarified by looking at the decrees of this Council. As for the use of the vernacular, the Council's Decree on the Liturgy may already be dated; but without it and without the Council the victory of the vernacular would be unthinkable. In secular terms, Latin had been the common cultural language for Western civilization, and for that reason it had been and with some procrastination remained the liturgical language of the Western Church. But Latin could not become the liturgical language of a world Church, since it was the language of a small and particular cultural region. The victory of the vernacular in the Church's liturgy signals unmistakably the coming-to-be of a world Church whose individual churches exist with a certain independence in their respective cultural spheres, inculturated, and no longer a European export. It also signals, of course, the new problems of a world Church whose non-European local churches, for all their relationship to Rome, may no longer be ruled from Europe and its mentality.

In *Gaudium et spes*, in an action of the entire Church as such, the Church as a totality becomes conscious of its responsibility for the dawning history of humanity. Much of the Constitution may be conceived in a European way, as far as details go, but the Third World is truly present as part of the Church and as object of its responsibility. The sensitization of the European Church to its world responsibility may move ahead only with painstaking slowness. But this responsibility, our political theology, can no longer be excluded from the consciousness of a world Church.

As far as the doctrinal decrees of the Council are concerned, those namely on the Church and divine revelation, it may be that they speak largely from a specifically European horizon of understanding and that they consider problems that are vital only for a European theology. And still we can say that these decrees strive for statements that are not entirely conditioned by the linguistic style of a Neo-Scholastic theology and can be made more easily understandable in the entire world. To make this clearer, we would have to compare these texts with the corresponding late Neo-Scholastic schemata that were prepared in Rome before the Council. One can also indicate that the Council's teaching on the whole episcopate and its function in the Church as well as on the significance of regional particular churches makes or clarifies doctrinal presuppositions which are fundamental for the self-understanding of the Church as world Church. It may well be that the Decree on Revelation, starting as it does with revelation in the Old Testament alone, with "Abraham," does not exactly propagate a concept of revelation that is easily accessible for African and Asian cultures, especially since hundreds of thousands of years between primordial revelation and Abraham remain unfilled. But we can also say that doctrinally the Council did two things which are of fundamental significance for a world-wide missionary effort. In the Declaration on the Relation of the Church to Non-Christian Religions, a truly positive evaluation of the great world religions is initiated for the first time in the doctrinal history of the Church. Furthermore, even from an infralapsarian perspective (as the Scholastics say), the documents on the Church, on the missions, and on the Church in the modern world proclaim a universal and effective salvific will of God which is limited only by the evil decision of human conscience and nothing else. This implies the possibility of a properly salvific revelation-faith even beyond the Christian revelatory word. As a result, in comparison with earlier theology roughly to our own time, basic presuppositions for the world mission of the world Church are fashioned which were not previously available. The Declaration on Religious Liberty can also be seen in this perspective, since for all situations throughout the world the Church expressly renounces all instruments of force for the proclamation of its faith which do not lie in the power of the gospel itself. Everyone knows how great an obstacle the ecclesial division of Christendom also constitutes for the spread of Christianity in all the world, in the so-called "mission countries." For that reason, whatever ecumenical activities the Council itself develops or approves and encourages must also be evaluated as contributions to Christianity's becoming a world religion. In short: at least in a rudimentary way the Church at this Council began doctrinally to act precisely as a world Church. Under the still widely prevalent phenotype of a European and North American Church, we begin to notice, so to speak, the genotype of a world Church.

EPOCHS IN CHURCH HISTORY

But perhaps we can grasp even more profoundly this process of a world Church coming into being. So let us consider, secondly, the question of epochs in the Church's history. In writing Church history, people have puzzled again and again over a theologically appropriate division of the material. It is indeed quite clear that dividing European history into antiquity, Middle Ages, and modernity does not give us a theologically meaningful outline for dividing Church history. Here I am leaving aside, of course, questions about theologically appropriate subdivisions of Church history's major epochs. In addition, I am persuaded that, for history in general and especially for the history of the Church, the individual phases of chronologically measured history do not contain events of equal moment; rather, a chronologically limited time can still bear within itself a historically major epoch.

With these presuppositions, I say: theologically speaking, there are three great epochs in Church history, of which the third has only just begun and made itself observable officially at Vatican II. First, the short period of Jewish Christianity. Second, the period of the Church in a distinct cultural region, namely, that of Hellenism and of European culture and civilization. Third, the period in which the sphere of the Church's life is in fact the entire world. These three periods signify three essential and different basic situations for Christianity and its preaching. Within them, of course, there can be very important subdivisions: for example, in the second period, through the caesuras or breaks which occur with the transition from antiquity to the Middle Ages and with the transition from medieval culture to European colonialism and the Enlightenment. In all this one would have to clarify the causes of these multiple and yet interrelated breaks. Nevertheless, I believe that this tripartite division of Church history is theologically correct, even if the first period was very short. This first period, Jewish Christianity, with the expanding influence which Jewish proselytism brought it, is in fact distinguished in its fundamental, characteristic, and unique quality by the fact that its human historical situation was that of the fundamental Christian salvation event, the death and resurrection of Jesus himself; this event was proclaimed *within* its *own* historical situation and not in one different from it; it was proclamation precisely in Israel and to it.

On *that* basis something like a mission to the Gentiles would indeed have been possible. Consequently, we can see that it was not theologically self-evident for Paul to inaugurate the transition from a Jewish Christianity to a Christianity of Gentiles as such. Rather, this introduced a radically new period in Church history, a Christianity that was not the export of Jewish Christianity to the Diaspora but instead a Christianity which, for all its relationship to the historical Jesus, still grew on the soil of paganism. I know that I am speaking dimly and darkly. But I think the difficulty derives ultimately from the theological problems involved in this transition from Jewish to Gentile Christianity, problems that are by no means so simple as people think, theologically difficult problems still to be worked out correctly; it is not yet reflectively clear to us what Paul "brought about" when he declared circumcision and everything connected with it superfluous for non-Jews (and perhaps only for them). However that may be, if we want to make, in fundamental fashion, a more precise and authentically theological division of previous Church history, then the proposed triple division seems to me the only correct one. This means that in the history of Christianity the transition of Christianity from one historical and theological situation to an essentially new one did happen *once,* and that now in the transition from a Christianity of Europe (with its American annexes) to a fully world religion it is starting to happen for a second time. Of course, one can dare to make this assertion only if one considers that the transition from the ancient Gentile Christianity in the Mediterranean area to the medieval and modern Christianity in Europe is theologically less decisive than both the breaks with which we are here concerned. But that seems entirely justified, considering the unity of the Roman-Hellenistic Mediterranean culture and its transmission to the Germanic peoples—although I cannot show this in more detail here and now.

If what I have said is more or less correct, a twofold theological question arises: In what more precisely does the theological and not only the cultural historical character of such a transition, such a caesura or break, consist? And what results if we apply the theology of this transition to the one in which we are living today, a transition for which Vatican II implies something like an ecclesiastically official beginning?

As for the first question, we can start by saying at least that it concerns an event of importance not only for the history of culture but for theology and the history of salvation. This seems to me to be evident in Paul. He proclaims abolition of circumcision for Gentile Christianity, an abolition which Jesus certainly did not anticipate and which can scarcely be cogently derived from Jesus' own explicit preaching or from the preaching about the salvific meaning of his death and resurrection. And yet for Paul this principle belongs to his gospel and means revelation in some sense. It is the interruption of a salvation-history continuity which a human being cannot undertake on personal authority alone. Thus the properly theological question arises which Paul himself did not adequately pursue: What can still remain and must still remain from the Old Testament salvation history and from the Church, if circumcision could be done away with, one of the realities that pertained to the final substance of salvation existence for a Jew of that time, something that according to Paul could and in fact should have remained for the Jewish Christians of the time? This transition, for him, constitutes a genuine caesura or break. We must furthermore consider that many other abolitions and interruptions of continuity in the history of salvation were connected with this change: abolishing the Sabbath, moving the Church's center from Jerusalem to Rome, far-reaching modifications in moral doctrine, the rise and acceptance of new canonical writings, and so forth. And for the moment it does not concern me whether these turning points can be referred to Jesus or explicitly to Paul or happened somehow and somewhere in the apostolic age. Today, as a matter of fact, perhaps even in contrast to patristic and medieval theology, we do not have a clear, reflective theology of this break, this new beginning of Christianity with Paul as its inaugurator; perhaps that will only gradually be worked out in a dialogue with the Synagogue of today. And so I hope no one will hold it against me if I cannot say anything beyond the suggestions already given. And yet I would still venture the thesis that today we are experiencing a break such as occurred only once before, that is, in the transition from Jewish to Gentile Christianity.

Can one venture this thesis and through it determine the meaning of Vatican II in the sense that there the Church, even if only initially and unclearly, proclaimed the transition of the Western Church to a world Church in a way that had previously happened only once, when the Church changed from a Church of the Jews to a Church of the Gentiles? To repeat: I think one can and should answer this question affirmatively. Of course, this cannot mean that in content these two caesuras and transitions are simply the same. No historical event occurs twice. Nor would I contradict someone who is convinced that the break inaugurated by Paul also had characteristics of a formally theological nature which are not repeated, so that the transition to a world Church is really not comparable in every respect with the transition from the Christianity of the Jewish Jesus to the Christianity of Paul. I also do not doubt that such transitions happen for the most part and in the final analysis unreflectively; they are not first planned out theologically and then put into effect, but are unreflectively realized through a finally hidden instinct of the Spirit and of grace that remains mysterious—even though the element of reflection borne along with the action should certainly not be disregarded or considered superfluous. But with these provisos I would want to affirm and defend the thesis I proposed.

Next I venture to affirm that the difference between the historical situation of Jewish Christianity and the situation into which Paul transplanted Christianity as a radically new creation is not greater than the difference between Western culture and the contemporary cultures of all Asia and Africa into which Christianity must inculturate itself if it is now to be, as it has begun to be, genuinely a world Church. Today's difference may to some extent be hidden, inasmuch as a leveling layer of rational-industrial culture from Europe and the United States lies over these other cultures, so that the difference between our culture and the other cultures is veiled, and one might expect Christianity still to be well received throughout the world as a Western export ware wherever it coincided with the dubious blessings of the West. Antiquity did indeed have an analogue for this, namely, the Diaspora of the Jews with their proselytizing across the ancient world, on which foundation a Jewish Christianity apparently could also have been exported to that world. But, prescinding from some minor exceptions, modern missionary history shows that Christianity as a Western export actually succeeded neither with the high cultures of the East nor in the world of Islam, precisely because it was Western Christianity and sought in that way to establish itself in the rest of the world, without risking a really new beginning or breaking with many continuities that seem self-evident to us. This showed in the different rites controversies; in the export of Latin as a liturgical language to countries in which Latin was never a historical reality; in the unquestioning way that Western, Roman law was exported through canon law; in the naive, unquestioning way that an effort was made to impose the bourgeois morality of the West in all its detail on people of different cultures; in the rejection of religious experiences of other cultures, and so forth. This, then, is the issue: either the Church sees and recognizes these essential differences of other cultures for which she should become a world Church and with a Pauline boldness draws the necessary consequences from this recognition, or she remains a Western Church and so in the final analysis betrays the meaning of Vatican II.

SOME FURTHER IMPLICATIONS

Thirdly and finally, if such a claim is made for the meaning of Vatican II, what are its further implications, somewhat more concretely? It is a third question, of course. First of all, because in material terms the second break, towards a world Church, naturally has or must acquire a completely different content than the first break, towards the Gentile Church of antiquity and the Middle Ages. Then secondly, because it is an open and unclarified question whether and to what extent the Church in the postapostolic age still has the creative powers and authority that she had in the period of her first becoming, the apostolic age. At that time, in making irreversible or seemingly irreversible basic decisions which first concretely constituted her essence, she claimed such authority over and above what came to her directly from Jesus, now the Risen One. The open question is whether, during such historical breaks as the second one we are discussing, the Church can legitimately perceive possibilities of which she never made use during her second major epoch because those possibilities would have been meaningless in that epoch and consequently illegitimate. Thirdly, because despite all modern futurology, no one can correctly predict the secular future to which the Church must do justice in the new interpretation of her faith and of her essence as world Church. To that extent, of course, Vatican II is only a very abstract and formal model of the task the Church as world Church is meeting. But let us still try to say something about the image of the Church as world Church, about the task that is still to be addressed. This, I think, pertains to the theme we are considering, because a theological interpretation of the fundamental nature of Vatican II must in the last analysis be undertaken from its final cause, namely, from the Church's future, to which this Council committed itself.

First, there is the Christian proclamation. None of us can say exactly how, with what conceptuality, under what new aspects the old message of Christianity must in the future be proclaimed in Asia, in Africa, in the regions of Islam, perhaps also in South America, if this message is really to be present everywhere in the world. The people in these other cultural situations must themselves gradually discover this—and here, of course, it cannot remain a question of formally declaring the necessity of such other proclamations, nor simply of deriving them from an inherently problematic analysis of the special character of these peoples. For this task, whose solution is not yet at hand and which does not really belong to us Europeans, it will be necessary to appeal to the hierarchy of truths of which the Council spoke and to return to the final and fundamental substance of the Christian message, in order to formulate from it anew the whole of ecclesial faith with the natural creativity that corresponds to the actual historical situation. This reduction or return to the final and fundamental substance as the first step towards a new expression of the whole content of faith is not easy. In the course of it we will have to take account of efforts made in recent years to discover basic formulas of faith. But we will also have to ask a question which has scarcely been addressed: Is there a formal criterion for deciding what really can and what really cannot belong primordially to a supernatural revelation in the strict sense? If this task were fulfilled, we would have a pluralism of proclamations, in fact the authentic pluralism, which is much more meaningful than a pluralism of proclamations and theologies within the Western Church. Since all human beings can in principle speak with one another and make themselves understood, these different proclamations would not be simply disparate realities. They could criticize and enrich one another. But each of them would still constitute a historical individuality, which would be ultimately incommensurable with every other.

A further question arises: How can a unity of faith be maintained and verified when you have plural proclamations, and how can the highest ecclesial body in Rome work for this, since the task is apparently entirely different from what the Roman authorities on faith have previously assumed within a common Western horizon of understanding? It is also self-evident that a significant pluralism with respect to canon law (and other ecclesial praxis as well) must be developed in the great local churches—even apart from the fact that genuine progress towards ecumenical unity cannot otherwise be expected. Quite often it has been observed that a similar pluralism of liturgies is needed, one that cannot consist merely in the use of different vernaculars. Granted, these are all formal, abstract statements which are scarcely expressive of the concrete form which the future world Church will take. But can more be said?

Let me also draw attention to a characteristic of Vatican II that I have discussed elsewhere and cannot pursue here. At least in *Gaudium et spes* the Council unreflectively used a mode of expression that has the character neither of a permanently valid dogmatic teaching nor of a canonical regulation, but must rather be understood as the expression of "pastoral instructions" (*Weisungen*) or appeals.[1] (This requires a theological treatment of official Church statements, a treatment which is not at all explicit now, since we have previously been familiar only with *doctrinal* statements and official Church *regulations* and orders.) Does this other sort of statement have more urgent significance for the future? Under what assumptions can such instructions be made effective? Once again I cannot go into these questions here, although from another perspective they would help to answer our question about the theological uniqueness of this Council.

Finally, it should be explicitly said or repeated: the Council was, with and under the pope, the active subject of the highest plenary powers in the Church, in all their usage and application. This is obvious, it was explicitly taught, and it was basically not disputed by Paul VI. But how can this highest plenary authority, borne by the pope "alone" *and* the Council, actually exist and be able to act in two subjects at least partially different? This has not really been theoretically clarified, nor is it apparent in practice what lasting and timely significance there is in the fact that the whole college of bishops is, with and under the pope, but really *with* the pope, the highest collegial leadership body in the Church. The still timely significance of this collegial constitutional principle in the Church remained unclear into our time and once again was more repressed than not by Paul VI after the Council. Will John Paul II change anything here? In a true world Church some such change is necessary, since a world Church simply cannot be ruled with the sort of Roman centralism that was customary in the period of the Piuses.

But let me conclude. All our considerations were supposed to be concerned with how the Second Vatican Council is to be interpreted theologically. I tried to interpret it as that event of Church history in which the world Church modestly began to act as such. I tried to make clear with a few problematic considerations that the coming-to-be of a world Church precisely as such does not mean just a quantitative increase in the previous church, but rather contains a theological break in Church history that still lacks conceptual clarity and can scarcely be compared with anything except the transition from Jewish to Gentile Christianity. This was the caesura or break which occupied Paul, although one need not think that he reflected with theological adequacy on this transition whose protagonist he was. This is all I really wanted to say. Everything else is but dimly envisaged, and developed perhaps without the necessary systematic clarity. But I did want to draw attention to problems that have scarcely been noticed in previous theology.

NOTE

1. Translator's note: cf. *Theological Investigations* 10 (New York, 1973) 293–317, 330–36; 12 (New York, 1974) 242–46.

John O'Malley, S.J.

VATICAN II:
HISTORICAL PERSPECTIVES ON
ITS UNIQUENESS AND INTERPRETATION

Some twenty years after the close of Vatican II, Roman Catholics still find themselves being exhorted from all sides to its implementation. Widely divergent interpretations of the Council, however, especially concerning Church order, pastoral practice and the exercise of theology manifest themselves ever more insistently and find echo even on the front pages of our daily newspapers. It is difficult to implement something whose directives are disputed. Interpretation of the Council is thus at present as burning an issue as it has ever been and, to many people, an increasingly distressing one.[1] Why is this so? That is the question that, from the perspective of a Church historian, I will address in this article.[2]

To contextualize the question, we must constantly remind ourselves of certain features that are special to Vatican II and that, when taken as a whole, make it quite different from any council that preceded it. Obvious among such features is the sheer number of participants with the right to vote, triple the number present at Vatican I and ten, twenty, or thirty times the number present at most sessions of Trent. Similarly disproportionate to both Trent and Vatican I was the far greater representation from countries outside Western Europe. It could be argued, moreover, that the Council was the longest in the history of the Church—not surely in the span of years over which it extended but in terms of continuous working hours, particularly if we should count the work of the commissions done between the four great periods of the Council. Never before at any council had such an elaborate and broadly representative apparatus of theological scholarship been devised and put into such effective operation. The decision to admit non-Catholic "observers" was unique in the annals of

22

such gatherings, at least in the arrangements and spirit with which it was carried out.[3]

Limitations of space do not allow me to elaborate on the implications of these and similar features, but even the simple enumeration of them substantiates a peculiar character for the Council and suggests that problems of interpretation might arise. There are other features, however, that are more pertinent for our purposes and upon which I would like to dwell. Two of them can be joined together to help explain why the Council has been unique in the way it has touched the lives of the faithful and caused them so much joy and in some cases so much concern. Those features are the relationship of the media to the Council and the content of many of its documents.

We take the media so much for granted that we forget what an immense influence it has on our lives and that it therefore perforce had on the Council and its aftermath. At least until the Council of Trent, the deliberations and decisions of councils were almost the private concern of those who participated in them. With the invention of printing, Trent and especially Vatican I had to contend with a more rapid diffusion of information and propaganda, but this dissemination was still confined to an extremely small percentage of the world's population. Most Catholics probably had no idea Trent was even in session, and the implementation of its decrees had its effect only over the course of many decades, even centuries.[4]

Radio and television were by 1962, however, capable of thrusting news about the Council upon the world at large almost at the very minute any newsworthy event occurred. In the stages preparatory to the Council, the Vatican adopted a decidedly cautious attitude toward the media, but pressure from a world accustomed to open dissemination of information was too great to be resisted.[5] "Public opinion" became a major issue, and, because of the media, participants in the Council were constrained both in Rome and at home to explain and justify the actions of the Council not only to the Catholic faithful but to the world at large. No thinking Christian concerned about the future of Christianity was deprived of information, and, indeed, such information was eagerly sought.

As it turned out, the information was not dull or without import for the daily life of every Catholic. This is another feature that makes Vatican II altogether unique in the history of ecumenical councils and helps account for the sometimes acrid debates about it. Councils in the past have with few exceptions dealt with abstruse doctrinal or disciplinary matters that had little immediate relationship to the devotion of the ordinary faithful or, at most, affected only a single territory or

level of society—certainly not true of Vatican II! First in order of immediate impact were the decree on the liturgy and the subsequent series of documents emanating from the Holy See that dealt with it.
Every practicing Catholic had to be aware of these changes—changes
that he saw taking place with his own eyes and at the very heart of what
Catholics had learned their lives should center upon, the Eucharist.

Within a few years after the close of the Council, the entire liturgy
of the Church was celebrated in the vernacular. This was only the most
obvious change, which had even deeper ramifications. In fact what
happened was a complete reorientation of Catholic devotional life. A
style of piety now came to be promoted that was based more directly
on biblical sources and on the public liturgy of the Church, replacing
the so-called devotionalism and the "paraliturgical" practices that had
characterized the late Middle Ages and had shown great vitality in the
nineteenth and early twentieth centuries. An extensive system of novenas, Stations of the Cross, Forty Hours, "miraculous medals," parish
missions and other usages passed out of existence almost overnight
and found partial replacement in Bible study groups, directed retreats, and liturgical workshops.

The decrees on ecumenism and on religious liberty had similar,
though not quite so immediately striking, repercussions. In some
countries the latter decree had important legal ramifications, as the
idea of an official religion of the state gradually lost ground. Concomitant with these developments was the gradual lifting of episcopal pro-
hibitions in the United States, for instance, of Catholics attending non-
Catholic colleges and universities. The Index of Forbidden Books, still
a subject of perturbation for some Catholics as late as the 1960s, was
now seen as outmoded and was soon forgotten, just as it had for long
been unenforceable.[6]

The list of changes in practice and attitude that were mandated
or encouraged by the Council could be lengthened, but enough has
been said to indicate why the Council was immediately perceived as so
important. From the viewpoint of Church history, it can be categori-
cally asserted that never before in the history of Catholicism had so
many and such sudden changes been implemented, often without adequate explanation, that immediately touched the lives of all the faithful, and never before had such a radical adjustment of attitude been
required of them.

The impact of the media and the very content of the documents
explain, therefore, why Catholics feel such a stake in the Council, and
they further indicate why the interpretation of the Council has become
so problematic. Christianity is by self-definition traditional. Its obli-

gation is to "tell the next generation" the message it has received. Any too sudden or too obvious change in practice or attitude is bound to be scrutinized for possible adulteration of that fundamental commission. Vatican II could not hope to be exempt from that law, and, given the wide variety of cultures that Catholicism embraces and the wide variety of expectations it encourages, some divergence in interpretation of the conciliar documents was inevitable.

These factors do not fully explain, however, the present situation, in which not this or that prescription of some particular document seems to be at issue but rather the whole meaning of the Council.[7] Was the Council just an "adjustment" of certain practices or attitudes, or was it a wholly new orientation that cannot be so neatly tied down? Is the Council over, in that we adhere rather literally—and somewhat selectively—to its statements, or has it only just begun, in that the very heart of the Council was its openness to future developments? Though crudely put, these seem to be some of the major issues in play today. Further considerations must be adduced, therefore, to explain adequately the breadth and the depth of the present crisis, which has been notably accentuated in the last five years or so.

The first such consideration concerns not the specific content of the documents of the Council but their general scope and their style. Among the elements that make Vatican II unique in the history of ecumenical councils is the scope of its concerns and the scope of the persons it addressed. The vague purposes for which John XXIII convoked the Council allowed and even encouraged a review of every aspect of Catholic life.[8] In this regard, only the Council of Trent provides a precedent, and an imperfect one at that. Although Trent undertook a general reform of the Church, its basic impulse, especially as the years rolled on, was to purify rather than change the status quo. Trent addressed, moreover, exclusively "churchy" issues, without ever embarking on an enterprise as daring as *Gaudium et spes*.

That document is unique in the annals of conciliar history not only in that it tried to deal with a broad range of social issues, thus breaking with the time-honored practice of dealing only with dogmatic or disciplinary matters, but also in that it addressed "all persons of good will," not just Roman Catholics.[9] With such a document we have, in effect, a partial redefinition of the function of the Church in the world, a long and extremely important codicil to *Lumen gentium*. In a less dramatic mode the documents dealing with ecumenism, the Eastern churches and similar matters do the same. This is a new phenomenon, one that expresses *in actu exercito* the richness of the message of the Council but that also points to its unique nature. We really have no historical precedents that will help us deal, not so much with particulars that these documents indicate, as with the fact of their existence in this context.

The very breadth of the issues that the Council chose to review and reformulate and the all-inclusive audience that the Council finally chose to address would seem to suggest that we are facing a major turning point in the history of Catholicism, at least in intent.[10] These facts would, then, further suggest that the burden of proof rests upon those who would propose a minimal interpretation of the Council, not upon those who see it as an event with more radical implications. Otherwise the massive documentation that the Council produced stands as a theatrically ostentatious exercise in announcing that nothing of great moment has happened.

What in fact did happen emerges only when we place the documents in their precise historical context and do not treat them as enunciations of eternally valid platitudes. If we follow such a methodology, a fair, but not exhaustive, list of the aims of the Council would go something like this: to end the stance of cultural isolation that the Church was now seen as having maintained; to initiate a new freedom of expression and action within the Church that certain Vatican institutions were now interpreted as having previously curtailed; to distribute more broadly the exercise of pastoral authority, especially by strengthening the role of the episcopacy and local churches vis-à-vis the Holy See; to modify in people's consciousness and in the actual functioning of the Church the predominantly clerical, institutional and hierarchical model that had prevailed; to affirm the dignity of the laity in the Church; to establish through a more conciliatory attitude, through some new theological insights and through effective mechanisms a better relationship with other religious bodies, looking ultimately to the healing of the divisions in Christianity and the fruitful "dialogue" with non-Christian religions; to change the teaching of the Church on "religious liberty" and give new support to the principle of "freedom of conscience"; to base theology and biblical studies more firmly on historical principles; to foster styles of piety along the lines I indicated above; to affirm clearly that the Church was and should be affected by the cultures in which it exists; finally, to promote a more positive appreciation of "the world" and the relationship of the Church to it, with a concomitant assumption of clearer responsibility for the fate of the world in "the new era" that the Council saw opening up before its eyes. Surprisingly enough for some of us, the present conflict over interpretation of the Council revolves around just how seriously and radically these goals are to be taken—and in certain instances, it seems, whether they were really goals at all.

Perhaps just as important as the comprehensive scope of the documents is their style. Even a cursory glance at them shows that Vatican II is notably more verbose than any council that preceded it and also less technical in its language. The traditional style of conciliar documents has been the terse form of the canon, which in a few words proscribed some belief or practice. The canons reflect by their form the presumption that a council is basically a judicial or legislative body, convoked to resolve some immediate and well-defined problem or set of problems. The language is, within certain limits, juridical and precise. The first real break in this tradition came with the Council of Trent, which decided to issue along with canons the so-called "chapters" that would present the positive teaching against which the ideas condemned in the canons erred.

In the documents of Vatican II, no canons appear. The fact is undeniable, its implications great. The Council forged almost overnight a new language for conciliar, even theological, discourse. That discourse attempted to appeal to affect, to reconcile opposing viewpoints rather than vindicate one of them, and was notably exhortatory, almost homiletical in its style. That style was calculated not so much to judge and legislate as to prepare individuals for a new mind-set with which to approach all aspects of their religious lives. The traditional function of a council thus in effect underwent a notable reformulation.

One might hesitate to apply here the axiom that the medium was the message, but I must say that I continue to be surprised at how little study has been directed to the rhetoric of the Council, when we have learned over and over again that content cannot be divorced from style or literary form. If the style is the man, can we not assume, at least for the sake of discussion, that to some extent the style is the Council—and then, by extension, that the style is the Church? If we wish to interpret the Council, we must begin to pay attention to this aspect of it, rather than focusing exclusively on the content proposed in certain documents or paragraphs. Here, if ever, proof-texting shows its well-known limitations.

This subject is so complex that not much more can be done here than call attention to it and to invite scholars from various disciplines to investigate it. The limitations of the style of discourse the Council adopted are many. I have elsewhere called attention to them and have termed that style as "soft rhetoric."[11]

The Council addressed almost every aspect of Christian attitude and affect and called for some radical revisions. Though it was marked by considerable optimism about the realization of those revisions, it also was cautious about now explicitly condemning what had been for so long normatively in place. Thus the documents have a kind of detached quality to them, suspended somehow above the historical situations that they were aimed at changing. Since enemies and abuses are not named as such, the documents have a vagueness that opens them to a variety of interpretations, especially by persons untrained in the exegesis of historical texts. Since they are committee documents, moreover, they evince a flaccid quality that, at least at the distance of twenty years, weakens the dramatic punch many of them in fact in their substance delivered.

More important than these limitations, however, are the positive implications of the new conciliar rhetoric. Vocabulary is an important constituent of style, and we could do worse in trying to interpret the Council than to draw up a list of characteristic words—characteristic in that they occur often and in that they occur for all practical purposes for the first time in official Church documents.

Surely important among these words is "dialogue."[12] It was so characteristically attributed to the Council that it turned into jargon, and one became almost ashamed to use it. That lamentable fact should not obscure for us, however, the profound implications of the term, especially for a Church accustomed to a "from-the-top-down" style of dealing with both its members and outsiders. Dialogue is horizontal not vertical, and it implies, if it is to be taken seriously, a shift in ecclesiology more basic than any single passage or image from *Lumen gentium*. But this fact emerges only when we stop concentrating on such passages and images and then look to the new style that pervades practically everything the Council said.

Other words must be added to the list—"cooperation," "solidarity," "service," "pilgrim," "dignity." Attention must also be given to traditional words or expressions that have disappeared, and to others that are in effect redefined, like "prophet," "king," and "priest." We hear much about the "spirit" of Vatican II, but that expression wallows in subjectivity and vagueness until rescued by studies that can ground it in the conciliar texts with a methodology along the lines I am suggesting. In other words, it is possible to retrieve some sense of the "spirit of Vatican II," but we must employ a methodology that until now has not been widely applied and is only imperfectly formulated.

The verbosity of the documents of the Council often makes them boring to read, almost impossible to teach, and further complicates their interpretation. This quality indicates, however, the growing awareness of the participants of the complexity of the issues, of the wide variety of positions possible concerning them, and of the necessity of not bringing them to a premature closure. Nothing, the Council seemed to say, should be more characteristic of Catholicism than its catholicity—that is, its ability to embrace different cultures, different spiritualities and even different theologies without losing its basic identity.

The very generality of many passages of the conciliar documents does not, therefore, manifest a weakness but a strength—the strength of a long tradition that need not be defensive and that has the time to be open to opinions that seem to contradict or seriously qualify the status quo. The documents of the Council, though not all subsequent events, seemed to indicate that the lessons of the Galileo case had finally been well learned. They seemed to indicate a Church open to the future, not closed in upon its history, not even upon so glorious a moment of it as the Council itself. Their generality does, however, open them to interpretative manipulation.

Besides the scope and style of the documents, another feature of the Council that was unique was the leitmotif of aggiornamento that it borrowed from Pope John XXIII. The word means, literally, updating. The basic idea underlying it was, according to the Pope, to make certain appropriate "emendations" or "adjustments" in the Church that would put it in more effective touch with the world in which we live.[13] On the surface this seems to be indeed a modest proposal, and persons favoring a "strict construction" of the Council can always point to these words. A recent study has argued, however, that at least by the time the Council opened Pope John had himself come to hope for much more.[14]

In any case, the term placed Vatican II in the tradition of those councils that dealt extensively and professedly with the reform of the Church, like Constance, Lateran V and Trent. Even in this regard, however, Vatican II evinces a unique character, for the basic impulses of Catholic reform until the Council sought their goals on more timeless, less historically aware principles. Once Vatican II decided to make changes in the Church to bring it into more effective correspondence with the times, it significantly reoriented the old principle of *ecclesia semper reformanda*.

At least since the Gregorian reform of the eleventh century, no idea has had a greater impact on the history of the Western Church than the persuasion that the Church must from time to time take itself to task. With increasing insistence in the High and Late Middle Ages, the idea began to pervade the thinking of serious Christians and resulted in any number of reform movements, most graphically illustrated perhaps by the founding of so many religious orders. Despite its immense impact on the Church, the phenomenon has been curiously neglected by theologians, as if the idea were clear and without need of analysis and study. Yet it deals with the complex and fundamental problem of how an institution that is by self-definition both traditional and radical, both incarnate and transcendent, both born into a particular culture yet missioned for all times and peoples, can manage neither to turn itself into a local museum nor lose itself by assimilation into its environment. It deals with and is an historical concretization of the problem of the relationship between nature and grace, between "reason" and revelation.

Distinctive of the aggiornamento of Vatican II in all its aspects was a keener awareness of cultural differences and the historical conditioning of all aspects of the "human side" of the face of the Church than any previous conciliar reform.[15] This was the result of the methodologies that many of the most influential periti brought to the formulation of the documents of the Council, whether their specialty was liturgy, the Bible, Church history, ecumenics, Church-state relations, social problems or even systematic theology. The training of most of these men had caused them to modify or move away from the so-called classicist mentality that had traditionally marked theological disciplines. The conflict between these two mentalities underlies many of the documents of the Council and is still operative today in the debate over how to interpret them.

Despite some ambivalence in the documents, awareness of historical differentiation and of the symbiotic relationship between the Church and the cultures in which it exercises its ministries is more strikingly manifest in Vatican II than in any other council. This fact again accentuates the uniqueness of the Council. For the first time, the Church officially began to take account in an across-the-board way of the profound implications of being a "pilgrim" in this world. A pilgrim is an alien, true, but also an alien on the move.

When the documents of the Council are viewed in this light, they imply an open-endedness, a certain sense of uncompleted business. If it is true that, as the times change, the Church must change with them, the process of aggiornamento is ongoing. By definition it cannot be statically frozen. It implies experimentation, adaptation and a keen attentiveness to the lessons of experience as we daily receive them. Those who read the documents thus must perforce clash with those whose approach is more classicist.

The turmoil into which the Church was thrown in the aftermath of the Council cannot be divorced from the cultural upheavals that took place world-wide in the late 1960s and 1970s. The blame, if it be such, for distress in the Church and for "certain excesses" cannot be laid solely at the door of the Council. Nonetheless, turmoil has rocked the Church at every moment of great crisis, which has generally coincided with a crisis in culture at large. We should not be surprised, therefore, at the disquiet and anguish that accompanied a Council that so expressly dealt with reforms that immediately touched the faithful and that even otherwise were so unique.

Here too we still lack adequate categories to deal with the phenomenon. I have attempted elsewhere to devise a few, but they are only faltering first steps toward a more adequate hermeneutic for interpreting the Council and for interpreting similar phenomena in the history of the Church.[16] We need, in other words, further reflection on these issues that will help us better find our way. We do not need power plays that, in the name of an "authentic" interpretation of the Council, would obstruct that reflection.

NOTES

1. See Karl Rahner, "Towards a Fundamental Theological Interpretation of Vatican II," *Theological Studies,* 40 (1979) 716–27. Worth reading is the article by Andrew Greeley, "The Failures of Vatican II after Twenty Years," *America,* 146, no. 5 (Feb. 6, 1982) 86–89, and the various responses in the same journal, 146, no. 23 (June 12, 1982) 454–61.

2. I have dealt more extensively with some of the issues I raise here in three publications: "Vatican II," in *New Catholic Encyclopedia,* XVII (1979) 687–90; "Reform, Historical Consciousness, and Vatican II's Aggiornamento," *Theological Studies,* 32 (1971) 573–601; "Developments, Reforms, and Two Great Reformations: Towards an Historical Assessment of Vatican II," ibid., 44 (1983) 373–406.

3. The admission of Lutherans at the second period of Trent, 1551–52, for instance, took place in an entirely different atmosphere. See Hubert Jedin, *Geschichte des Konzils von Trient,* 4 vols. (Freiburg, 1949–75), III, 292–314, 359–99.

4. See Giuseppe Alberigo, "The Council of Trent," in *Catholicism in Early Modern History: A Guide to Research,* ed. John W. O'Malley (St. Louis, 1987).

5. See, e.g., Xavier Rynne, *Vatican Council II* (New York, 1968) 51–52.

6. See, e.g., the last paragraph of the article (1967) on "Index of Forbidden Books," in *New Catholic Encyclopedia,* VII, 434–35. On the origins of the Index, see Agostino Borromeo, "The Inquisition and Inquisitorial Censorship," in *Catholicism.*

7. See, e.g., Alberto Abelli, "Ein Grundgesetz der Restauration? Zum Entwurf einer 'Lex fundamentalis' der Kirche," *Herder Korrespondenz,* 33 (1979) 36–43.

8. See *Acta Apostolicae Sedis,* 54 (1962) 788.

9. See *Documents of Vatican II,* ed. Austin P. Flannery, rev. ed. (Grand Rapids, 1984) 904.

10. See my "Developments, Reforms," 392–95.

11. See ibid., 385–88, 395–98.

12. See *Documents of Vatican II,* e.g., 325, 470, 744, 904, 924.

13. See *Acta Apostolicae Sedis,* 54 (1962) 788.

14. See Alberto Melloni, "Formazione, contenuto e fortuna dell'allocuzione," in *Fede Tradizione Profezia: Studi su Giovanni XXIII e sul Vaticano II* (Brescia, 1984) 187–222.

15. See my "Reform, Historical Consciousness."

16. "Developments, Reforms."

Jerome H. Neyrey, S.J.

INTERPRETATION OF SCRIPTURE IN THE LIFE OF THE CHURCH

This essay focuses on the interpretation of Scripture vis-à-vis Vatican II. So vast a topic is best treated by taking a particular example of interpretation, in this case, the interpretation of the Gospels. It is surely an understatement that the century before Vatican II witnessed an explosive development of scholarly interpretation of the Gospels, development which the Council presumed and endorsed. Since the importance of documents like *Dei Verbum,* the Dogmatic Constitution on Divine Revelation, lies in their place in this development, let us begin with a brief sketch of the history of Gospel interpretation in the pre-Vatican II period.

I
GOSPEL INTERPRETATION BEFORE VATICAN II

At the outset, it should be noted that the history of the interpretation of the Gospels which follows was neither stimulated by the Catholic Church nor favorably received by it initially. In fact, it was basically members of the Protestant churches of Germany who were first engaged in this enterprise, nor were their results readily received by their own churches. The churches, Protestant or Catholic, were rarely at peace with modern Gospel criticism, a tension which continues to exist even now. Why was this so and what effect did it have on the development of Gospel interpretation?

As a result of the Enlightenment, the nineteenth century saw the Church as the object of rational attack, an attack which would touch Gospel interpretation directly. Post-Enlightenment scholars came to realize that the churches' teaching and preaching about Jesus were heavily dogmatic and often overlaid with ecclesiastical ideology. Discoveries in languages, archeology and the like confirmed the perceived hiatus between what "history" (i.e. "reason") could tell us about Jesus and how he was preached according to Church dogma. With science and reason as trustworthy guides, authority and tradition came under attack as sources of "truth," which cast the churches in the role of reason's enemy. And so a split developed in Gospel interpretation between the Jesus of history (who spoke of the kingdom of God) and the Christ of faith (who left us an unenlightened Church). Reasonable scholars could only applaud the move to recover the genuine or historical Jesus, for this alone could be true. On this point alone, scholarship would travel 360 degrees in the course of the next century. Yet it should be obvious that critical Gospel scholarship was initially perceived as a way of attacking the Church, a perception which could hardly win it a favorable reception by the Church.

One of the chief results of nineteenth century Gospel criticism was the sorting out of Gospel sources. After realizing that there was indeed a "Synoptic problem," scholars settled on what is called the two-document hypothesis for explaining the sources of the Gospels: (1) the earliest or most original Gospel was Mark, (2) which, along with the Q source, a collection of parables and sayings found only in Matthew and Luke, was used by them in their gospels. If Mark was indeed the earliest, then it was presumed that he was the most reliable, most historical of the documents, and so for a while Mark enjoyed primacy of place in Gospel criticism. Such an initial critical move called into question the historicity of many Gospel passages as well as the value of divergent versions of events narrated, a move which was initially viewed with alarm and hostility by the Church.

Since source and literary criticism contributed notably to the way Gospels were interpreted, let us briefly evaluate aspects of this which set the agenda for subsequent decades of Gospel study. First, the focus was squarely on *Jesus*, not the Church. Inasmuch as scholarly criticism began as a *reaction to Church interpretations* of Jesus, it tended to value negatively all Church articulation of Jesus, whether that Church was a New Testament Church or the contemporary Church, for Church preaching even at its best is a filter which comes between Jesus and the individual believer. Value, then, was put primarily on the authentic words and deeds of Jesus, not on any later development of Christology. It was assumed, moreover, that we could in fact recover *Jesus' very words* and learn what he said of himself. This kernel of authentic material would be intrinsically more valuable than any secondary account or interpretation of him, just as historians value autographs over hearsay reports. Finally, this "historical" knowledge about Jesus would then become the *timeless deposit* of faith, applicable to all people, at all times, and in every circumstance. Christians would have to adapt to it, not vice versa. If this proved to be the case, then biblical scholars might tend to be the teachers and guardians of the churches' preaching about Jesus, not the traditional shepherds of the flock of Christ.

After the celebrated quest for the historical Jesus came to an impasse, Gospel criticism entered a new phase described as "form criticism." Studies of Mark indicated that it was heavily editorialized (e.g. the outline of the story was itself the evangelist's creation; the messianic secret owes more to Mark than to Jesus). The energy which formerly went into the quest was now turned on to the historical process whereby the early Church preached, prayed and taught about Jesus. What was yesterday's dross became today's treasure. If scholars could not study the historical Jesus, then they might investigate the history of the development of the early churches which preached Jesus. And so, the banner of form criticism was raised: "In the beginning was the preaching. . . . "

Form criticism had two foci, literary forms and the history of the early Church. As regards "forms," we know what degree of "truth" to assign to literary forms in our newspapers: hard news is found on the first page, soft editorials on the last; we would like the weather report to be "true," but plan flexibility; times of movies and TV shows must be fixed and exact, which is not what we expect from Ann Landers. Comparably, form critics indicated a variety of forms in the Gospel, logia (or sayings), miracle stories, legends, parables and preaching, each of which had a different claim to be "true" or "historical." Just as important, form criticism examined the growth and development of traditions about Jesus, giving us, if not a history of Jesus himself, at least a history of the early Church.

Evaluating the contributions of form criticism of the Gospels, we note, first of all, that the focus was squarely on the *apostolic churches;* interest in Jesus was limited to his titles, and only as these reflect the adapted preaching of the early churches. Second, as models of *historical development* arose, that of W. Bousset gradually gained dominance in seeking to explain the historical development of the early Church along specific lines. Development took place according to a three-stage process: first, Palestinian Jewish Christianity; then, Hellenistic Jewish Christianity; finally, Hellenistic Gentile Christianity. Yet critical problems abound even here, for in key points this model is both biased and inaccurate, inaccurate in its view of Palestinian Christianity and biased against what is Jewish and for what is Greek. Finally, while historical in one sense, the model of Bousset pays no attention to the *internal dy-*

namics of the early churches, their conflicts, disputes, anathemas, etc., in which different Christologies developed and were preached.

The initial reception of form criticism by the Church was slow and cool, for this way of viewing the Gospels demanded recognition of the necessary variety in the preaching of the early Church as well as an appreciation of the Gospels as specific historical attempts to articulate the meaning of Jesus, attempts which suggest that further development might be legitimate and necessary, points which were slow to gain a hearing in the Church. The Church, moreover, has tended to view form criticism as merely the latest version of the rationalism or modernism which plagued it in the nineteenth century, a perception which could not help but make its reception slow and painful.

In time, however, form criticism came to be perceived by the Church less and less as a threat and more and more as a useful and even necessary approach to Gospel interpretation, yet never without certain suspicion and ambivalence. For example, in *The Instruction on the Historical Truth of the Gospel* (1964), Gospel interpreters are mandated to use historical method: "He [the exegete] will diligently employ the new exegetical aids, above all those which the historical method, taken in its widest sense, offers him" (IV.1). In particular, form criticism was enjoined on the interpreter "prudently . . . to examine what contribution the manner of expression of the literary genre used by the sacred writer makes to a true and genuine interpretation." Yet this same document immediately warns against "inadmissible philosophical and theological principles . . . mixed with this method" (V), the remnants of rationalism. Form criticism is like an adopted child who sits uneasily at the family table.

As Vatican II began, a new scholarly focus was emerging, "redaction criticism." If form criticism acknowledged development in and by churches for the sake of preaching, redaction criticism continued this investigation into the final editions of the Gospels, not just their early history. It had long been acknowledged that the evangelists themselves, the final editors of the Gospels, added, deleted, arranged and changed materials as they produced their Gospels. Whereas this was once negatively evaluated, it became the valued data of scholarly research. Previously, it was thought that the evangelists' editing was as modest in scope as it was in value, but that judgment changed as considerable editorial scope was credited to them, so that redaction rose in value in the eyes of interpreters. And so three levels of historical development can be studied which affected Gospel interpretation:

1. Jesus himself   (source criticism)
2. the early Church   (form criticism)
3. the evangelists   (redaction criticism).

Interpretation of the Gospels, then, must take all three into account, even if contemporary scholarship gives greater salience to the last. Each of these foci, moreover, embodies a value as well as a bias, as the following diagram indicates.

BIBLICAL METHOD	AIM	VALUE	CHRISTOLOGY
source criticism	recovery of the very words/deeds of Jesus	1. early = best 2. late = bad	only authentic Jesus material
form criticism	history of tradition in apostolic churches	1. the quest is impossible; 2. early Church is all we can safely know; 3. this is a valuable contribution	development of Jesus' titles in life, preaching of early churches
redaction criticism	theology of the evangelists	1. more can be known; 2. value now placed on this contribution	full portrait of Jesus by the evangelist vis-à-vis his situation

This indicates a multiplicity of perspectives, which at times seem to be in competition, but which indicate more fundamentally how historical our approach to the Gospels must be and how particularistic our expectations of a specific Gospel. We have, after all, four Gospels, not one. Historical particularity and Christological diversity are the two themes sounded throughout pre-Vatican II Gospel interpretation.

As we noted earlier, however, modern Gospel criticism was initially resisted and only gradually came to have a rightful place in Scripture studies in the Catholic Church. For the appreciation of the Gospels as historical documents of the early churches which contain preaching adapted for the needs of those churches was met with positive Church hostility (see Pope Pius X's *Lamentabili*, 1907). With the condemnation of modernism, many of the results of Gospel criticism were held suspect, denied, etc., and so Gospel criticism in the Roman Church, at least, marked time for several decades, until Pope Pius XII's *Divino Afflante Spiritu* (1943) and *The Instruction on the Historical Truth of the Gospels* (1964) of the Biblical Commission, when most of the advances of earlier scholarship, once condemned, became the accepted and mandated approaches of Gospel interpretation: 1. acceptance of form criticism (but without its earlier rationalism), 2. requirement, finally, of the historical-critical method, 3. admission of the three stages of development (Jesus, early Church, evangelists), 4. appreciation of the nature of the apostles' preaching and the evangelists' theologizing, and 5. the admission of a fuller understanding of the historical Jesus by the apostolic churches as the "Christ of faith." *Dei Verbum*, which basically confirmed directions which were gradually approved between 1940–65, is no insignificant document, for it formally reflects the coming of age of the Church in regard to its foundational documents. What had been the provenance of scholars and the Biblical Commission became the heritage and the future of the pastoral Church at large. The approval and confirmation, moreover, came long after the consolidation of scholarly advances, but that seems to be the way institutions such as the Church operate (see T. Kuhn, *The Nature of Scientific Revolutions*).

II
DEI VERBUM AND GOSPEL INTERPRETATION

Turning to Vatican II, the document on revelation can be said to have embodied issues which had already been settled on a scholarly as well as an ecclesiastical level, but which were then presented in a pastoral form for an ecumenical audience. It must be remembered that *Dei Verbum* was not intended as a charter for the biblical guild, but as a pastoral guide for the Church and as an ecumenical search for common ground with the Christian churches of northern Europe. The great contributions of the German Protestant scholars of the last century to Gospel interpretation were finally acknowledged—truly a major ecumenical gesture.

While it is not necessary to comment on everything in that document, certain parts directly pertain to our topic, the interpretation of the Gospels. First, building on contemporary discussions of fundamental theology, *Dei Verbum* described revelation as God's self-communication, an affirmation which put stress on subjectivity rather than on objective creeds or dogmas. God, of course, is timeless, but the recipients of God's revelation are radically historical people whom God addresses in their particularity. Already a major theme has been sounded, divine adaptation to the receiving subject.

Second, in the description of the transmission of revelation, the form-critical emphasis on "preaching" came into its own. Christ *preached*, commissioned his apostles to *preach*, which commission was fulfilled by apostolic persons who committed the *preaching* to writing (#7). Not only "in the beginning was the preaching"; for preaching was the activity of all three periods of Gospel formation: Jesus, early Church, and evangelists. The Gospels, in short, are not biography or history, but preaching. Revelation, moreover, "was to be preserved in a continuous line of succession until the end of time" (#8).

Third, in some sense it was conceded that revelation "develops" (#8). This development was no Darwinian, organic evolution, but a supernatural phenomenon which occurred "with the help of the Holy Spirit." It is admitted, moreover, that revelation is not complete with the historical Jesus, but "the Church is always advancing toward the plenitude of divine truth," which will come only when humankind is face to face with God (1 Cor 13:12). These are important points because they imply that the task of the Church always was and will be to "develop" preaching about Jesus, thus affirming the radical historical nature of our human existence and its limitedness and incompleteness.

Fourth, in its remark that the sacred books have two authors, God and the human author (#11), *Dei Verbum* affirmed what had come to be a commonplace in biblical scholarship. It is the task of those who interpret the Gospels to engage in a project of objectivity, to discover "what meaning the sacred writers really had in mind," a phrase repeatedly mentioned in #12. While this gives due weight to the specialized task of the biblical guild, it also signals to the Church at large that it must be careful not to impose its own meaning on God's word or to make an ideology out of those writings, points which were the stuff of controversy in nineteenth century Gospel scholarship. Attention to "what the sacred writers really had in mind," moreover, implies a certain particularity in those writings, the individual stamp of a specific human author. Like the incarnation, God's word is historical, particular and specific.

In this same paragraph, another aspect of form criticism is affirmed, viz., that in the Gospels we must attend to "the customary and characteristic patterns of perception, speech, and narrative" of the

Gospel authors (#12), which the document had begun to treat under "preaching," the premier form for appreciating the Gospels. This remark, moreover, implies what has been stated by the social sciences all along, that all communication is culturally conditioned and time-bound to a specific culture. Implied here is a qualification of previous remarks about the timelessness of New Testament statements. Yet even as #12 speaks of particularity and diversity, it signals a concern for unity. Lest there be too much centrifugal thrust in our interpretation, which spins us individually apart, a centripetal energy is also at work in Gospel interpretation to see "the whole picture," the completeness of God's dealings with us.

Fifth, in the remarks on the formation of the Gospels, advance in scholarship is never more in evidence. What a century of scholarly investigation had taught us about the history of the New Testament documents is finally given salience here. The Gospel documents are the result of a long and complicated historical process, which can be said to have three clear moments to it. Jesus, of course, spoke, healed, argued and taught; memory of him lies at the foundation of our preaching (source criticism). His apostles and the early Church preached him for some forty years, the period which in Gospel criticism is the focus of form criticism. Finally the apostolic preaching was written down in documents we call Gospels, which contain the particular viewpoint and theology of the evangelist who composed them, which is the focus of what scholars now call redaction criticism. The dynamic character of the Gospel is never more in evidence than in the description in #19 of a general process which produced the final text of each Gospel:

> The sacred authors, in writing the four Gospels, *selected* certain of the many elements which had been handed on, either orally or already in written form, others they *synthesized* or *explained* with an eye to the situation of the churches, the while sustaining the form of preaching, but always in such fashion that they told the honest truth about Jesus.

No one Gospel contains all that could be said about Jesus—selectivity and particularity. Each Gospel spoke to a distinctive audience—specificity and diversity. It is the last point in the quote above which seems of great importance, the explication or adaptation of Gospel preaching "in view of the situation of each church," which may well be the most pastoral point made in this document.

Sixth, implicit in the schema, Jesus—apostolic Church—later evangelists, is an admission of development in revelation. It had long been an axiom in Gospel criticism that some distinction is warranted between the Jesus of history and the Christ of faith, that is, whereas Jesus himself preached the "kingdom of God," the apostles after Jesus' resurrection preached about God's Christ and his Church. It is an ongoing point of scholarly criticism to note that there is a distinction between Jesus before the cross and Christ after his resurrection, the only issue being the extent and importance of the distinction. *Dei Verbum* admits the fundamental distinction when it comments on how the apostles handed on the traditions about Jesus, an action they performed "with that fuller understanding which they, instructed by the glorious events of Christ and enlightened by the Spirit of truth, now enjoyed" (#19). The pastoral implications of this point ought not to be missed; for, together with the subsequent comment on synthesis or explication "with an eye to the situations of the churches," these remarks indicate a continuous process in the church both of understanding the mystery of Jesus and of preaching that mystery appropriately to specific times, places and peoples. Growth in understanding will continue in the Church until we see God face to face, and this growth will have to be communicated anew and in fresh ways to new generations of God's children. Herein lie the seeds of an appreciation of the radical historicity of faith, theology and preaching, which is truly a significant pastoral insight.

This document, moreover, marks a high point in our critical understanding of "history" vis-à-vis the Gospels. In the post-Enlightenment, "history," or "truth," was claimed by biblical scholars over against the churches which were said to engage in theological ideology and to celebrate myths and legends, an unfortunate distinction. To be scientifically respectable, Gospel interpreters had to pursue "history" or facticity, either that of Jesus' life or of the churches which produced the Gospels. It was assumed, of course, that "history" dealt with objective facts, not interpretations. In time "truth" claims were made for a variety of literary forms in the Gospels, so that "history" no longer enjoyed a monopoly on truth. In *Dei Verbum,* moreover, the Gospels could be described as preaching, not formal history; even here, it was maintained that they told "the honest truth" about Jesus, even if in a redacted form suited to a specific audience (#19). This sketch of the meanings of "history" and "truth" vis-à-vis the Gospels indicates the high degree of sophistication in Church and scholarly thinking which went into the document on revelation.

A quick summary of the high points of *Dei Verbum* seems in order. 1. "Preaching" is the technical term for describing the Gospels, a lasting contribution from form criticism; "preaching," moreover, inherently implies flexibility and diversity. 2. The historical process which resulted in the writing of the Gospels is affirmed: Jesus—early Church preaching—evangelists writing. 3. Development in the Gospels is admitted, as well as development in revelation. Just as the apostles by the light of the Spirit came to see more clearly after Jesus' resurrection, the Church will finally reach the fullness of God's revelation after its resurrection. 4. A qualified endorsement of form criticism is made in the insistence on appreciating literary forms, the role of the early Church, and the process of formation of the Gospels. 5. A qualified acknowledgment of the distinction between the Jesus of history and the Christ of faith is made. 6. The main thrust of redaction criticism is confirmed in the remark about the evangelist's selection, synthesis and explication of tradition. Although these may seem like academic matters, they have important implications attendant upon for the interpretation of the Gospels, especially pastoral implications.

III
CHALLENGES, NEW AGENDA

Since any student of the history of Bible scholarship knows that *Dei Verbum* could never be the last word in Gospel interpretation, we should ask: What has happened since the Council? What are the issues raised by Vatican II for further conversation? What might be the challenges facing us?

It is odd to speak of the reception of *Dei Verbum* (1965), for it was but reflecting what had already come to light in the 1964 document, *Sancta Mater Ecclesia* (otherwise known as "The Historical Truth of the Gospels"). Yet it is important to note several of the post-conciliar milestones which indicate the flowering of Gospel scholarship attendant upon it. The publication of the *Jerome Biblical Commentary* (1968) must surely stand as the most significant indication of the richness of critical Catholic biblical scholarship. Worthy of mention also are the numerous, recent Christologies which takes Gospel criticism seriously (e.g. Schillebeeckx, Sobrino). Furthermore, American Catholic scholars like Raymond Brown regularly address hard questions in Gospel interpretation; witness his *Jesus God and Man* (1967) and *The Virginal Conception and Bodily Resurrection of Jesus* (1973), discussions remarkable for their bold but respectful treatment of difficult issues. Joseph Fitzmyer recently published *A Christological Catechism* (1981), a sophisticated, pastoral statement of major Christological issues which reflects the maturation of Catholic Gospel criticism. Finally the recent document of the Biblical Commission on Christology (1985) must be viewed as a remarkably fresh way of continuing the conversation with biblical and theological scholarship. Surely the single most important result of Vatican II has been the exploding phenomenon of Catholics owning, reading and studying the Scriptures. Gospel interpretation since Vatican II is alive and well.

As we noted above, *Dei Verbum* was a pastoral document, not a set of guidelines for the biblical guild. It was, by all accounts, a modest document, but it gave salience to many new areas and perspectives of Gospel interpretation for the next several decades. It is well to reflect on *Dei Verbum* once more about what that document did *not* say or what it said *guardedly*, for herein lies the agenda for conversation with the contemporary church. 1. Concerning diversity in the Gospels, although #19 commented on "explication in view of the situation of the Church," nothing else was said to acknowledge what scholars are keenly aware of in the New Testament, viz., strong diversity of perspective in the foundational documents of our faith. From a critical standpoint, *Dei Verbum* might be said to have projected too much homogeneity into the Gospels. 2. While we can appreciate the Christocentric focus of the document, contemporary Gospel criticism is giving considerable attention to the churches of the New Testament, their diversity, their particular history, their internal fights, etc. Diverse Christologies, it is maintained, reflect diverse communities; Christ must be understood in terms of the churches who preached him. 3. Although some acknowledgement of development emerged in the document, that notion still seems suspect; and it was continually counterbalanced by the more dominant notion that the fullness of revelation was given in Jesus and by him. 4. And while there was qualified acceptance of some distinction between the Jesus of history and the Christ of faith, the explanation of that distinction was so guarded that it allowed little appreciation of the way the early apostolic churches learned from their own experiences and strove to reach a fuller understanding of Jesus. Oddly enough for a Church in solemn council whose banner was aggiornamento, it did not credit the same learning ability to the apostolic Church which it claimed for itself. 5. Even in commenting that each evangelist "explicated" the Church's tradition about Jesus in view of the situation of their churches, there was no clear appreciation of the particular viewpoint of each evangelist, no hint of coming to terms with the idea that an evangelist may have composed any materials (such as allegorical interpretations of earlier parables). Newness is still suspect, especially in terms of the foundational documents of our faith. 6. Although form criticism's major points were adopted, there was no recognition that all human language is inherently and radically limited to specific cultures, be it New Testament language or Church documents. But in all fairness to *Dei Verbum,* it was a pastoral document for an ecumenical council. It reflects so much of the advance of biblical scholarship, but it was not directed to the biblical guild as a charter or a set of statutes and regulations. The above remarks, then, should not be taken as criticisms of *Dei Verbum,* so much as indications where further conversation might profitably take place.

What, then, are the challenges for Gospel interpretation arising from Vatican II? The challenges as I see them are both intellectual and pastoral. While it is possible only to comment on one or two of these challenges, let us at least name what seem to be the areas for further conversation and development. 1. *Historicity:* It remains for us to study the nature of language as culturally specific and historically conditioned. 2. *Diversity/Pluralism:* The Gospels contain rather diverse portraits of Jesus, indicating a genuine pluralism in our foundational documents. 3. *Development:* Development of Christology and hence of revelation did take place in the New Testament documents. 4. *New Testament Ecclesiology:* As well as a Christocentric focus, the Gospels deserve to be treated in terms of their rich ecclesiology. 5. *Inspiration and Inerrancy:* Given the complex history of each Gospel, the shifting points of view in each, and the radical nature of historical language, fresh discussion of the meaning of the Gospels' inspiration seems warranted.

The discussion of "history" and "truth" is far from over. It remains for our Church to come to grips with the historical and particular character of language and communication. As the social scientists remind us, communication is exchange *from a social system.* The New Testament documents communicate from a first century, Mediterranean, peasant, Semitic culture, yet we live in twentieth century, postindustrial, U.S. culture; the difficulty of understanding, much less preaching, the Gospels to our culture is truly enormous. This is a scholarly task with enormous implications for the mission of the Church. Just as the apostolic churches learned to understand and preach Jesus differently to diverse cultures (1 Cor 9:19–22), so the pastoral mission of the Church today is the task of "adapted evangelization":

> It [the Church] profits from the experience of past ages, from the progress of the sciences, and from the riches hidden in various cultures, through which greater light is thrown on the nature of man and new avenues to truth are opened up. The

Church learned early in its history to express the Christian message in the concepts and language of different peoples and tried to clarify it in the light of the wisdom of their philosophers; it was an attempt to adapt the Gospel to the understanding of all men and the requirements of the learned, insofar as this could be done. Indeed, *this kind of adaptation and preaching of the revealed word must ever be the law of all evangelization* (*Gaudium et Spes* #44, emphasis added).

Since the Gospels are themselves "accommodated preaching," we have a model and a warrant for contemporary, pastoral preaching which is fully in accord with the best of our scientific knowledge of language and culture.

Accommodation, however, implies pluralism and diversity. It is no surprise to anyone that our modern world is radically diverse, with competing East-West ideologies, competing Christian groups, competing Muslim-Christian factions, competing first and third worlds, etc. Yet it would help to acknowledge that in the New Testament there is radical diversity in the apostolic churches, even a fundamental pluralism in the New Testament itself. One need only read texts like 1 John 4:1–3, Galatians 2:1–14, James, and 2 Corinthians 10–11 to realize the diverse and pluralistic character of the apostolic churches and their preachings about Jesus. Gospel scholars, then, should be encouraged to continue the task of carefully describing the diversity even in the Gospel accounts, diversity which tells us as much about the particular character of the early churches as it does about diverse Christologies in those documents. The centripetal motion of contemporary Gospel studies is evidently not a bad thing, for centrifugal unity may be less thematic in the Gospels than the Council indicated.

At stake in all of this is renewed appreciation of the nature of Christ's Church, not simply as the conserver of Gospel traditions but also as the fashioner of tradition and the shaper of its preaching. The post-conciliar Church might well continue to look at the dynamic processes of the first century churches for clues to its own tasks, powers and responsibilities vis-à-vis the study and preaching of the Gospel of Jesus Christ. If redaction criticism has taught us anything, the role of the Church in the transmission of the Gospel has always been dynamic and inventive. These critical questions, moreover, are not inimical to the nature of the Church itself, if the thrust of Vatican II is not to be lost.

A SELECT BIBLIOGRAPHY

Bousset, Wilhelm, *Kyrios Christos: A History of the Belief in Jesus from the Beginnings of Christianity to Irenaeus* (Nashville: Abingdon, 1970)
Brown, Raymond E., *Biblical Reflections on Critical Issues Facing the Church* (New York: Paulist, 1975)
———, *The Critical Meaning of the Bible* (New York: Paulist, 1981)
———, *Jesus God and Man* (Milwaukee: Bruce, 1967)
———, *The Virginal Conception and Bodily Resurrection of Jesus* (New York: Paulist, 1973)
———, *Biblical Exegesis and Church Doctrine* (New York: Paulist, 1985)
Collins, T. A. and Brown, R. E., "Church Pronouncements," *Jerome Biblical Commentary* 72:1–36
Fitzmyer, Joseph A., "The Biblical Commission and Christology," *Theological Studies* 46 (1985) 407–79
———, "The Biblical Commission's Instruction on the Historical Truth of the Gospels," *Theological Studies* 25 (1964) 386–408
———, *A Christological Catechism* (New York: Paulist, 1982)
Hurtado, Larry W., "New Testament Christology: A Critique of Bousset's Influence," *Theological Studies* 40 (1979) 306–17
Kselman, John S., "Modern New Testament Criticism," *JBC* 41:7–20
Kümmel, Werner G., *The New Testament: The History of the Investigation of Its Problems* (Nashville: Abingdon, 1972)
Neyrey, Jerome H., *Christ Is Community* (Wilmington, Del.: Glazier, 1985)
Rome and the Study of Scripture (St. Meinrad, Ind., 1962).

Daniel J. Harrington, S.J.

WHY IS THE CHURCH
THE PEOPLE OF GOD?

"He called a race made up of Jews and Gentiles which would be one, not according to the flesh, but in the Spirit, and this race would be the new people of God" (*Lumen Gentium* 9).[1] The description of the Church as the people of God has become popular since the Second Vatican Council. In fact, if any single phrase or idea has served as the slogan for capturing the spirit and direction of Vatican II, the title "people of God" for the Church has done so. The title has been attractive for several reasons. It underlines the continuity between the Old Testament people of God and the New Testament Church. It captures the social, communitarian identity of the Church. It is a dynamic, open-ended idea that expresses the historical dimension of the Church and its pilgrimage toward the kingdom of God.

The fundamental theological insight underlying the title is related to the person of Jesus: Jesus the Messiah makes us the people of God. Insofar as Jesus has fulfilled God's promises to his people, those gathered around Jesus and sharing in his life—whether they be Jews or Gentiles—make up God's people. Christ is the *lumen gentium* ("light of nations"), which shines out visibly from the Church; he constitutes the people of God.

The Council's understanding of the Church as the people of God has been warmly received by most Catholics. At least, many instinctively like the phrase and have taken to using it themselves. Nevertheless, the phrase has often been used carelessly and without much depth of understanding. Some have used it apart from its context in the Dogmatic Constitution on the Church (*Lumen Gentium*) as if it suggested opposition to the hierarchy or served as an alternative to the idea of the Church as the body of Christ. Others have tried to ignore it and pass over it as a poetic fancy devoid of genuine theological significance.

47

As a way of giving to the idea of the Church as the people of God the theological depth that it deserves, this paper will first lay out the scriptural foundations for calling the Church the people of God.[2] Then it will examine what the texts of the Second Vatican Council (*Lumen Gentium* 9 and *Nostra Aetate* 4) say about the Church as the people of God. The final section will consider some of the challenges that the idea of the Church as God's people poses to the Church today and reflect on a possible refinement to the theological approach taken by the Council to this title. That refinement has arisen principally from developments in Jewish-Christian relations since the Council.[3]

SCRIPTURAL FOUNDATIONS

Even though the New Testament provides no lengthy discussion of the Church as the people of God, the idea seems to be an assumption in practically all the documents. The focus of the New Testament is Jesus of Nazareth—the Jewish teacher who gathered twelve disciples around him to represent the twelve tribes of Israel, the one whose death was seen by his followers not as a hopeless defeat but rather as the beginning of a new age, the one whose life and teachings inspired a movement destined to spread quickly throughout the world but always cognizant of its roots in Judaism.

The New Testament assumption that the Church is the people of God owed its major contours to the rich Old Testament tradition of Israel as the people of God. The great liturgical confessions of faith, the psalms, the covenantal sections, the prophets, and even some wisdom books all contribute to the overall picture of how ancient Israel understood its identity as God's people.[4]

Fundamental to Israel's consciousness of its nature as a people was the conviction that God had taken the initiative in this relationship: "The Lord your God has chosen you to be a people for his own possession, out of all the peoples that are on the face of the earth" (Dt 7:6). This choice was made not because of Israel's greatness as a people but simply "because the Lord loves you" (Dt 7:8). God showed his love especially in liberating the people from bondage in Egypt and in entering into a covenant relationship with them. Israel's God is "the faithful God who keeps covenant and steadfast love with those who love him and keep his commandments to a thousand generations" (Dt 7:9). The obligations laid upon Israel in the covenant are best understood as its divinely appointed way of responding to God's initiative of love.

The picture of ancient Israel as God's people that emerges from the Hebrew Scriptures can be summarized in the following three expressions: divinely initiated, covenantal in structure, and a response to God's gracious love. This set of descriptions also seems to have shaped the identity of those whom Jesus called to be with him and shared in his mission. Such a development was to be expected in a movement that was thoroughly Jewish in personnel and in values.

The problems regarding the Church as the people of God arose more sharply after Jesus' death and resurrection, when the early Christian movement began to develop its own identity especially with reference to other Jews who refused to confess Jesus as Messiah. Why did not all Jews accept Jesus as some did? How could Gentiles accept Jesus and thus become part of God's people? Were those Jews who rejected Jesus still part of God's people? These were the kind of questions that emerged in the time after Jesus' death and resurrection. The different answers to them can be divided into three categories: the organic model, the replacement model, and the conflict model.[5]

The organic model of thinking about these issues is represented by Paul in his undisputed epistles, especially in Galatians 3 and Romans 9–11. Galatians 3 presents a long and complicated argument about the law. But this argument is really an element in a larger reflection on how Gentiles can be part of God's people. At the beginning of that reflection, Paul asserts that the children of Abraham are people of faith (Gal 3:7,9). At the end, he states: "And if you are Christ's, then you are Abraham's offspring, heirs according to promise" (Gal 3:29). Immediately before this last assertion, Paul had affirmed that in Christ "there is neither Jew nor Greek" (Gal 3:28). Thus faith is the principle by which persons become part of the people of God. The identity of the people of God is traced through Jesus the Jewish Messiah back to Abraham.

Romans 9–11 develops some of the ideas raised in Galatians 3. At the outset, Paul reaffirms the privileges of Israel as the people of God: " . . . to them belong the sonship, the glory, the covenants, the giving of the law, the worship, and the promises; to them belong the patriarchs, and of their race, according to the flesh, is the Christ" (Rom 9:4–5). Later in Romans 11:29 he insists that the gifts and the call of God are irrevocable. To explain how it is that some Jews have rejected Jesus and some Gentiles have accepted him, Paul uses the analogy of an olive tree: " . . . some of the branches were broken off, and you, a wild olive shoot, were grafted in their place to share the richness of the olive tree" (Rom 11:17). Jews who have rejected Jesus are portrayed as branches broken off the olive tree, while Gentiles who have accepted Jesus have been grafted onto the olive tree. As in Galatians 3, Gentile Christians are understood to have been incorporated into the people of God whose lineage can be traced through Jesus of Nazareth back to Abraham.

Even though Paul's primary concern was to explain how Gentiles could be part of God's people, he also looked toward a time when "the natural branches will be grafted back into their own olive tree" (Rom 11:24). He envisioned three phases in God's plan: "a hardening has come upon part of Israel, until the full number of Gentiles come in, and so all Israel will be saved" (Rom 11:25–26). His description of unbelieving Israel's acceptance of Jesus as "life from the dead" (Rom 11:15) suggests that this will take place in the eschaton. At any rate, both Gentile Christians and unbelieving Jews exist in continuing relationship to the olive tree, which is God's people descended from Abraham through Jesus of Nazareth.

In New Testament letters generally acknowledged to be later than the Pauline epistles, the organic model proposed by Paul yields to a replacement model. Some texts in Paul's letters (e.g., Gal 4:21–31; 2 Cor 3:1–18; Phil 3:2–11; Rom 9–10) may have even provided the basis for the idea of replacement. For example, in 1 Peter 2:9–10 a largely Gentile Christian community is addressed in terms used to describe ancient Israel at Sinai: "But you are a chosen race, a royal priesthood, a holy nation, God's own people, that you may declare the wonderful deeds of him who called you out of darkness into his wonderful light. Once you were no people but now you are God's people; once you had not received mercy but now you have received mercy." The description of the addressees as once having been no people and having not received mercy identifies them as Gentiles by birth. Now through baptism (a major motif in 1 Peter) they have become God's own people and so can be addressed with the epithets given to Israel in Exodus 19:5–6. The passage suggests that the Church has replaced Israel as the people of God.

The replacement model also seems to underlie the description of what has happened in Christ for Jews and Gentiles in Ephesians 2:15: ". . . that he might create in himself one new man in place of the two, so making peace." The author of Ephesians (probably a later admirer of Paul rather than Paul himself) lays the foundation here for talking about the Church as a "third race," different from Jews and Gentiles. The idea is that both Jewish and Gentile identities have been by-passed in Christ. Another form of replacement thinking emerges in the Letter to the Hebrews with its contrasts between the institutions connected with the "first covenant" and the "new covenant" mediated by Christ. The Old Testament people of God serves as a negative warning to the

Christians on their way to the genuine sabbath rest for the people of God (see Heb 4:9).

Other New Testament documents illustrate a conflict model when dealing with the identity of the people of God. Indeed, conflict seems to have been an inevitable consequence of the Church's claims about replacement. The conflict model is expressed most clearly in the Gospels of Matthew and John. Both Gospels were composed after A.D. 70, when the split between Church and synagogue was becoming definitive. With the loss of Jerusalem and the destruction of the temple, the question of Judaism's spiritual center became a matter of fierce controversy. Both evangelists viewed the community gathered around Jesus as the true Israel and denied that other Jewish groups could validly make such a claim. Thus Matthew speaks of "their synagogues" (see Mt 4:23; 9:35; 10:17; 12:9; 13:54), which are also called the synagogues of the hypocrites (6:2, 5; 23:6, 34). John uses the expression *aposynagōgos* (see Jn 9:22; 12:42; 16:2), thus suggesting a sharp division between Moses' disciples and Jesus' disciples (see Jn 9:28). Both evangelists attempt to show that the promises to God's people have been fulfilled in Jesus of Nazareth, and in no one or nothing else. In the parable of the vineyard, Matthew asserts that Israel's elect status as the recipients of God's coming kingdom has been revoked and given to a new *ethnos* made up of those who confess Jesus: "The kingdom of God will be taken away from you and given to a nation producing the fruits of it" (Mt 21:43). Hostility and even contempt mark the evangelists' portrayals of Jesus' opponents. The heat of these polemics is understandable in the confused atmosphere that prevailed in Jewish circles after A.D. 70. But when taken out of their historical context, the polemics in Matthew and John have often given anti-semites an excuse for their foul deeds.

VATICAN II ON THE PEOPLE OF GOD

The most extensive treatment of the Church as the people of God comes in chapter two of the Dogmatic Constitution on the Church (9–17). The first chapter reflects on the Church's place in the mystery of salvation and on biblical images of the Church (sheepfold, field, building, body of Christ, bride of Christ). Then the document in chapter two identifies the Church as the people of God (9), shows how the people of God shares in Christ's priestly office (10–11) and prophetic office (12), and explains the Catholic unity of the people of God (13–17) with regard to the Catholic faithful (14), others who believe in Christ

(15), and all others called by God to salvation (16). The chapters that follow the section on the people of God concern (3) the hierarchical nature of the Church, (4) the laity, (5) the universal call to holiness in the Church, (6) religious life, (7) the pilgrim Church, and (8) Mary.[6]

This survey of the contents of *Lumen Gentium* indicates the pivotal nature of the chapter on the Church as the people of God. Among the biblical images it is singled out for separate and extensive treatment. Within chapter two, it is used as the framework for explaining priesthood, the sacraments, the teaching office of the Church, the charisms, and ecumenism. Within the document as a whole, it provides the framework for understanding the relationship of clergy, religious, and laity. The idea that the Church consists of the hierarchy plus the people of God (= laity) is rejected. Rather, the people of God consists of hierarchy plus laity and religious.

The paragraph that identifies the Church as the people of God (9) is thoroughly biblical, to the point of constituting a kind of midrash or anthology of biblical quotations. It affirms that God chose Israel to be his own people and made a covenant with it, that in Christ God has called a new people made up of Jews and Gentiles, and that Christ reigns in heaven and his messianic people on earth is a most sure sign of unity, hope, and salvation for the whole human race.

In this midrash, those New Testament texts that represent the replacement model are prominent (1 Pet 2:9–10; Heb 13:14). The idea of a "new" covenant glimpsed in Jeremiah 31:31–34 and reiterated in 1 Corinthians 11:25 is stressed. The understanding of the Church as the "new" people of God is emphasized twice: "This race would be the new people of God . . . the new Israel which advances in this present era in search of a future. . . . " All these features point toward the conclusion that the Church has replaced Israel as the people of God.

The relationship of the Church as the people of God to non-Christian religions is treated in more detail in *Nostra Aetate*. After establishing that all humans ultimately form one community and observing that people look to religion for answers to the problems of human existence, the document considers the positive values of Hinduism and Buddhism, pleads for a new relationship with Islam, takes up the Church's relationship to Judaism, and concludes by affirming that, since all humans are created in God's image, all forms of religious and racial discrimination are to be rejected.

Nostra Aetate is really a development of paragraph sixteen in *Lu-*

men Gentium. It shows a positive spirit toward other religions, expresses an eagerness for theological dialogue, and seeks to foster mutual respect. In this spirit, it treats in paragraph four the relationship of the Church to the Jewish people today.

The most dramatic development in this section was the rejection of a conflict theology loosely based on an ahistorical reading of statements in the Gospels of Matthew and John. It rejects the idea that all Jews indiscriminately in Jesus' time or Jews today can be charged with the crimes committed during Jesus' passion. It condemns all hatreds, persecutions, and displays of anti-semitism. In avoiding the conflict model of the Church's relationship to Judaism, the Council document followed the approach to Scripture outlined in the Dogmatic Constitution on Divine Revelation (*Dei Verbum*) 12 with its emphasis on reading biblical texts in their historical setting. It also began a new era in Jewish-Catholic relations, thus marking what one Jewish spokesman has called an irreversible moment in a not-very-happy history.

Elements of Paul's organic model found their way into paragraph four of *Nostra Aetate.* The document acknowledges the spiritual heritage of the Church in Israel by calling on Paul's analogy of the olive tree: "Nor can she forget that she draws nourishment from that good olive tree onto which the wild olive branches of the Gentiles have been grafted" (Rom 11:17–24). It repeats Paul's list of Israel's prerogatives (Rom 9:4–5) and even adds to it mentions of Mary, the apostles, and other early disciples of Jesus. It affirms that the Jews remain very dear to God because God's gifts to Israel are irrevocable (Rom 11:28). It awaits the day when Jews and Christians will call on God with one voice and serve him "shoulder to shoulder."

Even though Paul's organic model exercised positive influence on *Nostra Aetate* 4, the dominant concept is still the replacement model. The opening sentence recalls "the spiritual ties which link the people of the new covenant to the stock of Abraham." Later on, in the context of rejecting universal or continuing Jewish responsibility for Jesus' passion and death, the document asserts: "It is true that the Church is the new people of God, yet the Jews should not be spoken of as rejected or accursed as if this followed from holy Scripture." Both statements identify the Church as the new people of God while trying to be positive about Judaism as a continuing phenomenon.

Why then is the Church the people of God, according to Vatican II? Our examination of the biblical basis for this identification has revealed three different approaches: Paul's organic development model, the post-Pauline idea of the Church replacing Israel, and the conflict model reflected in the struggles of the Matthean and Johannine communities with their fellow Jews.

The Council fathers refused to accept the conflict model as an appropriate way of carrying on the relationship between Jews and Christians. They have inserted some perspectives from Paul's organic model of relationships. But their predominant approach is the replacement model, whereby the Church is understood to have taken over Israel's prerogatives as the people of God. The church is the *new* people of God for the *new* covenant.

THE CHALLENGES AHEAD

The first and most obvious challenge arising from Vatican II's teaching about the Church as the people of God is its assimilation. At the beginning of the paper, I noted that even though "people of God" has become a popular expression in Catholic circles, it is seldom used with much theological depth. An educational program attempting to remedy that defect would feature first of all an immersion in the Hebrew Scriptures and other Jewish writings. Since these documents constitute our heritage as God's people, we need to know what is in that heritage. Then there is need to appreciate and welcome the scandalous particularity of the Jewishness of Jesus, through whom all peoples can become part of the people of God. He is the principle of continuity with the movement begun by Abraham and the fundamental point of unity for people all over the world. Finally there is need to grasp the historical, dynamic, "on the move" nature of the people of God as it continues its pilgrimage to God. These are but a few elements that seem necessary for a more profound assimilation of the idea of the Church as the people of God.

The second challenge flows from the first. Many have used "people of God" as a slogan for Vatican II and proceeded to disregard practically everything else in the documents. "People of God" is a framework, not the whole story; it was not intended to deny the traditional aspects of teaching about the Church. *Lumen Gentium* must be read in its entirety. It does not deny the hierarchical nature of the Church, nor does it dismiss the idea of the Church as the body of Christ. The best antidote to the danger of "sloganeering" is to take the "people of God" idea as it was intended—as a framework in which all the documents of Vatican II can be read. On the other hand, it is a serious theological idea, which is not to be dismissed by those who see it as an unfortunate innovation. The second challenge therefore is not to allow "people of God" to function simply as a mindlessly repeated slogan.

The third challenge is less obvious but potentially very important. It involves the question, *Why* is the Church the people of God? It concerns the new relationship that has arisen (the "irreversible moment") between Catholics and Jews. As that new relationship proceeds, it is important for Catholics to become sensitive to the variety of approaches to the Church-and-synagogue issue in the New Testament. In particular, we must acknowledge the terrible effects that the conflict model has exercised on our relationship throughout the centuries. We must ask whether even in embracing a replacement model we thereby evacuate Judaism of its ongoing religious significance. We must join in what has been a rediscovery of Paul's organic model of relationships and ask ourselves whether this biblically based concept may be a more appropriate way to approach the issue. Adoption of Paul's approach would encourage Christians and Jews to look upon one another as spiritual kin bound together by a common religious heritage and caught up in the unfolding of God's mysterious plan. Judaism would cease to be simply another "non-Christian religion." The third challenge then involves further reflection on the question, Why is the Church the people of God? This reflection is best carried on in the spirit of *Nostra Aetate* 4: "Since Christians and Jews have such a common spiritual heritage, this sacred Council wishes to encourage and further mutual understanding and appreciation. This can be obtained, especially, by way of biblical and theological inquiry and through friendly discussions."

NOTES

1. All quotations of Vatican II texts are taken from A. Flannery (ed.), *Vatican Council II. The Conciliar and Post-Conciliar Documents* (Northport, NY: Costello, 1975).

2. See my book *God's People in Christ. New Testament Perspectives on the Church and Judaism* (Overtures to Biblical Theology 7; Philadelphia: Fortress, 1980).

3. See Franz Mussner, *Tractate on the Jews: The Significance of Judaism for Christian Faith* (Philadelphia: Fortress, 1984); Clemens Thoma, *A Christian Theology of Judaism* (Ramsey, NJ: Paulist, 1980).

4. Hans Joachim Kraus, *The People of God in the Old Testament* (New York: Association Press, 1958); P. D. Hanson, *The People Called.*

The Growth of Community in the Bible (San Francisco: Harper & Row, 1986).

5. Norman A. Beck, *Mature Christianity. The Recognition and Repudiation of the Anti-Jewish Polemic of the New Testament* (Cranbury, NJ: Susquehanna University Press, 1985), adopts another categorization for what he describes as the anti-Jewish statements in the New Testament: Christological, supersessionistic, and defamatory. See also A. G. Segal, *Rebecca's Children. Judaism and Christianity in the Roman World* (Cambridge: Harvard University Press, 1986); M. Simon, *Versus Israel. A Study of the Relations between Christians and Jews in the Roman Empire (135–425)* (New York: Oxford University Press, 1986).

6. For developments in ecclesiology, see Hans Küng, *The Church* (Garden City, NY: Doubleday, 1976); Avery Dulles, *Models of the Church* (Garden City, NY: Doubleday, 1978). A very useful bibliographic tool is Avery Dulles and Patrick Granfield, *The Church: A Bibliography* (Theological and Biblical Resources 1; Wilmington, DE: Glazier, 1985).

Lucien Richard, O.M.I.

VATICAN II AND THE MISSION OF THE CHURCH: A CONTEMPORARY AGENDA

"The blind recover their sight, the lame walk. . . . The dead are raised to life and the poor are hearing the good news" (Mt 11:5). And what was accomplished by God's own apostle is to be prolonged and continued: "As the Father sent me so I send you" (Jn 20:21). "Go forth therefore and make all nations my disciples" (Mt 28:19). These words have never ceased to be heard in the Church, although at times in conflicting ways. Never before was a more complete discussion of the Church's mission provided than at Vatican II. Yet here also one encounters different emphases, inconsistencies, and at times conflicting views.

In order to get an idea of the development that took place relative to the nature of mission at Vatican II, I will first of all consider briefly the context in which the debate took place. I will follow this with a brief study of the pertinent documents of Vatican II, which will indicate the tensions and lack of clarity concerning the meaning of mission. Some of these tensions were dealt with in the years that followed the closing of Vatican II: in 1969 at the gathering of Latin American bishops at Medellín, in the 1971 Synod of Bishops in Rome, and in 1976 when Paul VI addressed the basic problem of the relationship between evangelization and humanization in the apostolic exhortation *Evangelii Nuntiandi*. The tracing of this debate will lead us to the last question to be dealt with: the nature of mission in contemporary theology beyond Vatican II.

At Vatican II a profound transformation of the Church's self-understanding as missionary Church took place. Karl Rahner saw this change in terms of the Church becoming for the first time the world Church.[1] At Vatican II "mission" is a concept in transition. The transformation of language is indicative of a change in reality. There is a

57

movement from "missions" in the plural to mission in the singular; from evangelization to development, to humanization; from inculturation to liberation, to preferential option for the poor. Every change involved conflicts and tensions.

The transformation that took place at Vatican II did not occur in a vacuum. Sociocultural and theological developments were already challenging basic assumptions about the Church's missionary activity.[2] The period between the two wars was one of intensive missionary activity and of systematized study of the Church's mission and of the ways in which this mission is to be carried out. A series of missionary encyclicals promoted the idea of "mission" as a task given to the whole Church: *Maximum Illud* of Benedict XV (1919), *Rerum Ecclesiae* of Pius XI (1926), *Evangelii Praecones* (1951) and *Fidei Donum* (1957) of Pius XII.

The understanding of mission prevalent before and during Vatican II was influenced by an ecclesiology in which the governing question was that of the foundation of the Church.[3] Jesus founded a Church to which he gave specific constitutive elements. Most importantly he gave this Church the same purpose and goal he himself had received from the Father: the salvation of humanity. This was a supernatural goal distinct from the natural goals of humanity.

MISSION IN THE DOCUMENTS OF VATICAN II

Although all of the conciliar documents are relevant to the concept of mission, the most important contributions are to be found in the dogmatic constitution *Lumen Gentium*, the pastoral constitution *Gaudium et Spes*, and the decree on the Church's missionary activity *Ad Gentes*. In these documents several themes related to the nature of mission are presented. The mission of the Church is inserted within the larger framework of the mystery of the Trinity.[4] No belief is more central to the Christian tradition than the Trinity. It is the organizing principle of the Christian faith, the most basic interpretation of God as the mystery of salvific love, of God's universal salvific will. The Church must necessarily be intrinsically involved with the question of salvation. The Church has the mission to be obedient to the divine and salvific will of God. In *Ad Gentes* this divine will is said to be twofold. First, "God . . . graciously calls us to share in his life and glory" so that, through his divine goodness, "he who is Creator of all things might at last become all in all." "It pleased God to call men to share in his life and not merely singly, without any bond between them, but he formed them into a people, in which his children who had been scattered were gathered together (cf. Jn 11:52)."[5] The sharing of God's glory and the unity of his children therefore express both the meaning of salvation and the end of the Church's mission.

The origin of the mystery of salvation lies within the Father, is manifested in the incarnation of the Son, and is present and operative in the gift of the Spirit. Central to the mission of the Church is the person of Jesus Christ. "Since this mission continues and, in the course of history, unfolds the mission of Christ, who was sent to evangelize the poor, then the Church, urged on by the Spirit of Christ, must walk the road Christ himself walked, a way of poverty and obedience, of service and self-sacrifice even to death. . . . "[6] The Church is a sacrament of Christ's presence in history. " . . . the Church, in Christ, is in the nature of sacrament, a sign and instrument, that is, of communion with God and of unity among all men."[7]

In the decree *Ad Gentes* that mission constitutes the basic nature of the Church, although this affirmation is somewhat obscured because of a more traditional concern for "foreign missions." "The Church on earth is by its very nature missionary. . . . "[8] "It is clear, therefore, that missionary activity flows immediately from the very nature of the Church."[9] Mission is not to be conceived as something going on at the periphery of the Church; it is at the very center of its inner life.

Since the Church continues the mission of Christ and Christ's mission is the result and the manifestation of the Father's universal salvific will, the Church's mission is also universal. For all are to be converted to Christ: "Everyone, therefore, ought to be converted to Christ, who is known through the preaching of the Church. . . . "[10] The Church, as the sacrament of Christ's salvific presence, " . . . is even more urgently called upon to save and renew every creature."[11]

TENSIONS IN THE DOCUMENTS

A tension arises in Vatican II's understanding of the mission of the Church vis-à-vis the salvation of "all" and God's universal salvific will. The fundamental unity of the human community and its common destiny is rooted in its common origin. "All men form but one community. This is so because all stem from one stock which God created to people the entire earth (cf. Acts 17:26), and also because all share a common destiny, namely God. His providence, evident goodness, and saving designs extend to all men."[12] Similarly in *Lumen Gentium:*

"All men are called to this catholic unity . . . all mankind is called by God's grace to salvation."[13]

While this concern for all reflects God's universal salvific will, such a concern comes into tension with the affirmation that the Church is necessary for salvation. " . . . the Church, a pilgrim now on earth, is necessary for salvation: the one Christ is mediator and the way of salvation. . . . He himself explicitly asserted the necessity of faith and baptism (cf. Mk 16:16; Jn 3:5), and thereby affirmed at the same time the necessity of the Church which men enter through baptism as through a door."[14] The tension emerging from these affirmations of the necessity of the Church cannot be resolved by affirming with Ad Gentes that "in ways known to himself God can lead those who, through no fault of their own, are ignorant of the Gospel to that faith without which it is impossible to please her (Heb 11:6)."[15] The question of the relation of the Church to salvation presents us with the first tension in Vatican II teaching on mission.

Since the Church is "mission" by nature, every member in the Church, the whole people of God through baptism, is called to continue Christ's mission. Yet the fact that the Church is hierarchically structured diversifies somehow the nature of such a call. "In the Church there is diversity of ministry but unity of mission. To the apostles and their successors Christ has entrusted the office of teaching, sanctifying, and governing in his name and by his power. But the laity are made to share in the priestly, prophetical, and kingly office of Christ."[16] The hierarchical structure of the Church is basically constituted by the existence in the Church of ordained and non-ordained members. The basic mission of the Church inherited by all, through baptism, is then diversified through the sacrament of orders. This diversification in structure leads to a diversification in ministry: the ministry of the ordained is sacred ministry; to the laity is given an "apostolate" of witnessing in the world.[17] These distinctions lead to tensions relative to the nature of mission, tensions that are related to the question of sanctification as the primary purpose of the Church.

THE MISSION OF THE CHURCH AND MISSIONS: THE ESTABLISHMENT OF LOCAL CHURCHES

Another source of tension pertains to the affirmation that the Church by nature is missionary, yet the decree Ad Gentes affirms that the proper meaning of mission is "preaching the Gospel and implanting the Church among people who do not yet believe in Christ."[18]

There is a proper meaning for the missionary task of the Church: "The special end of this missionary activity is the evangelization and the implanting of the Church among peoples or groups in which it has not yet taken root."[19] This understanding is also affirmed in the new Code of Canon Law.[20] The "mission" of the Church becomes the "missions" of the Church. A distinction is maintained between the pastoral function of the Church "inside" and the missionary function "outside." Evangelization is understood as the first preaching of the Gospel and is concerned mainly with formation of individual Christians. This is followed by the "planting" of the Church which is the establishment of local churches.

The establishment of local churches, the "proper" missionary task of the Church, is understood as the transformation of a culture by the implanting of the Gospel. Such a transformation is likened to the mystery of the incarnation. The Church " . . . must implant itself among all these groups [those who have not heard the Gospel message] in the same way that Christ by his incarnation committed himself to the particular social and cultural circumstances of the men among whom he lived."[21] Not only is the missionary task of the Church likened to the mystery of the incarnation, but because the Church brings Christ to those who do not yet know him, the missionary task leads to a form of humanism. For, according to *Gaudium et Spes,* in the person of Jesus Christ we have not only a revelation of who God is, but also a revelation of what it means to be human. "The Church likewise believes that the key, the center, and the purpose of the whole of man's history is to be found in its Lord and master."[22] " . . . Christ, the new Adam, in the very revelation of the mystery of the Father and of his love, fully reveals man to himself and brings to light his most high calling."[23]

THE MISSION OF THE CHURCH TO THE WORLD

From seeing its "special" mission as that of transforming a specific culture, a process modeled on the incarnation, there is a natural transition to the question of the Church's mission to the world. In *Gaudium et Spes* the Church sees itself as confronting the "world" even where it is already established. The Church's mission is to all of humanity in all of its dimensions.

"Missionary activity is intimately bound up with human nature and its aspirations. In manifesting Christ, the Church reveals to men their true situation and calling, since Christ is the head and exemplar of that renewed humanity. . . . "[24]

Jesus Christ is the revelation of authentic humanness for all times and places. "The good news of Christ continually renews the life and culture of fallen man."[25]

SALVATION AND HUMANIZATION

Vatican II provided the Church with an extensive, broad, yet incomplete and at times fragmented and inconsistent understanding of mission. The most controversial issue to emerge out of the various documents has to do with the primary purpose of the Church's mission. A certain dichotomy is present between the Church's concern for those realities that are conceived to be essentially "religious," and others that have more to do with the secular realm. This dichotomy has been understood by certain interpreters of Vatican II as simply the residue of pre-conciliar ecclesiology. The emphasis of Vatican II on the primacy of sanctification as the Church's goal and mission precludes this interpretation.[26] In the decree on the apostolate of the laity where the Council deals with the Church's involvement with the secular realm, it is affirmed: "The Church's mission is concerned with the salvation of men; and men win salvation through the grace of Christ and faith in him. . . . The principal means of bringing this about is the ministry of the word and of the sacraments."[27] Yet this primary religious function cannot be exercised without influencing the secular realm, for the Gospel functions as a leaven that penetrates the temporal realm. In a sense it appears that according to Vatican II it is somewhat indirectly that the Church is concerned with the secular realm. To preach Jesus Christ and to administer the sacraments is the proper mission of the Church; to bring about a just society is not the proper mission of the Church except as this relates to salvation. "Whether it aids the world or whether it benefits from it, the Church has but one sole purpose—that the kingdom of God may come and the salvation of the human race may be accomplished."[28]

This approach of Vatican II gave rise to a dichotomizing of the Church's mission in "official" and "unofficial mission."[29] Such a dichotomy emphasizes the distinction between the ordained and non-ordained members of the Church. The ordained have the "official" mission while the lay person must be concerned with the "unofficial" mission. Most fundamentally, the discussion on the primary and secondary mission of the Church raises the fundamental theological problem of the nature of that which is religious, and therefore the relation between the Church's religious identity and the nature of its mission. Religious identity becomes the focusing point. Is what is religious a separate and isolated experience, a specific realm, or is it an intrinsic dimension of this human realm?

THE CHURCH AND THE SOCIAL-POLITICAL REALM: THE POST-VATICAN II DEBATE

Since Vatican II, official Church documents have especially concerned themselves with the question of the Church's religious identity and its mission in the social and political realms.[30] The document produced at Medellín (1968) became the charter for those who were working for a radical renewal of the Church in Latin America. The document underlines the Church's commitment to the evangelization of the poor, an evangelization that can only be realized in solidarity with the poor. This solidarity is made concrete through criticism of injustice and oppression and demands that the Church be actively involved in the reform of situations of oppression and injustice. The Medellín documents constantly speak of the Latin American situation as marked by structural injustice that can be called institutionalized violence. It emphasizes the need to "conscientisize" the "popular sectors" in order to inspire dynamic action. There is a recognition of the need to stimulate action for justice from the grassroots. The word "liberation" is often used and is closely linked to "humanization."

Rome was deeply affected by Medellín. The major documents concerned with social justice issued by Rome the following decade should be understood as being, to some extent, reactions, at times positive and at times negative, to the ideas of Medellín. Clearly, the document *Justice in the World*[31] of the Bishops' Synod of 1971, reflects the preoccupations of Medellín. The document proclaims: "Action on behalf of justice and participation in the transformation of the world fully appear to us as a constitutive dimension of the preaching of the Gospel, or, in other words, of the Church's mission for the redemption of the human race and its liberation from every oppressive situation."[32] The important word here is "constitutive." According to F. Schüssler Fiorenza, "The mission to transform the world is not secondary, improper, or derivative; it is constitutive of gospel proclamation. The document goes beyond previous affirmations, beyond viewing justice and liberation as only prerequisites or consequences of the Church's mission."[33] The use of the word "constitutive" led to a controversy which brought to a head closely related theological issues that emerged relative to the Church's action to promote justice: What is the nature of salvation and how is it related to political, economic, and cultural liberation?

The debate on the above quoted passage continued at the next Synod in 1974. Paul VI opened the Synod with the challenge to define more accurately the relationship between evangelization and the human effort toward development. The Synod produced two documents: "On Human Rights and Reconciliation" and "Evangelization of the Modern World." In the first document it is affirmed that "the promotion of human rights is required by the Gospel and is central to [the Church's] ministry";[34] the second not only affirms "the intimate connection between evangelization and liberation" but also that the "Church in more faithfully fulfilling the work of evangelization will announce the total salvation of man or rather his complete liberation, and from now on will start to bring this about."[35] The documents do avoid a simple affirmation of identity between salvation and liberation, salvation being much more than liberation. However the documents stress that there is a mutual relationship between evangelization and the integral salvation or complete liberation of the person and peoples.

In *Evangelii Nuntiandi* (1976), Paul VI made it clear that evangelization is not limited to preaching or to ministries of the literal word. In words that appear surprisingly radical, he identifies the scope of evangelization with the transformation of the human realm: "It is a question not only of preaching the Gospel in ever wider geographic areas or to ever greater numbers of people, but also of affecting and as it were upsetting, through the power of the Gospel, mankind's criteria of judgment, determining values, points of interests, lines of thought, sources of inspiration, and models of life, which are in contrast with the word of God and the plan of salvation."[36] Evangelization will clearly have a counter-cultural thrust for, as Paul VI affirms, "what matters is to evangelize human culture and cultures (not in a purely decorative way as it were by applying a thin veneer, but in a vital way, in depth, and right to their very roots)."[37] This counter-cultural thrust of evangelization is not without difficulties, yet "the split between the Gospel and culture is without a doubt the drama of our time . . . every effort must be made to ensure a full evangelization of culture, or, more correctly, of cultures. They have to be regenerated by an encounter with the Gospel."[38]

For Paul VI evangelization is not identical with human liberation because evangelization entails more than liberation. It is more encompassing insofar as the establishment of God's kingdom is much more universal than any improved social or political order. Evangelization goes more deeply, for it reaches the personal depths of human life and strikes at sin. Paul VI's understanding of the relationship of evangelization to liberation is dialectical. Evangelization is incomplete without liberation in the same way that liberation is incomplete without evangelization. Evangelization includes liberation in a transformative way; while action for justice is constitutive of evangelization, such action and such justice because they are related to evangelization have a depth that they would not otherwise have. The liberation announced by Jesus cannot fail to take account of the deepest dimensions of what it means to be human—social and political concerns are not of secondary importance for the Church: they are to be taken more seriously than by any other social institution.

A similar dialectic is present in the writings of John Paul II. Evangelization is presented as the essential mission of the Church, yet it must touch upon all the dimensions of human existence. John Paul II's dialectic has deep Christological roots—at the core of all political and social distortions lies a false image of human personhood, an image that is not that of Jesus Christ. "Following the teaching of the Second Vatican Council and paying close attention to the special needs of our times, I devoted the encyclical 'Redemptor Hominis' to the truth about man, a truth that is revealed to us in its fullness and depth in Christ."[39] John Paul II's emphasis on a Christological model of personhood leads him to emphasize much more what evangelization contributes to action for justice than what action for justice contributes to evangelization.

AGENDA: DEFINING THE NATURE OF THE
RELIGIOUS AND THE SECULAR REALMS
—A CHRISTOLOGICAL TASK

In all of these post-Vatican II documents there is an on-going attempt to come to terms with the question of the relationship of evangelization to liberation, of the relation between religious identity and the Church's social and political mission. The question about the specificity of the Church's presence, of its message and gifts, is constantly posed. This same challenge is posed by Bryan Hehir: "To determine precisely how justice can be described as properly belonging to the work of the Church and to describe precisely what is the style of a religiously based social-political ministry is one of the questions of the *Gaudium et Spes* decade."[40]

The fundamental question about the nature of the Church's mission is a question about religious identity, within which the Christian context is clearly a question about Christology. The question about the Church's mission cannot be resolved at the level of ecclesiology, as W. Kasper has written:

> If we are to find a way out of this impasse and the related polarizations in the Church, we have to reflect more profoundly on the real basis and meaning of the Church and its task in the modern world. The basis and meaning of the Church is not an idea, a principle, or a program. It is not comprised in so many dogmas and moral injunctions. It does not amount to specific Church or social structures. All these things are right and proper in their setting. But the basis and meaning of the Church is a person. And not a vague person, but one with a specific name: Jesus Christ.[41]

Contemporary Christology has emphasized the fullness of Jesus' humanity. In Jesus God has accepted for himself the dimension of the human including all the limitations—social, historical, psychological—of human existence. In Jesus the divine is Jesus-like. The humanity of Jesus is the epiphany of the divine and the limitations of the Holy Mystery. Nothing is alien to God except sin. Contemporary Christology affirms that the transcendent is truly in our midst. God is not to be limited to a spiritual realm, but is fully present to all historical reality. God can be equally encountered in the rituals of a religious tradition and in busy worldly activity. World-affirmation does not necessarily lead to materialism while world-rejection always results in the destruction of the human. Docetism in Christology has always been most detrimental to the valuation of human existence. The distinction made between the Christ of faith and the Jesus of history emphasizes the importance of history. The only way we encounter Jesus is through a thoroughly historical process. We arrive at our Christian identity through a process of socialization. As W. Thompson writes, "Owing up to the Jesus of history is owing up to our own historical makeup, an affirmation of the thoroughly historical character of our faith too."[42]

Related to this new consciousness in Christology, there are in ecclesiology two movements which affect our understanding of the Church's mission.[43] First, the Church is thoroughly historical, an empirical phenomenon of history. Such a historical point of view raises the fundamental question: What is the relation of this human community, this movement of people, to God's activity in the world? The historical dimension of the Church entails another element affecting our understanding of the Church's mission: the religious pluralism of the world. The fundamental question here is again about God's relationship to such a pluralism. Is such a pluralism positively wanted by God?

Both of these cultural elements demand an ecclesiology in which the basic question is no longer "What is the Church?" but "Why the Church?" The question of the nature of the Church is no longer a question about a static essential structure but more a question of the dynamic relationship the Church bears in relation to God's salvific will. The "divine" nature of the Church is determined by its relation to God's salvific action in history. The nature of the Church must be defined in functional symbols. The basic symbol here is that of mission which answers directly the question "Why the Church?" The nature of the Church is determined by its role, its mission, to and for the world. "Mission" as a religious symbol for the Church, with deep roots in the New Testament, points to a level of the Church that goes deeper and somehow transcends the empirical community; "mission" points to a dimension that goes beyond and is prior to the community itself. According to J. Moltmann: "What we have to learn . . . is not that the Church 'has' a mission, but the very reverse: that the mission of Christ creates its own Church. Mission does not come from the Church; it is from mission and in the light of mission that the Church has to be understood."[44] The priority of this mission not only harks back to the salvific will of the Father but also historically to Jesus' own sending of his disciples.

The Church is not for its own sake. "Mission" encompasses its whole nature. First there was the mission; and it is because of the mission that the Church exists. The Church must serve and express the mission. If it fails to do this, it fails to be the Church. There is not a first moment in which the Church comes to be as a distinct community of faith and grace and then a second moment in which the Church decides to be an instrument of God's salvific will. It is this will that is the ultimate source of mission and the ultimate catalyst for the Church's constant moving beyond the boundaries of a particular culture or national group. This fundamental conviction about the salvific will of God remains the most provocative challenge to the contemporary Church. Any claim to exclusivity or religious triumphalism will eventually run aground on this all-englobing vision of God. This vision of God demands a dynamic and developmental view of world history. God moves humanity forward; God's salvific will is progressive, inclusive in nature; not only Israel, nor the Church, but all nations and even the cosmic powers are caught up in this divine will. The ultimate word is life and not death; the final action is fulfillment not frustration.

The Church as mission sacramentalizes God's salvific will in human history. Such sacramentality occurs precisely in its visible, organized, and institutional forms in history; as such this sacramentality is concrete, practical and existential. It also involves a critical relevance; sacramentality demands visibility so that action becomes a necessary element of the Church's nature. Ministry is the very substance of the Church.

Ministry makes the Church what it is as sacramental reality. The praxis of the Church not only discloses the validity and truth of its mission but it is also a source of the discovery of such value and truth. This praxis cannot be limited to some exclusive "spiritual sphere"; it embraces the whole sphere of secular existence. Sacramental, whether applied to Jesus Christ, the Church, or the lives of individuals, includes within itself the tension of the transcendent-in-our-midst and implies simultaneously the impossibility of collapsing one into the other. There can be no strictly "religious" nor "this-worldly" ministry. God's salvific will, the eschatological promise, is operative in the totality of this life.

The sacramental nature of the Church's mission also implies that the Church is not "religious" nor "clerical" but the people of God; thus the Church is "mission" and realizes that its sacramentally ordained ministers belong first to that people and that ordination does not set them apart from their original community.

CONCLUSION

"Mission to the world" sums up adequately the purpose of Vatican II. Defining the words "mission" and "world" was not an easy task for the Council—the past twenty years have seen the Church and theologians grappling with the same basic questions. The agenda for the next decade is determined by such questions. The question about that which constitutes the realm of the religious must be dealt with. The hierarchical structure of the Church with its emphasis on the distinction between the ordained and non-ordained must be reconsidered. Ultimately the question of the mission of the Church will be clarified once the full implications of calling itself "the people of God" is realized.

NOTES

1. K. Rahner, "Basic Theological Interpretation of the Second Vatican Council," in *Theological Investigations*, Vol. 20, pp. 77–89.

2. Cf. A. M. Henry, O.P., art. "Mission" in *Catholicisme*, Vol. IX, 1982, coll. 298–374.

3. For a good exposition of this view, cf. F. Schüssler-Fiorenza, *Foundational Theology. Jesus and the Church* (N.Y.: Crossroad, 1984), pp. 57–192.

4. All references to Vatican II documents are from Austin P. Flannery, ed., *Documents of Vatican II* (Grand Rapids, Michigan: Eerdmans, 1984), A.G., No. 3, p. 351.

5. A.G., No. 2, p. 814.

6. A.G., No. 5, p. 818.

7. L.G., No. 1, p. 350.

8. A.G., No. 1, p. 814.

9. A.G., No. 6, p. 820.

10. A.G., No. 7, p. 821.

11. A.G., No. 1, p. 813.

12. N.A., No. 1, p. 738.

13. L.G., No. 13, p. 365.

14. L.G., No. 14, p. 365.

15. A.G., No. 7, p. 821.

16. A.A., No. 2, p. 768.

17. Cf. L.G., No. 28, pp. 384–387; No. 30, p. 388; A.A., No. 2, pp. 767–768.

18. A.G., No. 6, p. 819.

19. A.G., No. 6, p. 819.

20. Canon 786 affirms: "Missionary activity, properly so-called, by which the Church is implanted among peoples and groups in which it has not yet taken root, is accomplished by the Church especially by sending heralds of the Gospel until the young churches are fully established to the point that they are able to perform the work of evangelization on their own with their own resources and sufficient means."

21. A.G., No. 10, pp. 824–25.

22. G.S., No. 10, p. 911.

23. G.S., No. 22, p. 922.

24. A.G., No. 8, p. 822.

25. G.S., No. 58, p. 963.

26. On the question of the interpretation of Vatican II, see A.

Dulles, "Vatican II and the Church's Purpose," in *Theology Digest* 32:4 (Winter 1985), pp. 341–351.

27. A.A., No. 6, p. 772.

28. G.S., No. 45, p. 947.

29. Cf. F. Schüssler-Fiorenza, *Foundational Theology*, op. cit., pp. 195–212.

30. Cf. Y. Congar, "The Role of the Church in the Modern World," in Herbert Vorgrimler, ed., *Commentary on the Documents of Vatican II* (N.Y.: Herder and Herder, 1969), pp. 200–223.

31. *De Justitia in Mundo*, AAS 63 (1971) 923–942. English translation: *Justice in the World*, in Joseph Gremillion, ed., *The Gospel of Peace and Justice: Catholic Social Teaching Since Pope John* (Maryknoll: Orbis, 1976), pp. 513–529.

32. J. Gremillion, *The Gospel*, op. cit., p. 514.

33. F. Schüssler Fiorenza, *Foundational Theology*, op. cit., p. 208.

34. *Catholic Mind* 73, No. 1291 (March 1975), p. 51.

35. Ibid., pp. 55–56.

36. On "Evangelization in the Modern World" (Washington: USCC, 1976), No. 19, p. 16.

37. Ibid.

38. Ibid., p. 17.

39. "Rich in Mercy" (Washington, D.C.: USCC, 1981), No. 1, p. 1.

40. Bryan Hehir, "The Church in Mission: Canonical Implications," *Canon Law Society Proceedings* 37 (1975), p. 6.

41. Walter Kasper, *Jesus the Christ* (N.Y.: Paulist Press, 1977), p. 15.

42. William Thompson, *The Jesus Debate* (N.Y.: Paulist Press, 1983), p. 22.

43. See Roger Haight, "Mission: Symbol for Church Today," *Theological Studies* 37 (1976), 620–649.

44. Jurgen Moltmann, *The Church in the Power of the Spirit* (N.Y.: Harper & Row, 1975), p. 10.

Peter E. Fink, S.J.

THE CHURCH AS SACRAMENT AND THE SACRAMENTAL LIFE OF THE CHURCH

The most obvious and tangible result of the Second Vatican Council has been the new ways of worship set forth in the revised rites for the Eucharist and the other sacraments of the Church. These represent, in many ways, a dramatic and radical change from the patterns of liturgical prayer established by the reform that followed the Council of Trent. Prayer in the vernacular, the recovery of the word as integral to the liturgy, the recognition and reinstatement of a variety of true liturgical ministers and ministries, the restoration of ancient liturgical texts and the creation of new and original forms of prayer are but a few of the developments that have served to reshape the way in which Catholic Christians of the West worship in liturgical assembly.

Less obvious, perhaps, though no less dramatic and radical, is the understanding of sacrament that the Constitution on the Sacred Liturgy (*Sacrosanctum Concilium* [SC]) set forth, and which the new liturgical texts themselves embody. Theology before Vatican II had for centuries viewed sacraments somewhat objectively, as sacred signs, vehicles of grace, holy things, administered to the many through the ministry of a few. Each was defined in terms of its own special grace, and each was named a sacrament *of* the Church insofar as the Church was the dispenser of the mysteries of Christ. Each was considered to be on a par with the others, and little was said of the relationship that exists among them. The 1917 Code of Canon Law treated the sacraments under the heading "de rebus" (on things), and, in accord with the decision first formulated at the Second Council of Lyons (1274), and solidly reaffirmed at the Councils of Florence (1439) and Trent (1547), there were exactly seven sacraments, no more, no less. The term was not used to identify anything else.

In contrast to this theological tradition, Vatican II recaptured and endorsed the understanding that sacraments are *liturgical acts*, the action prayer of the Church gathered in assembly. This is true not only of the Eucharist, where its application is somewhat easy to grasp, but also of the other sacraments where the role of the gathered assembly as integral to their enactment has been much less immediately evident. The revised Code of Canon Law now speaks of the sacraments under a different heading, namely, "The Office of Sanctifying in the Church," and the Constitution on the Sacred Liturgy gives a richer meaning to the statement that the sacraments are sacraments of the Church. Each sacrament in its own way expresses and manifests "the mystery of Christ and the real nature of the true Church" (SC 2).

In addition, the sacraments are presented as ordered to the Eucharist, which is itself primary. Lines of relationship are drawn, as, for example, with the initiation sacraments of baptism and confirmation leading to and completed by the Eucharist, or with reconciliation seen as restoration to the Eucharist. And in accord with certain theological developments in the middle twentieth century, notably those of Karl Rahner and Edward Schillebeeckx, the term sacrament is employed in both the Constitution on the Sacred Liturgy and the Dogmatic Constitution on the Church (*Lumen Gentium* [LG]) to name the very reality of the Church itself and its relationship to the risen Christ. In Vatican II the term "sacrament" has clearly undergone development and transformation.

In this brief essay I would like to explore some of the main lines of this development in understanding which Vatican II brought to the sacraments, a shift which now allows us to speak of the Church as sacrament of Christ, and of the traditional seven sacraments as constituting the sacramental life of this sacramental Church. I will sketch this development under six headings: (a) the Church as sacrament of Christ, (b) sacraments as liturgical acts, (c) sacraments as signifying acts, (d) sacraments as expressive of the mystery of Christ, (e) the sacramental life of the Christian, and (f) the sacramental life of the Church.

(a) THE CHURCH AS SACRAMENT OF CHRIST

The Dogmatic Constitution on the Church speaks of the Church as being "a kind of sacrament or sign of intimate union with God, and of the unity of all mankind" (LG 1). It seeks here to identify the intimate relationship between the Church and the risen Christ. In like manner the Constitution on the Sacred Liturgy names the Church "sacrament" in its very coming to be: " . . . it was from the side of Christ as he slept the sleep of death upon the cross that there came forth the 'wondrous sacrament of the whole Church' " (SC 5). As Christ is the sacrament of God in history, namely, God's visible manifestation, tangible presence, and embodied saving grace, in like manner the Church is Christ's own sacrament in history until he shall come again. This extension of the word sacrament to the Church is crucial both to Vatican II's theology of sacraments and to the ritual revisions which have come about as a result of its mandate for liturgical reform.

By naming the Church *sacrament,* the Council expanded the meaning of the term well beyond its familiar application to the liturgical acts of baptism, confirmation, Eucharist, anointing of the sick, reconciliation of sinners, orders and marriage. It is not as though an eighth sacrament were being named in addition to the traditional seven. Church as sacrament is more fundamental. It is a statement of the Church's identity and mission, and one which serves to link the traditional seven to the Church precisely in terms of its identity and mission.

The sacramentality of the Church is central to the theology of Vatican II, and the extension of the word to name the Church serves to illuminate both the reality of the Church and the true sacramentality of the traditional seven liturgical acts. "The liturgy is thus the outstanding means by which the faithful can express in their lives, and manifest to others, the mystery of Christ and the real nature of the true Church" (SC 2). The truth of the Church is that it is an expression, a visible manifestation, of the risen Christ and an effective agent of Christ's own saving work. The truth of the seven sacraments is that they visibly portray and effectively enact this deepest truth of the Church itself. The Church in assembly expresses its identity and carries out its mission as the sacrament of Christ whenever it baptizes, confirms, does Eucharist, anoints the sick, reconciles the sinner, consecrates ordained ministers or blesses married love.

As applied to the Church, therefore, the term "sacrament" is descriptive. It names something essential to the Church's mission and ministry, namely, that this community of believers is both the manifestation and effective agent of Christ's own presence and on-going saving work. When the Church gathers in assembly to carry out this mission and ministry through the medium of its ritual actions, it embodies, makes present, and effectively continues the saving work of Christ. These ritual actions are called sacraments precisely for this reason. They are not independent of the sacramentality of the Church. They are sacraments of the Church precisely because they bring the Church's sacramentality to expression.

(b) SACRAMENTS AS LITURGICAL ACTS

With the primary sacrament of Christ identified as the Church, and more concretely the Church gathered in liturgical assembly, the Constitution on the Sacred Liturgy proceeds to speak of sacraments as *liturgy*, that is, actions of the Church in liturgical assembly. Immediately the understanding and imagination are invited to expand beyond the traditional and more restricted focus on matter, form, minister and recipient alone, and to call into view, as the primary focus for each sacrament, the whole assembly and its total liturgical action. This is a remarkable enough recovery for the Eucharist, which had for centuries been viewed as the act of the priest, with the people in passive attendance. It is truly astonishing with regard to baptism, or reconciliation, or orders, or even marriage, where an assembly, if one was gathered at all, was gathered exclusively to watch the sacrament take place.

It is clear from the Constitution that the normative enactment of each sacrament is that which is done by the Church in assembly: " . . . whenever rites, according to their specific nature, make provision for communal celebration involving the presence and active participation of the faithful, this way of celebrating them is to be preferred, as far as possible, to a celebration that is individual and quasi-private" (SC 27). Because sacraments are actions of the Church, it is important that everyone act: "In the restoration and promotion of the sacred liturgy, the full and active participation by all the people is the aim to be considered before all else" (SC 14). And because the enacted ritual is itself the living expression of the sacrament, the ritual text and directives must foster, not hinder, this participation by all: "In the revision of liturgical books, it should be carefully provided that the rubrics take the role of the people into account" (SC 31), and, "The rites should be . . . within the people's power of comprehension, and normally not require much explanation" (SC 34).

A note should be made here about one of the more obscure, yet vitally important, tenets of Scholastic sacramental theology. Sacraments are effective enactments of the saving work of Christ, and they achieve their effect in the very doing of them (*ex opere operato*). The two essential pieces of this tradition required that (a) the ritual be done according to the mind of the Church ("do what the Church intends"), and (b) that people be open to what is done ("put no obstacle in the way"). As long as the focus remained on sacrament as thing, administered by a special minister, and received by the faithful, it was almost impossible to avoid the accusation that sacraments behaved like magic.

Once the full and active participation of all the people is restored as essential to sacramental action, however, the puzzlement yields to something quite simple and quite obvious. People are affected by what they do, and what they do determines the effect. Provided they are open to what they are doing in sacraments, the entire assembly will be affected accordingly. What faith adds to the equation is that these effects, through the gracious action of God in Christ, are themselves redemption.

(c) SACRAMENTS AS SIGNIFYING ACTS

Drawing on the insight of Augustine that when someone baptizes it is Christ who baptizes, Scholastic theology secured for Catholic faith the effectiveness of sacraments. Christ himself, present in the act, is the source of all sacramental effectiveness. What the Scholastics mentioned, but did not develop, however, was the mode of this effectiveness: how sacraments work. The Constitution on the Sacred Liturgy brought forward this neglected dimension of sacramental effectiveness by remembering and reaffirming that sacraments achieve their effect "by signifying." Signifying is a specific way of making something happen, and proper signification is crucial if sacraments are to be properly effective.

This is made clear in the strong insistence throughout the Constitution on the Sacred Liturgy that the liturgical texts and rites express more clearly the holy things which they signify and signify more fully and accurately the holy realities they contain. If the pre-conciliar Church was content to affirm that sacraments effect what they signify, the post-conciliar Church has added a complementary concern: that sacraments signify all we believe they effect. The relationship between what sacraments accomplish, namely Christ's saving work, and the signifiers that constitute sacraments as such is clearly and boldly set out: "In the liturgy human sanctification is manifested by signs perceptible to the senses, and is effected in a way which is proper to each of these signs" (SC 7).

Sacramental actions involve the participants in the truth of Jesus Christ, and in their own deepest truth as that is revealed in and by him. Whether we stand in thanksgiving around the table of sacrifice and partake of Jesus' own offering, the Father's embrace and consecration of Jesus, and the fellowship in the Spirit which Jesus has brought about, or enact that same truth specifically in the face of sin, or sickness, or service, or love, or those whom we initiate into our midst, in sacraments we are drawn into Christ's own truth. Our imaginations become shaped by the truth of Christ. Our affections take on the affections of Christ. And the behavior we enact together is Christ's own behavior toward God (Abba) and toward those he names as friends. The power of our sacraments is that they make an appeal to our consciousness, to our affections, and to our behavior, that, in the words of Paul, we "put on Christ," and this appeal is made in the face of all other ways of imagining, all other ways of affection and behavior, that are rooted, not in Christ, but rather in our own sinfulness. What we do in sacraments places us in Christ's own way of being, and therefore calls us to conversion from our sins, and to transformation into Christ.

Doing what the Church intends places us in Christ's own truth. Putting no obstacle in the way renders us vulnerable to his power to transform us. And our act of consent, Amen, enabled by Christ's own power within us, an act which is so essential to the completion of our sacraments, is nothing less than our surrender into his own gracious ways. Sacraments achieve their effect by signifying, and their signifying power works to transform us into Christ, into Christ's way of being, Christ's way of praying, Christ's way of acting, Christ's way of loving, healing, forgiving, serving.

It is important to remember that signifying, where sacraments are concerned, is not a purely cognitive act. This would be true if Vatican II had not reversed the medieval understanding of liturgy as "sacred drama" observed by the assembly as if it were an audience. The catechetical method known as allegory which medieval theology spawned does rely on the cognitive precisely because it is a catechesis for watchers. In the wake of Vatican II, however, there are no watchers in sacraments, only doers, and the catechesis proper to doers, mystagogy, is intended to illuminate not only what one sees, but more deeply what one experiences with all of the senses. The awareness to which sacraments aim to lead the participants is not the "I understand" or "I see" of a cognitive appeal, but rather the "Amen," the surrender, of the whole person to the fullness of that in which we are engaged.

(d) SACRAMENTS AS EXPRESSIVE OF THE MYSTERY OF CHRIST

The rituals of our sacraments, including the prayers, the gestures, and the material elements such as food, water and oil, allow those who enact the sacraments to express the mystery of Christ (SC 2). This mystery of Christ is the truth of Jesus' own life, lived in obedient love toward the Father and in embracing love toward all creation. It is the truth expressed in the familiar hymn which Paul incorporated into his Letter to the Philippians: " . . . he humbled himself and became obedient unto death, even death on a cross. Therefore God has highly exalted him . . . " (Phil 2:8–9). This truth is presented with its challenging mandate, "Have this mind among yourselves, which you have in Christ Jesus . . . " (Phil 2:5). It is likewise the truth proclaimed in John: "No longer do I call you servants. . . . I have called you friends" (Jn 15:15). This too has its mandate: "Love one another as I have loved you."

The mystery of Christ is a mystery of love, a mystery of relationship. It is the love between Abba and Christ who is Son. It is the love between the First-born and all whom he calls and gathers into himself. This profound relational mystery finds expression in our ritual acts in word, where the assembly is addressed by God in Christ, in offering, where the assembly opens itself and gives itself over to God's ways revealed in Christ, in consecration, where the God who raised Jesus from the dead once again makes firm commitment to and covenant with those who are gathered with Christ and claims and consecrates them as God's own people, and finally in communion, where relationship with Christ and with the Abba of Christ sets all who enact the mystery into relationship with each other. These four, word, offertory, consecration, and communion, find expression not only in Eucharist but in all the sacraments of the Church.

Because the mystery of Christ is a personal mystery, the symbols that bring it to expression must include persons. Things alone cannot express a mystery of love. Thus it is that the people of the Church are said to make Christ present in their very gathering, that the presiding minister of liturgical prayer is said to act "in persona Christi," that the minister of the word gives human voice to the Christ who speaks in word, and that the consecrated food, that so tangibly makes Christ present in the Eucharist, remains, as the Council of Trent proclaimed, *ad manducandum*, that is, food shared by people through the ministry of people. Full and active participation of the people, and the ministries of liturgical ministers in the assembly, are required so that the personal mystery of Christ may be personally brought to expression.

(e) THE SACRAMENTAL LIFE OF THE CHRISTIAN

A clear thread running through the Constitution on the Sacred Liturgy is that sacraments aim at human transformation, a transformation that can be humanly described and humanly recognized. This transformation is not, and cannot be, understood as something taking place all at once. It is a human process, and therefore a slow process, one indeed which unfolds throughout one's life. Sacramental actions are not independent of life's journey. It is this very journey which they encapsulate, express, shape and deepen.

It is at this point that Vatican II stretches our imagination even further. The Scholastic theology of sacraments simply did not have a mechanism, or even the language, to relate participation in sacraments to the on-going transformation into Christ. It did, of course, name "sanctifying grace" as an increased share in the life of Christ, but, be-yond affirming it, there was little in Scholastic theology to describe just what that meant or how it took effect. It also spoke of "actual grace," which is the help sacraments give for living one's life, but even here there was little intrinsic connection drawn between the actual enact-ment of the sacrament and the grace that ensued. Sacraments were envisioned episodically, that is, as individual experiences with their own specific value and effect, and not within the process view that on-going transformation into Christ calls for.

Fortunately, one of the most remarkable achievements of the post-conciliar liturgical reform, namely the Rite of Christian Initiation of Adults (RCIA), brought forward such a mechanism and such a lan-guage. RCIA identifies the intimate relationship that exists between baptism, confirmation and Eucharist and calls for their celebration to-gether in a single ritual enactment. Much more, however, it locates these three sacraments within a life process which is Christian initia-tion. Initiation unfolds in stages, though the sacraments themselves do not constitute the stages. Instead, they emerge from the process al-ready underway for those being initiated, raise that process to a new level, and lead back into the process which must continue throughout one's life.

RCIA recaptures Augustine's insight into the Eucharist that the Eucharist itself is the repeatable sacrament of initiation. If one holds RCIA together with the restored rites of Christian burial, the full scope of initiation is made clear. The funeral rite calls on the baptism of Christians to proclaim that what was enacted throughout one's life in sacrament has finally been realized in Christian death. In death one passes through in fact what one has passed through ritually in baptism, in the Eucharist, and indeed in all of the sacraments enacted through-out one's life.

With the concept of initiation offered by RCIA it is possible to view each sacrament, and every enactment of the sacraments, as part of the initiation process, and part of the sacramental life of each Christian. It is a process that has a structure, a shape and a goal, captured and enacted in the sacraments that are *of* initiation. All who are placed with Christ (the primary symbolism of baptism) are anointed and consecrated by the Father (the primary symbolism of the anointing of confirmation) and set in union with Christ and with each other by God's own Spirit placed within us (the primary symbolism of the Eucharist). The sacramental life of each Christian is lived toward the achievement of this reality, and every enactment of the sacraments enacts this reality into our life and our history. This is the hope in which Christians live, and the destiny planned by God from the beginning to be realized by all at death. It is this goal toward which the Church's sacraments invite and lead us.

What both the Constitution on the Sacred Liturgy and the reformed liturgical rituals call for is nothing less than a sacramental spirituality. The language of journey, the language of process, a language which will relate sacramental enactments not only to each other but even more to the gradual transformation of human life into the truth which sacraments express, will be essential to such a spirituality and to a theology of sacraments which must underlie it. Sacraments truly deserve to be treated under the heading, "The Office of Sanctifying in the Church."

(f) THE SACRAMENTAL LIFE OF THE CHURCH

The final expansion of the term sacrament envisioned by Vatican II is in many ways a return full-circle to the point at which these reflections began. There the Church itself was named to be sacrament, and this naming was said to be foundational to both the theology and the praxis that has come from the conciliar reform. The liturgical acts that are named sacrament express this sacramentality of the Church. Moreover, these acts cannot be seen in isolation from life, but need to be seen as part of the transformative process of Christian initiation into which each Christian is invited by the Lord. This needs now to be taken one step further, beyond the individual Christian to the Church as a whole.

It is necessary to remember that what is proclaimed in sacraments involves Christians in a tension that is fundamental to the Church itself. What is proclaimed has both the finality of an accomplished fact, namely, the once-for-all redemptive act of Jesus Christ, and the unfinished-ness that attends the unfolding of that fact in human history. On

God's part, what is proclaimed in sacraments is complete; in human life, however, and indeed in the life of the Church, it is yet to be fully realized. For any Christian, this process of realization is the life-long venture that is Christian initiation. For the Church it is the same process writ large, the history of the Church as it moves toward the eschaton.

The Church is called the sacrament of Christ, and as noted above this is a statement of both its identity and its mission. This sacramentality of the Church is, on the one hand, an accomplished fact brought about in the death and resurrection of Christ and in the coming of the Spirit which that death and resurrection unleashed. The identity and the mission of the Church share in the once-for-all redemptive act of Christ. On the other hand, however, the truth that the Church is the sacrament of Christ is only partially realized by the Church at any point in its passage through human history. The Church too is on a journey of initiation and transformation which will not be complete until "he comes again."

The statement that the Church is the sacrament of Christ is, therefore, in addition to being a statement of identity and mission, a self-summoning statement. The very proclamation of it summons the Church more deeply into its own truth. Whenever it is proclaimed, as it is each time the Church enacts its sacraments, it calls the Church to be and become more deeply that which is proclaimed. It is not only the individual Christian, but the Church itself, which must undergo a continual process of transformation into Christ.

RCIA envisions the sacramentality of the Church to be most vividly displayed in the life of a local Church, and not exclusively in liturgical ritual moments. It envisions a people who pray, believe, relate to one another, and serve one another in the manner displayed in Jesus' own life. It envisions a people who do what Christ did, namely, speak of God, heal and forgive, call to reconciliation, and live the new life that belongs to the children of God. "By this all will know you are my disciples, if you have love for one another" (Jn 13:35). Echoing an insight from the sixteenth century Protestant reformation, Vatican II acknowledged that the Church must always undergo reformation. Transformation into the ways of Christ is the stuff of this reformation. As with the individual Christian, so too with the Church as a whole, sacramental life is larger than ritual moments. What goes on in assembly serves to foster what must go on in the Church's life as a whole if the Church will be faithful to the mission and ministry given it by Christ.

CONCLUDING REMARK

Vatican II was indeed a major moment in the history of the Church, and specifically in the history of liturgical worship and sacramental understanding. The six points outlined above capture at least in skeletal form the extent to which post-conciliar Catholic Christians, and any others who choose to be guided by Vatican II, are challenged to expand and deepen their understanding: how they understand themselves in relation to Christ, how they understand what they do when they enact that relationship in liturgical, sacramental act, and how they understand what they are summoned to become whenever they gather in assembly to "express in their lives and manifest to others the mystery of Christ and the nature of the true Church" (SC 2). The sacraments of the Church are not only vehicles of grace. Together they constitute the life of the Church and allow that life to grow and deepen.

Stanley Marrow, S.J.

VATICAN II:
SCRIPTURE AND PREACHING

An insufficiently remarked fact in the history of Christian theology is that, in the early centuries of the faith, the great saints were also the great preachers, the outstanding theologians and—more often than not—the illustrious bishops of the Church. They combined an admirable holiness of life with an exalted and manifest sense of mission in the Church. That mission was to present the Christian revelation whole and entire to the faithful of their time, planting dogmatics firmly at the very heart of the Church's life, and Scripture at the very core of their dogmatics.[1] They did all this, not as what we might call today "professional theologians," but as great preachers, interpreters of the Scriptures, and proclaimers of the word of life. Their expository tracts, their polemical works, even their correspondence were but the preaching of the word carried on by other means. But, above all, it was the life they led that gave substance to their preaching: "Sit eius quasi copia dicendi forma vivendi," said Augustine about the preacher of the word: let the eloquence of his teaching be the manner of his life.[2]

With the spread of monasticism throughout the Christian world, from about the fifth century, that situation was bound to change. There is a vast amount of information about monastic life in the Middle Ages, its use of Scripture, its preaching and its instruction. This, unfortunately, is offset by an equally vast ignorance of the lot of the faithful outside monastery walls: their contact with the word of God, the preaching practices of their clergy, and the Christian instruction of the believers. The rise of the mendicant orders in the thirteenth century is but a small indication of the negative overall picture. They attest the urgent need for Christians dedicated to the preaching of the word both in their lives and in their words, not within the confines of monastery walls but to the people of God at large.

It is baffling to note the almost total lack of preoccupation with

82

any aspect of preaching in the conciliar and ecclesiastical decrees that have accumulated over the centuries. There you will find heresies aplenty combated, numberless practices discouraged, hosts of causes espoused, but you will look in vain for an explicitly formulated concern about the preachers of the word, the practice and the quality of preaching, the preparation and education of future preachers. Indeed, it is no small glory of the Order of Preachers (the Dominicans) that they were among the first to devise and carry out the proper education and formation of those destined to preach the word of God to the Church.[3]

BACKGROUND TO VATICAN II

We have to wait several centuries later to find, in the eleventh session of the Fifth Lateran Council under Leo X (December 1516), one of the earliest instructions on preaching in a conciliar document. The Council required that preachers be not only competent but also fit as regards moral integrity, age, knowledge, uprightness, prudence, and exemplariness of life.[4] What they were to preach was "the truth of the Gospel and the Holy Scriptures."

The preachers, moreover, were warned against defaming the character of bishops, prelates and other superiors before the people.[5] One might well wonder, of course, whether those not fortunate enough to fall within the mentioned categories were fair game, or whether the warning tacitly allowed room for defamation of those same ecclesiastical dignitaries in private.

But there is in this exhortation—and this is the point to keep in mind—no appeal to any teaching of the Scriptures on this point such as, e.g., Galatians 5:15 or Philippians 2:3–5. On the other hand, in forbidding preachers to speculate about the end of time, the Council cites—out of context and out of sense—Acts 1:7, "It is not for you to know times or seasons."[6] This may well have reflected the way Scripture was commonly used, but it certainly was not a very salutary example for any preacher, and just as certainly could not have been conducive to preaching "the truth of the Gospel and the Holy Scriptures."

As is to be expected, the Council of Trent—in its fifth session (1546)—took up the subject of preaching, the principal task of bishops (*praecipuum episcoporum munus*), who are personally bound to preach "the holy Gospel of Jesus Christ."[7] Of course, the crisis of the Church in any age is, ultimately, a crisis of preaching. Therefore, the fact that in a time of grave crisis the Council of Trent took up the subject of preaching should come as no surprise. What is surprising is how little the Council did in fact say about the ministry of the word as such. To appreciate this paucity at its true significance, one has but to compare the section devoted to preaching with, for instance, the seventh session's discussion on the sacraments, the thirteenth session's on the Eucharist, or the fourteenth session's on penance and extreme unction.

There were, doubtless, good reasons for all of this insistence on the sacraments, but one has to wonder whether any of them was sufficient to countervail Paul's reminder that "Christ did not send me to baptize but *to preach the Gospel*" (1 Cor 1:17), and his handing on the tradition of the Eucharistic institution that "as often as you eat this bread and drink the cup, *you proclaim the Lord's death* until he comes" (1 Cor 11:26). Trent, in other words, could not very well avoid taking cognizance of the importance of preaching the word of God, but its real concerns lay elsewhere.

MODERN TIMES

Whether intended by Trent or not, preaching in actual practice came to mean not so much the preaching of the Gospel of Jesus Christ as the teaching of the articles of the creed, the explanation of the commandments, the giving of novenas, missions and the like. Preaching became almost synonymous with the exhortation to good living. The principal accent was on the virtues to be practiced and the vices to be eschewed as a means of salvation.[8] This is hardly what one might call *the* New Testament message. Moreover, it is hard to see how "the Gospel of Jesus Christ" figured in all these exercises as anything but an arsenal of quotations to serve a multiplicity of aims: instructional, apologetic, polemic, and the like.

This is not the dyspeptic judgment of yet another disgruntled theologian, but the conclusion evidently reached by the Supreme Pontiffs of recent times whose names figure in the revival of biblical studies in the Catholic Church: Leo XIII, Benedict XV, and Pius XII. In each of their respective encyclicals on the Bible (*Providentissimus Deus* in 1893, *Spiritus Paraclitus* in 1920, and *Divino Afflante Spiritu* in 1943), specific attention is paid to its primary role in inspiring, nourishing and fostering the living and active word of God (Heb 4:12).

Even when due allowance is made for the literary genre of such compositions, one has to recognize that the papal encyclicals felt the urgency to treat an endemic malaise whose deep-rooted causes lay in misunderstanding the role of the Scriptures in Christian preaching, and whose perduring effects they wished to alleviate, if not wholly eradicate. Thus they mark a decisive turn in biblical methodology which profoundly influenced theological reflection and—to a far lesser extent—modified the view of Christian preaching expressed in the documents of Vatican II.

But, even in these imposing documents of the Second Vatican Council, the primary concern was not so much the preaching of the word as its proper interpretation, the application of modern exegetical methods to its understanding, and the solicitude for the safeguarding of its truth. Aware as the encyclicals were of the need to encourage the "scientific study of Scripture," they remained mindful—as was Leo XIII's *Providentissimus Deus*—that "our Gospel came to you not only in word, but also in power and in the Holy Spirit" (1 Thes 1:5).[9] Thus, Pius XII expressed the hope that Sacred Scripture "will become for the future priests of the Church a pure and never failing source for their own spiritual life, as well as food and strength for the sacred office of preaching."[10]

Pius XII was reiterating, of course, the perennial conviction that neither the preaching function nor the actual life of the preacher can be divorced from one another, and that both are manifestations of the life of the Spirit in the community of believers. But for that life of the Spirit to be genuinely life and not the bloodless rote of moral prescriptions, the proclaimers of the word had to be conversant with and competent in the use of the tools that modern exegesis continues to put at their disposal. The one single victim of ignorance and incompetence in this regard is not the reputation of the Church or the fame of its exegetes, but the ministry of the word itself, without which the Church is not and cannot be an institution of salvation.

VATICAN II: THE MINISTRY OF THE WORD

If the modern papal encyclicals effected any change in the nature and quality of Christian preaching, that change eludes detection. For, when the Second Vatican Council issued its Constitution on the Liturgy, *Sacrosanctum Concilium* (4 December 1963), the first-fruits of its labors, it evidently felt the need, not so much to encourage or to improve the quality of the sermon, as simply to reinstate it in its rightful place:

That the intimate connection between rite and words may be apparent in the liturgy:

(1) In sacred celebrations a more ample, more varied, and more suitable reading from Sacred Scripture should be restored.[11]

(2) The most suitable place for a sermon ought to be indicated in the rubrics, for a sermon is part of the liturgical action. . . . The ministry of preaching is to be fulfilled most faithfully and carefully. The sermon, moreover, should draw its content mainly from scriptural and liturgical sources, for it is the proclamation of God's wonderful works in the history of salvation, which is the mystery of Christ ever made present and active in us, especially in the celebration of the liturgy.[12]

The Council's reminders of truths that scarcely need to be recalled should be seen as a reaction to the situation that prevailed in liturgical celebrations up to that point. One would have thought that reminders that the sermon is "part of the liturgical celebration," or an exhortation to practice with fidelity and care "the ministry of preaching," or a recall of the sources whence the sermon ought to derive its content, are alike unnecessary, being but elementary data of the life of the church.

Sceptics might regard such passages in the Constitution as pious makeweight. But the reminders must have been judged necessary by the reality of the situation prior to Vatican II. In other words, the fathers of the Council recognized the fact that the sermon was *not* part of the liturgical celebration, that the ministry of preaching was *not* practiced with "fidelity and care," and that what preaching did take place did *not* draw its content from "scriptural and liturgical sources." Those long enough in the tooth to remember attending novenas, preached retreats, parish missions, Lenten courses and the like hardly need any convincing about the justness of the Council's assessment of the situation.

But the Council, which strove to have a word for everyone and for each category in the Church and in the world, also issued a Decree on the Ministry and Life of Priests (*Presbyterorum Ordinis*, 7 December 1965). The Decree lists the ministry of God's word as the first in the list of the "functions of priests":

The people of God is formed into one in the first place by the word of the living God . . . it is the first task of priests as co-workers of the bishops to preach the Gospel of God to all men.[13]

No church could afford to forget or neglect this truth. So it comes as an unwelcome surprise to see added immediately after its statement:

In the Christian community itself on the other hand, *especially [praesertim] for those who seem to have little understanding or belief underlying their practice,* the preaching of the word is required for the sacramental ministry itself, since the sacraments are sacraments of faith, drawing their origin and nourishment from the Word.[14]

The addition of the emphasized phrase in this sentence defies comprehension. Is the conclusion to be drawn from this that those who have much "understanding or belief underlying their practice" can afford to do without the ministry of the word? Might one not be excused for supposing that, for all its assertion of the contrary in the opening sentence of n. 4 cited above, the Council was not entirely convinced of the primacy of the ministry of the word in the life of the Church?

The concern of the Council seems to have been the perennial one with the sacraments. It is not easy to avoid the suspicion that the concern with the word seems to be there because of its unavoidable presence in the New Testament itself, not because of any compelling conviction of its primacy in the life of the Church.

The Decree on the Apostolate of Lay People (*Apostolicam Actuositatem,* 18 November 1965) lends verisimilitude to this view:

The apostolate of the Church therefore, and of each of its members, aims primarily at the announcing to the world by word and action the message of Christ and communicating to it the grace of Christ. The principal (*principaliter*) means of bringing this about is *the ministry of the word and of the sacraments.*[15]

In other words, what the Council seems reluctant to say is what, for example, the Bishops' Committee on Priestly Life and Ministry did not hesitate to state. Having cited Vatican II's Decree on the Ministry, this episcopal committee adds, "The other duties of the priest are to be considered properly presbyteral to the degree that they support the proclamation of the Gospel."[16] The primacy of the ministry of the word is a premise not a theologoumenon, a principle from which all ministry derives and not a mere corollary to sacramental ministry.

As is to be expected, it is the Constitution on Divine Revelation (*Dei Verbum,* 18 November 1965) that best sums up the Council's understanding of the ministry of the word:

Therefore, the "study of the sacred page" should be the very soul of sacred theology. The ministry of the word too—*pas-*

toral preaching, catechetics and all forms of Christian instruction,
among which *the liturgical homily* should hold pride of place—
is healthily nourished and thrives in holiness through the
word of Scripture.[17]

Of course, where the "study of the sacred page" is not the "very
soul of sacred theology," theology itself is no more, and cannot pre-
tend to be anything other than human discourse on human affairs.
This is no less true of the other functions comprised under the "ministry of the word." Without "the sacred page," they would be at best
editorials on the current scene, and at worst empty chatter.

But the important thing to keep in mind is the Council's inclusive
definition of the ministry of the word. It embraces not only theology
and the liturgical homily but pastoral preaching, catechetics and *all*
forms of Christian instruction. If the Council really meant this, then
one might rightly wonder why only the first two continue to receive
any form of official recognition from the institution, whether by ordination or by mandate:

> But how are men to call upon him in whom they have not
> believed? And how are they to believe in him of whom they
> have never heard? And how are they to hear without a
> preacher? And how can men preach *unless they are sent?* (Rom
> 10:14–15).

To estimate rightly the effects of Vatican II on the life of the
Church—if such an estimate can indeed be made after a score of
years—the status of all ministries of the word has to be assessed. The
granting of academic or even of ecclesiastical degrees is not an index
of "they are sent," nor is the change in the configuration of parish ministries. The real norm for assessment has to be the true and recognized
status of catechists, religion instructors on all levels, and all those who
in any form or fashion exercise the ministry of the word in the Church
and the missions. Put graphically—but not misleadingly—the question
to ask is: How has the status in the Church of those who have taught
first-graders their catechism over the past thirty years changed at all?

VATICAN II: THE PROCLAMATION OF THE GOSPEL

The Gospel of Matthew, the perennial favorite of the Church,
concludes with one of the most frequently cited scriptural texts in the
acts of its Councils:[18]

And Jesus came and said to them, "All authority in heaven and on earth has been given to me. Go therefore and make disciples of all nations, baptizing them in the name of the Father and of the Son and of the Holy Spirit, teaching them to observe all that I have commanded you; and lo, I am with you always, to the close of the age" (Mt 28:18–20).

This is the text to which the Constitution on the Church (*Lumen Gentium*) refers when it describes the ministry of bishops:

> The bishops, inasmuch as they are the successors of the apostles, receive from the Lord, to whom all power is given in heaven and on earth, the mission of teaching all peoples, and of preaching the Gospel to every creature, so that all men may attain to salvation through faith, baptism and the observance of the commandments (cf. Mt 28:18; Mk 16:15–16; Acts 26:17f).[19]

"Preaching the Gospel" is accorded "pride of place" among the principal [*inter praecipua*] duties of bishops.[20] By the sacrament of orders, priests "are consecrated in order to preach the Gospel and shepherd the faithful as well as to celebrate divine worship as true priests of the New Testament."[21] Such statements make explicit what the Decree on the Means of Social Communication (*Inter Mirifica* of 4 December 1963) had already said:

> The Catholic Church was founded by Christ our Lord to bring salvation to all men. It feels obliged, therefore, to preach the Gospel [*evangelizandi necessitate compellatur*].[22]

Of course, preaching the Gospel is more than a matter of obligation or even of compulsion, whether juridical or moral. It is the very condition of the Church's life in the world. The text of Matthew 28:18–20 is not merely a command of the risen Lord but a description of the very nature of the Church. The proclamation of the Gospel is to be neither confused with, nor subordinated to, the "shepherding" of the faithful or the celebration of divine worship—necessary and important though both of these be. Preaching the good news of salvation cannot be reduced to drawing up an elenchus of the virtues and vices to be embraced and shunned by Christians. It is the proclamation of "the cross of Christ as the sign of God's universal love and the source of all grace."[23]

Whether or not Vatican II has succeeded more than the encyclicals which preceded it and, in many ways, prepared the way for it, remains to be seen. Perhaps a good place to start an assessment of its after-effects on preaching the word would be with what Trent had already stated and Vatican II reiterated: that preaching is the principal task of bishops.[24] When bishops throughout the world begin to embrace in practice their "principal task," then perhaps a right assessment of the preaching of the word in today's Church can begin to be undertaken. They do have in the Bishop of Rome a good example to follow.

NOTES

1. Hans von Balthasar, "Théologie et sainteté," *Dieu Vivant* 12 (Paris: Seuil, 1948) 17.

2. St. Augustine, *De doctrina christiana* IV.29.61, *Corpus Christianorum:* Series Latina, vol. 32, p. 165, 1. 3. This, thoroughly Christian view of the preacher though it be, is a classical topos. For, as Quintilian remarks, the orator by definition is a "vir bonus dicendi peritus" (*Institutiones Oratoriae*, XII.1; Loeb, volume IV, p. 354), eloquence and goodness of life being regarded as inseparable.

3. "The Dominicans were from the earliest days an Order organized for theological study. . . . The General Chapter of 1228 had laid down that every community in the Order should have a friar in charge of theological studies . . . it provided that no member of the Order should preach in public until he had studied theology for at least three years. . . . " R. W. Southern, *Western Society and the Church in the Middle Ages* (The Pelican History of the Church 2; Harmondsworth: Penguin Books, 1970), pp. 296–297.

4. "With the approval of the holy council we decree and ordain that no clerics, whether seculars or members of any of the mendicant orders or any other order to which the office of preaching [*facultas praedicandi*] pertains by right, custom, privilege, or otherwise, be admitted to exercise that office [*officium*] unless they have first been carefully examined by their respective superiors and found competent and fit as regards moral integrity, age, knowledge, uprightness, prudence, and exemplariness of life. Of this approved competency they must, wherever they may preach, acquaint the local ordinary by means of authentic letters or other instruments from those who examined and approved them for this work." Pope Leo X's Bull "Supernae Majestatis Praesidio," Session XI of the Fifth Lateran Council, December 19,

1516, in James J. Megivern, *Bible Interpretation* (Wilmington, N.C., 1978), no. 262, pp. 177–178. For the Latin text see J. Alberigo, J. A. Dossetti et al., eds., *Conciliorum oecumenicorum decreta*, editio 3ª (Bologna: Istituto per le Scienze Religiose, 1973), p. 636.

5. "But by divine command it is [the cleric's, whether regular or secular] duty to preach and explain [*enucleant et declarent*] the Gospel to every creature [Mt 16:15], to instill a hatred of sin and the cultivation of virtue, and to promote the peace and mutual charity so insistently counseled by our Redeemer. To realize this peace and charity, let him preserve undivided the seamless garment of Christ by abstaining from that scandalous practice of defaming the character of bishops, prelates, and other superiors before the people [*coram vulgo*]." Ibid., no. 263, p. 178. See *Concil. oecum. decreta*, p. 637.

6. See J. J. Megivern, no. 263, p. 178.

7. "But since the preaching of the Gospel is no less necessary to the Christian commonwealth [*christianae rei publicae*] than the reading thereof, and since this is the chief duty of the bishops, the same holy council has ordained and decreed that all bishops, archbishops, primates and all other prelates of the churches are bound personally, if not lawfully hindered [*legitime impediti*], to preach the holy Gospel of Jesus Christ." The Decree goes on to make explicit what the preachers are to teach the people: "those things that are necessary for all to know in order to be saved, and by impressing upon them with briefness and plainness of speech [*cum brevitate et facilitate sermonis*] the vices that they must avoid and the virtues that they must cultivate, in order that they may escape eternal punishment and obtain the glory of heaven." J. J. Megivern, no. 271, pp. 183–184. See Sessio V, "Decretum secundum: super lectione et praedicatione," no. 9, in *Concil. oecum. decreta*, p. 669. It has recently been pointed out that the content of the preaching as stated by Trent is practically a paraphrase of the Franciscan Rule.

8. See the above note.

9. *Acta Sanctae Sedis* 26 (1893–94), pp. 269–292; see *Enchiridion Biblicum*, editio 2ª (Napoli: d'Auria, 1954), no. 87. For the English text see J. J. Megivern, who prints all three encyclicals *in toto*.

10. "Sic Divinae Litterae futuris Ecclesiae sacerdotibus fiant et propriae cuiusque vitae spiritualis fons purus atque perennis, et sacri concionandi muneris, quod suscepturi sunt, alimentum ac robur." Pius XII, "Divino Afflante Spiritu," *Acta Apostolicae Sedis* 35 (1943) 297–326; see *Enchiridion Biblicum*, no 567. See J. J. Megivern, no. 772, p. 339.

11. That the lectionary we have as a consequence is "more ample" and "more varied" is evident to anyone who remembers the wearying

dominance of Matthew and the constricted segments of the Old Testament that made up the old scriptural selections in the liturgy. But, "suitability" being a highly arbitrary—not to say subjective—norm, the new lectionary, especially in its Old Testament parts, is less catholic and more "Marcionite" than it should be. This is all the more surprising in a Council whose aftermath saw such an increased awareness of the plight of "the poor." It is incomprehensible to see the strident advocates of the dispossessed so reluctant to let their cry be heard in the liturgy. It is highly doubtful whether those who would not admit, e.g., Psalms 35, 64, 70, or 75 to the liturgy, or so "expurgate" Psalms 109 and 137 as to render them inoffensive, can know who the "poor" truly are.

12. No. 35 in Austin P. Flannery, ed., *Documents of Vatican II* (Grand Rapids, MI: W. B. Eerdmans, 1975), p. 12.

13. No. 4; Flannery, p. 868.

14. No. 4; Flannery, pp. 869–870—emphasis added. The Decree goes on: "This is of paramount importance in the case of the liturgy of the word within the celebration of Mass where there is an inseparable union of the proclamation of the Lord's death and resurrection, the response of its hearers and the offering itself by which Christ confirmed the new covenant in his blood. In this offering the faithful share both by their sacrificial sentiments and by the reception of the sacraments."

15. No. 6; Flannery, p. 772—emphasis added.

16. The Bishops' Committee on Priestly Life and Ministry, *Fulfilled in Your Hearing: The Homily in the Sunday Assembly* (Washington, D.C.: U. S. Catholic Conference, 1982), p. 1.

17. No. 24; Flannery, p. 764—emphasis added.

18. The statement is based on the "Loci S. Scripturae" in *Conciliorum oecumenicorum decreta,* where for Matthew 28:18–20 there are nineteen references listed as compared to the eleven for Matthew 16:18–19.

19. *Lumen Gentium,* no. 24; Flannery, p. 378.

20. *Lumen Gentium,* no. 25; Flannery, p. 379. The Constitution refers here to the Council of Trent, Session V (17 June 1546; see above note 7) and Session XXIV (11 November 1563), which is the "Decretum de reformatione." The Vatican II footnote can be misleading on this point.

21. *Lumen Gentium,* no. 28; Flannery, p. 384.

22. *Inter Mirifica,* no. 3; Flannery, p. 284.

23. Declaration on the Relation of the Church to Non-Christian Religions (*Nostra Aetate* of 28 October 1965), no. 4; Flannery, p. 742.

24. See note No. 7 above.

Lucien Richard, O.M.I.

MISSION AND INCULTURATION: THE CHURCH IN THE WORLD

It is now twenty years since the close of the Council and ten years since Paul VI issued his apostolic exhortation on evangelization in the modern world, *Evangelii Nuntiandi*. This period in the Church's history brought about radical change in Roman Catholic mission theology and practice.[1] This change is felt most fully in Paul VI's surprisingly radical language in which he identifies the scope of evangelization with the transformation of humanity.

> It is a question not only of preaching the Gospel in ever wider geographic areas or to ever greater numbers of people (a preoccupation of evangelism) but also of affecting and as it were upsetting, through the power of the Gospel, humankind's criteria of judgment, determining values, points of interest, lines of thought, sources of inspiration and models of life, which are in contrast with the word of God and the plan of salvation.[2]

For Paul VI, evangelization has to do with culture: the Church's mission is to evangelize culture. "What matters is to evangelize human culture and cultures. . . ."[3] This approach to evangelization has led to a new vocabulary in mission theology such as enculturation, acculturation and inculturation. This perspective on the Church's mission has also sharpened the fundamental debate present in the major texts of Vatican II on the relation between evangelization and humanization, a debate which is basically about the nature of the religious and the secular.

The question of culture was of major importance for Vatican II. Since it is the total man/woman who is addressed by the Church and since culture is an essential dimension of the human, the encounter

between the Church and modern culture was at the heart of the debates at the Council. The Council understands culture in a broad sense
as the activity by which men and women, acting on and transforming
the world, transform themselves. Culture as such is an essential feature
of human existence. "It is one of the properties of the human person
that he can achieve true and full humanity only by means of culture,
that is, through the cultivation of the goods and values of nature.
Whenever, therefore, there is a question of human life, nature and
culture are intimately linked together."[4] But since context and history
are also essential features of human existence, culture is not mono-
lithic; there is not one single culture, but a variety of cultures.

As a process of human activity, culture expresses what humanity
can create and simultaneously be created by. Man/woman the author
of culture becomes a synonym for man/woman capable of transforming this world and bringing about a new and better future. *Gaudium et
Spes* has a very strong and optimistic sense of this capacity. "We are
witnessing, then, the birth of a new humanism where man is defined
before all else by his responsibility to his brothers and at the court of
history."[5] Because of the very nature of culture, there is an urgency
on the part of the Church to be concerned with culture, for culture
and Church mutually require one another. Culture can only find fulfillment when it is open to becoming Church, and Church needs culture as a point of insertion.[6]

The question of inculturation underlines the importance and
power of culture. Robert Schreiter writes about culture as represent-
ing "a way of life for a given time and place, replete with values, symbols, and meanings reaching out with hopes and dreams often
struggling with values for a better world."[7] According to Clifford
Geertz, culture "denotes an historically transmitted pattern of meanings embodied in symbols, a system of inherited conceptions expressed
by means of which men communicate, perpetuate, and develop their
knowledge about and attitudes toward life."[8]

Culture is the result of human interaction. It is the basic context
of all human creative activity and simultaneously the product of this
activity. Culture therefore distinguishes groups from one another; it
establishes the way such groups understand and construe the more
fundamental dimensions of their lives. Culture establishes the primary
dynamic of insider/outsider. It is always contemporary, a present process continually in the making yet always anchored in the past. Cultural
systems shape people by means of processes that result in support,
maintenance, communication and social control. All this indicates the
relevance of culture to the Church's own mission. According to

Thomas Clarke "What makes the evangelization of culture and cultures crucial to the Church's mission of peace and justice is the power and energy that reside there. All the greater for being hidden—as the wellspring of the most powerful resources of persons, groups, and peoples."[9]

THE CHURCH'S MISSION TO THE WORLD

On the question of mission it is essential not to isolate *Lumen Gentium* from *Gaudium et Spes*. *Lumen Gentium* is centered on the internal structure of the Church; it focuses on the nature of the Church. *Gaudium et Spes* presents the Church not as standing outside the world but as listening to the world from within the world. The Church is not considered primarily in itself but in its life and action in the world. In *Lumen Gentium* the Church is perceived as a sacrament of salvation; its primary function, its essential mission toward the world, is to convert it to the Gospel: the world needs to become the Church. In *Gaudium et Spes* the Church's mission includes active engagement to enhance human dignity and to achieve just societies. It fulfills such a mission while respecting the autonomy of earthly realities. Clearly then the concepts of mission in *Lumen Gentium* and in *Gaudium et Spes* are not exactly the same: one focuses on the Church as sacrament of salvation; the other sees the Church as an agent involved in and with the world. Yet nothing is said about the relation which must be established between these two activities. Yet this relation has to be very close. In the realization of the total mission of the Church, working for welfare or humankind and preaching the Gospel are not easily separable. The tendency present in some Vatican II documents is to emphasize one over the other, to assign the preaching of the Gospel to the ordained and the welfare of humankind to the laity. Yet the reason given in *Gaudium et Spes* for the Church's concern for human realities leaves no space for separation or dichotomy in its mission.

The basis of the relation of the Church to the world according to *Gaudium et Spes* is humanity itself, for it is for humanity that Christianity exists. The preface of the Constitution declares: "It is man himself who must be saved; it is mankind that must be renewed. It is man therefore, who is the key to this discussion, man considered whole and entire with body and soul, heart and conscience, mind and will."[10] Chapter IV of *Lumen Gentium* repeats with greater emphasis what it had already stated in the preface.

All we have said up to now about the dignity of the human
person, the community of mankind, and the deep significance of human activity provides a basis for discussing the relationship between the Church and the world and the
dialogue between them. The Council now intends to consider
the presence of the Church in the world, and its life and activity there, in the light of what it has already declared about
the mystery of the Church.[11]

The Church here is the people of God, a social body in the midst
of the world, which owes its origin to the person of Jesus Christ and
from whom it has received a mission for the world within the world.
The world in question is the totality of humanity's activities perceived
as having their own intrinsic values. The Church's concern and mission is to work for and somehow assure the success of the human future. While the Church's concern is directly related to the same earthly
realities with which all humanistic movements are concerned, the
Church perceives a transcendent depth to such realities and is conscious of the power of sin. Both transcendence and sin are located in
the midst of the human, and while humanity created in the image of
God proves to be religious, so does religion prove to be human. In its
mission to the world, the Church does not attempt to reduce this world
to a simple means for an otherworldly end.[12]
    If there is to be any valid meaning to the expression "other-
worldly," this must be understood as the eschatological dimension of
human reality—and while the eschatological is totally from the salvific
love of God, expressed and manifested in Jesus Christ and operative
through the presence and action of the Holy Spirit, it is not foreign to
human reality, unrelated to creation, external to earthly realities. The
eschatological dimension of human existence leaves no place for contempt of the world; the eschatological gives meaning and ultimate integrity to the human and earthly realm. In its mission to "sanctify" and
"consecrate" the world the Church does not take over the world or
eliminate its autonomy; it respects its otherness. In this respect everything can be sacred for the Church; the only profane reality is sinfulness.
    Gaudium et Spes sees this approach to earthly realities and human
destiny as revealed in the person of Jesus. It presents Christ as the re-
vealer of the truth about humanity and humanization.[13] And while the
Constitution does not develop or emphasize the connection between
its Christology and its affirmation of the Church's relation to the

world, there is nevertheless a strong Christological understanding of the human nature.

Jesus Christ is presented as the true answer to the question of being human. This Christological emphasis leads necessarily to some fundamental question relative to non-Christians. How necessary is it to know Christ in order to know what it means to be human? Is there any difference in being human as human, and being human as Christ is human? Does the position taken by the Council not lead to some form of sectarianism which divides humankind into those who "know" Christ and those who do not? Or does it lead to a collapse of Christology into anthropology? These questions are not answered by the Constitution or by Vatican II, and yet they are quite crucial for any understanding of the full implications of the Church's mission to the world. The situation becomes more acute as *Lumen Gentium* emphasizes the role of the Church relative to cultures.

THE CHURCH AND THE TRANSFORMATION OF CULTURES

While *Gaudium et Spes* perceives the Church as being of the world, the emphasis is on the Church for the world. The Church claims for itself a culturally redemptive presence.

> The good news of Christ continually renews the life and culture of fallen man; it combats and removes the error and evil which flow from the ever-present attraction of sin. It never ceases to purify and elevate the morality of peoples. It takes the spiritual qualities and endowments of every age and nation, and with supernatural riches it causes them to blossom, as it were, from within; it fortifies, completes and restores them in Christ. In this way the Church carries out its mission and in that very act it stimulates and advances human and civil culture, as well as contributing by its activity, including liturgical activity, to man's interior freedom.[14]

The Church's transformative insertion into cultures is similar and analogous to the mystery of incarnation in which the Divine Logos accommodated itself to human reality and necessity.

> In his self-revelation to his people culminating in the fullness of manifestation in his incarnate Son, God spoke according to the culture proper to each age. Similarly the Church has

existed through the centuries in varying circumstances and
has utilized the resources of different cultures in its preaching to spread and explain the message of Christ, to examine
and understand it more deeply, and to express it more per-
fectly in the liturgy and in various aspects of the life of the
faithful.[15]

This insertion of the Church into various cultural frameworks can
have different results depending on the purpose. If the immediate intention of such insertion is conversion, the result will be the emergence
of a local church.

The seed which is the word of God grows out of good soil
watered by the divine dew; it absorbs moisture, transforms
it, and makes it part of itself, so that eventually it bears
much fruit. So too indeed, just as happened in the economy of the incarnation, the young churches, which are
rooted in Christ and built on the foundations of the apostles, take over all the riches of the nations which have been
given to Christ as an inheritance (cf. Ps 2:8). They borrow
from the customs, traditions, wisdom, teaching, arts and
sciences of their people everything which could be used to
praise the glory of the Creator, manifest the grace of the
Savior, or contribute to the right ordering of Christian
life.[16]

The concept of local church is also intrinsically related to the
Church's transformative encounter with different cultures when the
immediate purpose of the Church's insertion in culture is not immediate conversion. The encounter with cultures in this case is more
directly concerned with the manifestation of the truly human as revealed in the person of Jesus Christ. "In manifesting Christ, the
Church reveals to men their true situation and calling."[17] Relative
to this second purpose, the language used by the Council continues
to view the Church's mission as separate from the world in which
we live, above the fray of the day to day struggle to create a more
human world. Within this perspective the world's mission is separate
("Christ did not bequeath to the Church a mission in the political,
economic, or social order: the purpose he assigned to it was a religious one"[18]) although the world needs the Church to complete its
own task. The insertion of the Church in world culture takes on the

characteristics of a prophetic mission. The Church "is to be leaven and as it were the soul of human society";[19] the Church's role is "to encourage the employment of human talents in the service of God and man."[20]

Although some of the language of *Gaudium et Spes* emphasizes the Church as being *of* this world, when the same Constitution speaks of the Church as being *for* the world, when it speaks of the Church's mission *to* the world, it sees the Church as separate. "By its nature and mission the Church is universal in that it is not committed to any one culture or to any political, economic, or social system."[21] This text resurfaces the fundamental question about the Church's "incarnation" in the world: Can one be truly "incarnated" yet not committed to a particular historical or social reality? The question is basically that of the relation of the universal to the particular, the historical and the contextual. The task of harmonizing the full embodiment of what is perceived as the transcendent message of the Gospel in a particular culture is a difficult one and clearly, while sensing the problem, Vatican II was unable to realize it.

Gaudium et Spes senses that there is a new situation that demands the proclamation of the Gospel in a new way, yet the use of an older language emphasizes the dichotomy of the earthly/heavenly realms, and therefore falls short of really incarnating the Gospel in the human context. Somehow only through the mission of the laity is the Church fully incarnated in the world; but as such the laity is considered as having a secondary role in the mission of the Church. The laity seeks the kingdom of God by directing temporal affairs according to God's will, thus fulfilling a special vocation in which they make the Church "present and fruitful in the places and circumstances where it is only through them that she can become the salt of the earth."[22]

The Church does not emerge at Vatican II as knowing how to be "faithful to its tradition" and at the same time coming to terms with its "universal mission." It appears to be too conscious of the transcendence of its message, and not enough of the limitations of the medium of communication. As A. Dondeyne correctly affirms, "To say that Christianity is a saving message which comes from God does not mean that Christianity is a magic power which acts upon humanity by force from outside. Message means speech (logos) and speech means culture. All genuine speech by which reality is brought forth and made public and thus becomes truth, which makes humanity free, is a cultural event."[23]

INCULTURATION, DEVELOPMENT AND LIBERATION:
THE POST-VATICAN II YEARS

The decade following Vatican II witnessed a crucial debate on the nature of the Church's mission to the world. A good deal of the debate centered on the question of the Church's attitude toward and action for the poor. In that debate the concept of "development" emerged, a concept which posed in a different way the question of the Church's involvement and embodiment. Poverty is presented as a problem to be solved by "development." While this approach to the situation of poverty proved to be inadequate, it provided a basis for what took place in the Latin American Church. According to Donal Dorr, "It was *Gaudium et Spes* that provided the foundation on which was built, three years later at Medellín, the Latin American Church's formal commitment to taking 'an option for the poor.' "[24] In the Latin American situation what was at stake was the Church's commitment to its values, to its sacramental and prophetic mission. The Church's action or lack of action, her commitment or lack of commitment to a particular situation of injustice, becomes in light of her teaching a test of credibility. At Medellín the Latin American bishops insisted on the need for "a poor Church," a Church in solidarity with the poor, committed to their liberation. In a situation of poverty and harshness such as in Latin America, the Church could not remain content above the fray with a universal message about justice, but had to choose sides and be involved in particular situations. The Church was faced with the urgency of taking a stand; it could no longer take refuge in vagueness or generalities. The move from seeing the situation of poverty in Latin America as one not simply of a lack of development but of liberation implied the centrality of political action; there was a shift from economics to politics, and therefore to the particular. This move is evident in Paul VI's *Octogesima Adveniens* and, according to several authors, indicates a radical departure from previous Church pronouncements.[25] According to Donal Dorr this shift in the Church's approach has implications for the teaching role of the magisterium, for theological method, and fundamentally for the Church's mission to the world. "As a moral teacher the Pope cannot hope to be familiar with situations all over the world; so he must respect the discernment done at local or regional level as regards theological method; Paul VI is far more willing than earlier Popes to adopt an inductive approach; that means accepting that if one is to discover universal principles about social morality one must start from the variety of cultural and geographical situations in which issues arise."[26] The necessity for concreteness and realism demanded of an authentic insertion of the Church in the real world is also evident in the documents of the synod of bishops which took place in Rome in 1971. Again according to Dorr, "A genuine attempt is made to begin from the real situation in the world, in order to discern there 'the signs of the times,' the specific ways in which God is speaking to today's world and calling people to respond."[27] In its document "Justice in the World," the synod affirms: "While the Church is bound to give witness to justice, she recognizes that anyone who ventures to speak to people about justice must first be just in their eyes. Hence we must undertake an examination of the modes of acting and of the possessions and lifestyle found within the Church herself."[28]

For the Church to be present to a "world of poverty" more than development was needed. Because of its sacramental and prophetic nature, the Church had to address the situation of structural injustice and the need for liberation as part of a process of transformation.

PAUL VI AND THE EVANGELIZATION OF CULTURES

Paul VI's apostolic exhortation *Evangelii Nuntiandi* aimed at making "the Church of the twentieth century better fitted for proclaiming the Gospel to the people of the twentieth century."[29] The document begins its reflections with three questions that had been centerpieces for the discussion at the synod:

1. In our day, what has happened to that hidden energy of the good news, which is able to have a powerful effect in man's conscience?

2. To what extent and in what way is the evangelical force capable of really transforming the people of this century?

3. What methods should be followed in order that the power of the Gospel may have its effect?[30]

These three questions are concerned with the ineffectiveness of the Gospel's engagement with the world. According to the exhortation, the principal cause of this ineffectiveness is the persistent temptation to perceive evangelization in fragmentary ways. The dynamic of evangelization is a rich and complex one. It includes proclamation; it penetrates all strata of society[31] and permeates cultures.[32] Paul VI relates the Church's mission of evangelization to everyone: to the de-Christianized, to those of other religions, to non-believers, even to all Christians. He also links evangelization to the struggle for a just society, for if evangelization "did not take account of the unceasing interplay of the Gospel and of man's concrete life, both personal and social," it would be incomplete.[33] Although evangelical liberation "cannot be contained in the . . . restricted dimension of economics, politics, social or cultural life, it must envisage the whole man in all his aspects, including . . . openness to . . . the Divine Absolute."[34] And while the Pope considers the Church's role in the liberating of oppressed people as essentially linked and part of evangelization, the two are never identified "because she knows . . . that all temporal liberation . . . carries within itself the germ of its own negation . . . whenever its final goal is not salvation."[35] While liberation can easily be restricted to just one area of human life, evangelical liberation offered by the Gospel engages the whole person and demands not only structural changes but also attitudinal changes. This understanding of evangelization establishes the proper interpretative context for the Pope's affirmation of the need to evangelize culture. To evangelize culture is to bring about "a conversion of the hearts and minds of those who live under these systems (i.e., of oppression) and of those who have control of the systems."[36] To evangelize "means affecting the standards by which people make judgments, their prevailing values, their interests and thought patterns, the things that move them to action and their models of human living."[37]

When the Pope affirms that "it is necessary to evangelize and to permeate with the Gospel, human culture and cultures," what is being affirmed as human liberation must touch not only political and social structures but the mind and the heart. Culture is understood as referring to the common understanding and valuing of a specific group of people, although such shared understanding may cut across various groups. Culture in this sense is made up of patterns or structures of perceiving and valuing and is handed down from generation to generation in traditions.

By affirming that human liberation implies more than changing political and social structures and is concerned essentially with the conversion of the mind and the heart, Paul VI is not advocating individualism or private morality. By emphasizing the importance of culture as D. Dorr points out, Paul VI is affirming "that perhaps the most important structures in our world are our patterns of thinking and feeling and valuing. These are deeply personal; yet in many respects they transcend the individual."[38] A change in culture should lead to a change in valuing which may lead in turn to changes in political and social structures.

The most dangerous oppression is that of the mind and the heart by cultural structures, an oppression which finds expression in social, political, and economic structures of society. The Pope advocates the liberation from such an oppression but he does not develop the relation between culture and political, social, and economic structures, or indicate how oppression in the former feeds into the latter and vice versa. A certain imbalance favors the cultural liberation over structural change, while in fact the two are intrinsically linked.

In its mission to evangelize cultures the Church is in possession of the Gospel which belongs to no specific cultures and which, while in need of being embodied in different traditions, can never be fully incarnated in any specific one. While the Gospel is compatible with all cultures, it poses a challenge to every culture and demands *metanoia*, conversion. Evangelization means the intimate transformation of authentic cultural values through their integration in Christianity in a process of "inculturation." In an address to the African bishops assembled in Kampala, Uganda in 1969, Paul VI describes this process.

> The expression, that is, the language and mode of manifesting this one Faith, may be manifold; hence, it may be original, suited to the tongue, the style, the genius, and the culture, of the one who professes this one Faith. From this point of view, a certain pluralism is not only legitimate, but desirable. An adaptation of the Christian life in the fields of pastoral, ritual, didactic and spiritual activities is not only possible, it is even favored by the Church. The liturgical renewal is a living example of this. And in this sense you may, and you must, have an African Christianity. Indeed, you possess human values and characteristic forms of culture which can rise up to perfection such as to find in Christianity, and for Christianity, a true superior fullness, and prove to be capable of a richness of expression all its own, and genuinely African. This may take time. It will require that your African soul become imbued to its depths with the secret charisms of Christianity, so that these charisms may then overflow freely, in beauty and wisdom, in the true African manner.[39]

What the Pope is advocating here is the Africanization of Christianity and not the Christianization of Africa. Evangelization as "inculturation" leads to the emergence of local churches.

EVANGELIZATION AND CONTEXTUALIZATION

From Paul VI's understanding of the mission of the Church as evangelizing cultures comes an emphasis on the need for contextualization. The Latin American bishops, meeting at Puebla, spelled out that process in a language that is in continuity with Vatican II and Paul VI. They begin by noting that "the Church has been acquiring an increasingly clear and deep realization that evangelization is its fundamental mission and that it cannot possibly carry out this mission without an on-going effort to know the real situation, adapting the Gospel message for today's man in a dynamic, attractive, and convincing way."[40]

The starting point then for a reflection on mission is a reading of the signs of the times that yields an awareness of the aspirations of a people involved in an on-going struggle for justice. The very real cries of the poor and oppressed can be neither ignored nor diluted by a purely spiritual mission. The Church is forced to reflect upon new ways of evangelization, since the Church's pastoral work faces a great challenge "in trying to help human beings move from less human to more human conditions."[41]

From the Puebla document, it is clear that the Church is not the primary agent of humanization. Its activities in the area of human promotion entail "those things that help arouse human awareness in every dimension . . . making men themselves the active protagonists of their own human and Christian development."[42] The bishops add that the Church "*educates* people in living together, *gives impetus* to organization, and *fosters* Christian sharing of goods."[43] The Church, through its efforts of evangelization, is a kind of *pre-humanizer, enabling* men and women to be active agents in their own integral liberation. The role of the Church is to train and educate free men and women capable of forging history, just as Jesus forged history.[44] According to the Latin American bishops, the most appropriate service of evangelization is the training and education of people that disposes them "to fulfill themselves as children of God, liberating themselves from injustice."[45]

The best way to fulfill this task of evangelization as education "is to proclaim clearly the mystery of the incarnation, leaving no room for doubt or equivocation, the divinity of Jesus Christ . . . and the full force of his human and historical dimension." It is the work " . . . of bearing witness to God, announcing the good news of Jesus Christ, engendering faith, leading people into the community, sending them out to actualize . . . " the Gospel message as protagonists of their own human history.[46]

In the preceding pages I have attempted to summarize the Church's recent understanding of its mission relative to the development and future of earthly realities. At Vatican II, the Church became more aware of the connection between the aspirations of the human community and its own mission to evangelize the world. More and more, especially in the Latin American Church, the Church appears as willing to identify itself with these aspirations. The consideration of these hopes, functioning as a concrete starting point, has enabled the Church to develop its mission in light of the concrete circumstances affecting this world, and has opened the door to the use of social analysis in the shaping of its mission. Contextualization has become for many in the Church an essential *mode* of acting, if not of being.

THE NATURE AND DIFFICULTIES OF INCULTURATION

The contextualization of the Church and of its message poses the question of the nature of its mission as inculturation.[47] Inculturation has been defined as "the process of a deep, sympathetic adaptation to and appropriation of a local cultural setting in which the Church finds itself in a way that does not compromise its basic faith in Christ."[48] While inculturation is a word which became current in circles concerned with evangelization only after 1975, yet the reality of inculturation has been with the Church from the very beginning: Paul addressed the Church in Rome, Corinth, etc. Over the centuries Christianity achieved a mutually fulfilling encounter with different cultures; it has penetrated them, found identity and concrete form in them. In fact the past success of inculturation is a problem for the Church today; the Church is seen as the Western Church and missionaries have often been considered as representatives of a Western mentality. In the breakdown of colonialism and the emergence of new nationalities, inculturation has become a major problem.[49]

So, the process of inculturation is problematic because of the nature of culture itself and of the Church. Culture has to do with values, ideas, customs. As such culture is transmitted and not freely chosen. We belong to our culture before it belongs to us; we are not culturally neutral beings. Culture is transmitted primarily by language and other symbolic media; as cultural beings we are shaped by such language and symbols. Our capacity to construe the world is affected by our cultural situation, and so is the experience of our potentialities and limitations. Societies protect their cultures by systems of rewards and punishments. Counter-cultural attitudes and behavior are threatening to societies as well as to one's own sense of reality and of belonging. Humans are involved in webs of significance that they themselves have spun. The personal world is the cultural world; culture is the womb in which personhood grows and is transformed and, in its turn, transforms. The personal world is cultivated within cultural forms.

One of the fundamental assumptions of this point of view is that human behavior is understandable only in terms of a dynamic social reference. Culture always exists as a web of dynamic social relations.[50] The inherited culture forms the individual's identity. Human identity is the result of a process of socialization. Socialization involves the process of being inserted into a social-cultural environment which in fact produces one's self-identity. That process of insertion demands the internalization of the society's self-understanding, self-image, and valuing. Thomas Groome, paraphrasing Herbert Mead, writes:

> Having externalized ourselves into culture and society, and culture and society having taken on a life of their own, the empowerments and limitations of that world are now taken back into our consciousness as our own. The possibilities and parameters that our social/cultural context appears to offer become our own perception of our possibilities and parameters. In other words, the objectified culture and society created by us and our predecessors become internalized as the basis of our own self-identity.[51]

The process of socialization determines the process of self-interpretation. Joseph Cahill explains that "in many instances this self-interpretation is really a misnomer since the interpretation is really done by others rather than by a genuinely autonomous or inner-directed self."[52]

In a real sense, there is nothing human—values, concepts, religious beliefs—that is not in some way socially determined. Yet this is not simple determinism. There is always place for individual dissent and change. Yet change is no easy process. One of the major obstacles to inculturation is the process of socialization which is an essential element of culture itself. The concerns of both inculturation and socialization lie always with the dimensions of individuation and that of social incorporation, the linking of symbol systems with social and behavioral structures.

Evangelization as inculturation is problematic not only because of the nature of culture, but also because a religious tradition does not escape the influence of culture. Christianity, according to Avery Dulles, is like a culture: " . . . it is a system of meanings, historically transmitted, embodied in symbols, and instilled into new members of the group so that they are inclined to think, judge, and act in charac-

teristic ways."[53] That Christianity is like a culture is made even clearer
when one realizes that culture is essentially tradition.

In Romans 10:13–15, Paul outlines the basic process that gov-
erns access to Christian existence: "Everyone who invokes the name
of the Lord will be saved." How could people invoke one in whom
they had no faith? And how could they have faith in one they had
never heard of? And how hear without someone to spread the news?
And how could someone spread the news without a commission to
do so? And that is what Paul affirms: "How welcome are the feet of
the messengers of good news!" Faith in Christ, and therefore Christian existence, is essentially ecclesial. It is as recipient of the Gospel
that the Church is Church. It is in connection with the Church that
later generations have access to the revelation of God in Jesus Christ.
Accepting Ernest Troeltsch's important insight, David Tracy claims:
"It is the tradition of the Church that *is* our central mediation to the
actual Jesus—the Jesus remembered by the Church; it is our present
experience of the mediated Christ-event which impels our belief in
Jesus Christ."[54]

The present experience of the Christ-event is mediated through
the tradition. Trust in the reality of the Christ-event as made present
to us implies essentially trust in the mediation itself.[55] The tradition is
an essential structure in the emergence of Christian existence and
identity. "We live in the Christ-event in and by the tradition, the community, the Church."[56]

Jesus Christ brought to life a movement, and it is through this
movement that we are confronted here and now with Jesus the Christ.
The movement which Jesus set afoot remains the medium for any approach to His meaning for us. "The only knowledge we possess of the
Christ-event reaches us via the concrete experience of the first local
communities of Christians who were sensitive of a new life present in
them."[57]

The Christ-event is mediated through the particular historical
form that is the Christian Church. The Church as tradition provides
for the organization of human experience as Christian. This systematic organization is a communal possession which provides stability
and an effective way of living for the believer. As Christians, individuals are socialized and constituted by the Christian tradition. It is the
Christian tradition which enables the individual to remember the past
Christ-event, celebrate its actual presence and anticipate its future fulfillment. The tradition plays an integrating role by uniting past, present, and future. The ecclesial communities are, therefore, in Ghislain
LaFont's words,

at once theological place and hermeneutical place. They are the former because if the conduct and the objectives which define a community are in conformity with the Gospel in a given situation they deliver by themselves something of the evangelical message which can be read and revealed only there. They are a hermeneutical place because the objective gift of faith is never perceived except from the angle from which each of the communities, in fact, receives and lives it.[58]

It becomes clearer as we focus on the cultural nature of Christianity and of Christian identity, why the Church's mission of evangelization as inculturation is problematic. In the process of inculturation two cultures encounter one another. The process of inculturation encounters the process of socialization. In any situation this is always problematic. It is more so when the Church claims, as we have already seen, to be supra-cultural and its mission as that of regenerating and inwardly renewing cultures. To invite people to enter a specific religious tradition is to ask them to reject other possible ways of interpreting and conducting a life both individually and socially. Christianity as a tradition serves the role of what David Tracy calls a "classic." Such a "classic" functions as "an expression of Christian meaning and value which initially stands over and against a person or whole culture, with the power to evoke fundamental questions about human existence and to place a person or culture before an ineluctable choice."[59]

CONCLUSION

We have already seen that in Vatican II evangelization is understood as modeled on the incarnation. What God has done in Jesus of Nazareth is paradigmatic for what the Church is sent to accomplish among the people of all times and places. The incarnation is considered as the origin and model of all authentic missionary work. The incarnation also appears in the Church's documents as the primary motivation and pattern for inculturation.[60] Yet there is clearly a danger in using the incarnation as a model for inculturation. The first danger arises out of the possibility of understanding the incarnation in a distorted way, in which the humanity of Jesus is no longer considered as fully human but as divinized.

The emphasis of the Council on pluriformity, freedom of conscience, respect for the values in non-Christian religions, and the availability of God's grace outside the visible Church was tempered by the dichotomy constantly implied between the earthly and heavenly realms. Behind some of this dichotomy, with implications for the process of inculturation as modeled on the incarnation, lies a somewhat triumphalistic understanding of the incarnation and therefore of the Church and its mission. The incarnation can be understood from a kenotic perspective as a descent into the authentic poverty of humankind. It involved the deliberate setting aside of any pretension to superiority. According to Jose Comblin:

> Jesus Christ addressed himself to the whole of the world, to each individual as a totality. He did not propose or live some parallel existence alongside the world; instead he embodied a way of acting in the world. His mission represents a way of living in this world that is designed to penetrate and transform everything. Christ plunged into the world to alter it by his mission. . . . Just as Christ does not stay on the sidelines of the outside world, so those who carry on his work are plunged into the world; instead they work to shape and transform it.[61]

But the main reason for hesitation in using the incarnation as a model is that the incarnation applies to the relation between the human and the divine, while inculturation applies to the passage of culture into culture. While we do believe that God is truly at work in the Church, it is the Church which must inculturate itself in ever new ways. Christian inculturation is not nor can it be the unceasing reincarnation of a nucleus of divine truths and realities as if they were taken out of history and abstractly isolated into a pure state and applied to always new historical cultural contexts. Inculturation does not move from a world of essences to history but *from history to history*, from Jerusalem to the ends of the earth.

The Church cannot be understood as a cultural entity standing apart from the cultural groups in the world, with which it has to enter into dialogue. Yet the Church, although historical in its origin, and particular in its nature, has a universal mission. It must reach out to the whole world in its diversity and in doing so must empty itself of ongoing historical accretions and cultural baggage, opening itself thus to ways of understanding and modes of expression that did not belong to it previously. To truly perform its mission the Church must be willing to reduce itself to what is truly essential. According to Karl Rahner, "The Church is changeable in all its structures to a far greater extent than people thought during the Pian epoch."[62] The world Church, envisioned by Rahner, demands a search for what is essential in Christianity.

Authentic inculturation demands on the part of the Church a willingness to dialogue with all cultures. Dialogue demands concern and hospitality toward the other, as well as respectful acceptance of the other's identity, modes of expression and values. True dialogue does not invade; it does not manipulate, for dialogical manipulation is a contradiction in terms. Dialogue achieves a communion of horizons which leads to mutual self-disclosure and self-understanding. The task of the Church in the coming decades is to be faithful to its mission of preaching the Christ-event in such a way as to transform and penetrate the various existing cultures but to do so in such a manner as to be opened itself to transformation. The nature of the Church is in the making. We do not yet know what it is to be.

NOTES

1. Cf. E. Dunn. *Missionary Theology. Foundations in Development* (Lanham, Maryland: University of America, 1980).
2. Apostolic Exhortation *Evangelii Nuntiandi,* Eng. trans., United States Catholic Conference (1976), No. 19, p. 16.
3. Ibid., No. 20, p. 16.
4. G.S. No. 53, p. 958.
5. G.S. No. 55, p. 960.
6. Cf. No. 57, p. 962.
7. R. J. Schreiter. *Constructing Local Theologies,* (Maryknoll: Orbis Press, 1985) 21.
8. Clifford Geertz. *The Interpretation of Cultures* (London: Hutchinson, 1973) 89.
9. T. Clarke. "To Make Peace Evangelize Culture," *America* 150/21 (1984) 415.
10. All references to Vatican II documents are from Austin P. Flannery, ed., *Documents of Vatican II* (Grand Rapids, Michigan: Eerdmans, 1984) G.S. No. 3, p. 904.
11. G.S. No. 40, p. 939.
12. Cf. G.S. No. 36, p. 935.
13. Cf. G.S. No. 10, 22, 38.
14. No. 58, p. 963.
15. No. 58, p. 962; cf. also A.G. No. 10, pp. 824–25.
16. A.G. No. 22, p. 839.

17. A.G. No. 8, p. 822.
18. G.S. No. 42, p. 942.
19. G.S. No. 40, p. 940.
20. G.S. No. 41, p. 941.
21. G.S. No. 42, p. 942.
22. L.G. No. 33, p. 390.
23. Quoted in Roberto Tucci, "The Proper Development of Culture," *Commentary on the Documents of Vatican II*, H. Vorgrimler, ed., Vol. V (N.Y.: Herder and Herder, 1968) 278.
24. Donal Dorr, *Option for the Poor* (Maryknoll: Orbis Press, 1983) 138.
25. Cf. Marie Dominique Chenu, *La Doctrine Sociale de L'Eglise Comme Idéologie* (Paris: Cerf, 1979).
26. D. Dorr, *Option for the Poor*, op. cit., 169.
27. Ibid., 178.
28. *Justice in the World* (Vatican Press, 197) 40.
29. Apostolic Exhortation *Evangelii Nuntiandi*, Eng. trans. op. cit., 6.
30. No. 4, p. 7.
31. Cf. No. 18, pp. 15–16.
32. Cf. No. 20, pp. 16–17.
33. No. 29, p. 22.
34. No. 33, p. 24.
35. No. 35, pp. 24–25.
36. No. 36, p. 25.
37. No. 19, p. 16.
38. Donal Dorr, *Option for the Poor*, op. cit., 202.
39. Quoted in Robert J. Schreiter. *Constructing Local Theologies*, op. cit., 11.
40. Third General Conference of Latin American Bishops: *Evangelization at Present and in the Future of Latin America: Conclusions* (official English edition) (Middlegreen and London: St. Paul Publications, 1980), No. 85.
41. Puebla, No. 90.
42. Puebla, No. 477.
43. Ibid.
44. Puebla, No. 279.
45. Puebla, No. 1145.
46. Puebla, Nos. 356–360.
47. On inculturation see the following:
A. Dulles. "The Emerging World Church: A Theological Reflection," in *CTSA*, Vol. 39 (1984) 1–12.

W. Reiser. "Inculturation and Doctrinal Development," *Heythrop Journal* 22 (1981) 135–48.

A. Roest Crollius. "What Is So New About Inculturation?" *Gregorianum* 59 (1978) 721–38.

Marcello Azevedo. *Inculturation and the Challenges of Modernity* (Rome: Pont. Biblical Inst. and Pont. Gregorian Univ. Press, 1982).

Y. Congar. "Christianity as Faith and Culture," *East Asian Pastoral Review* 18/3 (1981) 304–319.

B. Lonergan. "Revolution in Catholic Theology," *A Second Collection* (Philadelphia: Westminster, 1974) 233.

48. William Reiser. "Inculturation and Doctrinal Development," *Heythrop Journal* 22 (1981) 135.

49. Ibid.

50. Edmund Sullivan. *A Critical Psychology: Interpretation of the Personal World* (N.Y.: Plenum Press, 1984) 25.

51. Thomas Groome. *Christian Religious Education* (San Francisco: Harper & Row, 1980) 112.

52. Joseph Cahill. *Mended Speech: The Crisis of Religious Studies and Theology* (N.Y.: Crossroad, 1982) 154.

53. Avery Dulles. "The Emerging World Church: A Theological Reflection," *CTSA*, Vol. 39 (1984) 6.

54. David Tracy. *The Analogical Imagination* (N.Y.: Crossroad, 1981) 323.

55. Ibid.

56. Ibid.

57. Edward Schillebeeckx. *Jesus: An Experiment in Christology* (N.Y.: Crossroad, 1979) 47.

58. Ghislain LaFont. "Monastic Life and Theological Studies," *Monastic Studies* 12 (1976) 4.

59. Joseph Komonchak, "The Ecclesial and Cultural Roles of Theology," *CTSA* Vol. 40 (1985) p. 31.

60. Cf. L.G. No. 13.

61. Jose Comblin, *The Meaning of Mission* (Maryknoll, New York: Orbis Books, 1984) 11.

62. K. Rahner, "Structural Change in the Church of the Future," *Theological Investigations* Vol. 20 (N.Y.: Crossroad, 1981) p. 118.

David Hollenbach, S.J.

THE CHURCH'S SOCIAL MISSION IN A PLURALISTIC SOCIETY

The involvement of the Roman Catholic Church in social and political affairs has been undergoing a qualitative transformation since the close of the Second Vatican Council. The fact of such involvement is nothing new. For example, the special place granted the Church in the Roman Empire by Constantine, the investiture controversy of the Middle Ages, and the history of the Papal States all show that the Church has not been a stranger to the world of politics in the past. Similarly the Church has long been deeply involved in responding to pressing social ills through direct Christian service. Hospitals, orphanages, schools, and efforts to aid the poor have historically been part of the Church's understanding of its own mission. Since the Council, however, the mode of the Church's engagement in social and political life has entered a distinctive new phase whose contours are still in the process of taking shape.

The thesis of this essay is that the Council launched this new phase through its recognition that the context for Christian social ministry is an inherently pluralistic world. The reality of religious, ideological, and cultural diversity was taken with great seriousness by the Council, particularly in the two most important conciliar documents dealing with the social role of the church: the Pastoral Constitution on the Church in the Modern World and the Declaration on Religious Liberty.

The consequences of this new acknowledgement of pluralism have been multiple. First, it has pressed the Church to a deeper reflection on how its social mission is rooted in the core of Christian faith and identity. Second, it has opened new questions about how to pursue this mission while also respecting the religious freedom of those who do not share the Church's faith and tradition. These two issues will be the focus here. Other consequences of the new recognition of the pluralistic context for social mission are of equal importance. For example, this context calls for careful discernment of the relation between the Christian vision of society and contemporary political ideologies and careful reflection on how the universal mission of the Church is to be embodied in the particular circumstances of the diverse nations and cultures of the globe. It is hoped that the importance of the two questions discussed will justify the omission of these other matters that remain crucial in post-conciliar discussion of the social mission of the church.

I
SOCIAL MISSION AND THE IDENTITY OF THE CHURCH

J. Bryan Hehir, an astute interpreter and practitioner of the Church's social ministry, has argued that "the decisive contribution of Vatican II was to provide a description of the Church's role in the world which was properly theological and ecclesial in tone and substance."[1] Hehir's point is evident if one compares *Gaudium et Spes* and subsequent post-conciliar social teachings with the social encyclicals issued by the Popes from Leo XIII to John XXIII. These earlier social teachings were almost exclusively framed in concepts and language of the natural law ethic of Scholastic philosophy. One searches in vain the writings of the Popes during the hundred years before the Council for careful consideration of the biblical, Christological, eschatological or ecclesiological basis of the Church's social role.

There were several reasons for the pre-conciliar social encyclicals' almost exclusive reliance on philosophical rather than biblical and theological categories. This emphasis is in line with the Catholic tradition's high estimate of the power of human reason to discover the broad outlines of God's design for social life through reflection on human experience. This is the gist of the notion of natural law. At the same time the particular historical circumstances in which the Church found itself following the French Revolution and the Enlightenment gave this appeal to reason and natural law a markedly defensive tone. The Enlightenment philosophers often appealed to the autonomy of human reason in a way that challenged the authority of the Church and in some cases religion itself. In response Vatican I (1869–70) strongly affirmed the full compatibility of faith and reason. In his 1879 encyclical, urging renewal of the study of Thomas Aquinas, Leo XIII added that Christian faith does not detract from the dignity of human reason but rather "adds greatly to its nobility, keenness and stability." Therefore those who follow St. Thomas in combining the guidance of faith with the use of reason "are philosophizing in the best possible way."[2]

This way of seeing the complementarity of faith and reason put the Church in a position to declare that anyone who rejected the Popes' conclusions about the proper ordering of society was not only unfaithful but also unreasonable. In addition, for this essentially apologetic strategy to be effective, it was necessary to avoid *direct* and *explicit* appeal to biblical and theological perspectives in proposing the Catholic vision of social life. In the words of Johann Baptist Metz, nineteenth and early twentieth century Catholic social teaching did not seek to *mediate* between faith and society but sought rather to *defend* Christian tradition against the corrosive currents of modernity. This defense "was carried on just in front of the fortress Church, on the territory of pure social ethics" (i.e., strictly natural law ethics).[3] The Catholic insistence on the complementarity of faith and reason thus ironically came to be interpreted in a way that saw them moving on two parallel tracks only extrinsically related to each other. It became difficult to give properly *theological* reasons for the social teaching of the Church or to give an account of how the deepest meaning of Christianity could speak directly to the problems of post-Enlightenment society.

During the decades immediately prior to the Council, it became increasingly clear that this solution to the problem of the relation of the Church and the modern world was both historically anachronistic and theologically unsatisfactory. On the historical level, the early social encyclicals had Western Europe implicitly in mind as the "world" to which the Church's mission was to be directed. Further, they assumed that this world shared a unified intellectual heritage in which Christianity and culture had been harmoniously synthesized. Therefore new secular movements such as liberal democracy in the eighteenth century and socialisms of various stripes in the nineteenth century were regarded not only as betrayals of faith but as cultural heresies as well.

This reading of the historical context of the Church's mission is no longer accurate in the twentieth century (if it ever was fully accurate). Differences of class, race, economic status, and political tradition have made the West a far from unified society with a harmoniously integrated culture. When one views the Church's social mission in its full global scope this anachronism is even more evident. Cultural pluralism and social conflict are more adequate descriptions of the context of the Church's social mission than the organic model of society assumed by neo-Scholasticism. The Council clearly recognized this:

There is on the one hand a lively feeling of unity and of compelling solidarity of mutual dependence, and on the other a
lamentable cleavage of bitterly opposing camps. We have not
yet seen the last of bitter political, social, and economic hostility, and racial and ideological antagonism, nor are we free
from the spectre of a war of total destruction. If there is a
growing exchange of ideas, still there is widespread disagreement about the meaning of the words expressing our key concepts.[4]

In addition the Council was also cognizant of the methodological specialization of modern intellectual life and the fact that this has led to
competing conceptions of the human person.

The realities of modern social conflict and scientific specialization
have produced a kind of crisis of moral reason itself.[5] It has become
increasingly difficult to sustain the natural law tradition's robust confidence that intelligent exercise of reason by persons in different social
locations, from diverse cultures, and with differing intellectual back-
grounds will lead to identical conclusions about the way society should
be organized. Therefore if the Church is intent on making a contribution to debates about social, political, and economic life, it must state
forthrightly and publicly its own most basic convictions about the nature and destiny of human beings. It must respond to the most basic
questions about the meaning of human life in its social teaching as well
as in doctrinal theology. The Council highlighted a few of these questions:

What is man? What is the meaning of suffering, evil, death,
which have not been eliminated by all this progress? What is
the purpose of these achievements, purchased at so high a
price? What can man contribute to society? What can he expect from it? What happens after this earthly life?. . . What
measures are to be recommended for building up society today? What is the final meaning of man's activity in the universe?[6]

These are religious questions, demanding religious and theological
answers.

During the decades preceding the Council, Catholic theologians
had been at work seeking to respond to these perennial questions in
ways that spoke to the context of modern pluralism and skepticism.
Far from abandoning the Catholic conviction about the complemen-

tarity of faith and reason, however, these theologians sought to appropriate the meaning of this complementarity more thoroughly. They sought to *mediate* the meaning of Christianity to a modern pluralistic and often conflictual society and to appropriate the positive values of this society into the life and thought of the Church. For example, thinkers such as John Henry Newman, Maurice Blondel, Pierre Teilhard de Chardin, and Karl Rahner (each in a different way) argued that God's grace is not *extrinsic* to human experience, understanding, society or culture. Grace is immanent within history, beckoning it to transformation and redemption. It was but a short step from this retrieval of a more authentic understanding of the relation of nature and grace to the conclusion that the response of Christians to grace in faith should have a transformative and redemptive impact on history, society and culture. In the years immediately preceding the Council important theologians began publishing books with titles such as *The Theology of Earthly Realities* (Gustav Thils), *Catholicism: A Study of Dogma in Relation to the Corporate Destiny of Mankind* (Henri de Lubac), and *The Theology of Work* (Marie-Dominique Chenu).[7] It had become clear, as Metz put it over a decade after the Council, that the task of expounding the theology of the Church's social mission "has to be carried on by using the very substance of the Christian faith."[8] The social mission is not a propaedeutic to or extension of the Church's real purpose but is integral or essential to this purpose.[9]

The first result of the Council's willingness to acknowledge the social and intellectual dividedness of the contemporary world, therefore, was to move the discussion of the Church's social mission to the level of fundamental affirmations about Christian identity. The "social question" became a properly theological question. From one perspective this is a surprising result, for willingness to acknowledge the pluralism of contemporary society is often regarded as the first step toward religious indifferentism. But at the Council the result was just the opposite. The Church's social mission was more tightly linked to the Bible, Christology, eschatology, ecclesiology, and other central doctrinal perspectives than at any time in recent centuries.

For example, *Gaudium et Spes* stated that the religious mission and identity of the Church is a "source of commitment, direction, and vigor to establish and consolidate the community of men according to the law of God."[10] More specifically the Council spelled out three dimensions of this social mission: the healing and elevation of the dignity of the human person, the building and consolidation of bonds of solidarity in society, and the endowment of daily human activity with a deeper meaning and worth.[11] The first three chapters of *Gaudium et*

Spes take up the themes of human dignity, human community, and the value of human activity in the world and develop them as the basis of the Church's social mission. These three chapters all contain explicitly theological discussions of why the matter at stake is a religious and not purely secular concern.

Thus human dignity is rooted in the creation of human persons in the image of God. Though *Gaudium et Spes* reaffirmed the natural law argument that human dignity is evident apart from faith in the intelligence, freedom and conscience possessed by all persons, it sought to make the direct links between these philosophical considerations and biblical and theological notion of the *imago Dei*. Also, in a passage that has become central in the writings of John Paul II, the Council went on to provide a Christological basis for the Church's defense of this dignity. "Christ the Lord, Christ the new Adam, in the very revelation of the mystery of the Father and of his love, fully reveals man to himself and brings to light his most high calling."[12] In defending and promoting human dignity, therefore, the Church is engaged in a properly religious task. Social mission is part of the religious mission of the Church.

In the same way, while the Council reaffirmed the traditional natural law argument that human beings are social by nature, it went on to specifically theological arguments for the Church's mission to build up the bonds of community and mutual interdependence among all people. This mission is founded on the command to love God and all one's neighbors. It reflects the Christian faith in God as a trinitarian unity of persons, which implies that personality is essentially relational. And social mission manifests the fact that God's saving grace draws persons into a communion of solidarity with each other, a communion that "must be constantly increased until that day when it is brought to fulfillment" in the kingdom of God.[13] The task of forging such bonds of reciprocal interdependence is not only intra-ecclesial but societal. The Church, the Council maintains, is a sacrament, a sign and instrument, of "communion with God and of unity among all men." Therefore the Church's effort to promote "progress toward unity, healthy socialization, and civil and economic cooperation . . . is in harmony with the deepest nature of the Church's mission."[14]

The Council also affirmed the religious significance of all human endeavor, however secular it might conventionally be regarded. Even daily labor, when it is properly ordered, can be regarded "as a prolongation of the work of the Creator . . . and a personal contribution to the fulfillment in history of the divine plan."[15] The fulfillment of this plan will only be accomplished by God's definitive act of establishing the kingdom and the creation of a new heaven and a new earth. This eschatological hope, however, does not decrease the importance of Christian engagement in the world. "Far from diminishing our concern to develop this earth, the expectancy of a new earth should spur us on, for it is here that the body of a new human family grows, foreshadowing in some way the age which is to come." In fact all struggles to build a more just and humane social order are a participation in the paschal mystery of Christ's death and resurrection and in the activity of the Holy Spirit in our world.[16]

These are but a few of the explicitly theological perspectives that the Council brought to bear in its reflections on the social mission of the Church in the world. They show that this social mission is a religious one that flows from the heart of Christian faith. They have been developed and refined in the post-conciliar teaching of the magisterium and in movements such as liberation and political theology. They represent the distinctive contributions that the Church seeks to bring to the debates about social existence in a world increasingly conscious of itself as divided and pluralistic.

II
SOCIAL MISSION AND RELIGIOUS LIBERTY

The movement of these religious and theological themes to the forefront of the Church's understanding of its social mission has had a powerful effect on the level of social engagement by numerous Catholic groups. Since the Council, the Catholic Church has become an increasingly vigorous actor in the affairs of the polis. Base communities in Brazil, men's and women's religious orders, lay persons and lay groups, bishops' conferences in various nations, and the Pope in his worldwide travels have all intensified their engagement in the task of promoting justice and peace out of explicitly religious motivation. But it is not only the motivation of this activity that is Christian; the basic goals and objectives of social action are religiously based as well. The Christian vision of the kingdom of God is the overarching perspective shaping the Church's public role in society on these various levels of activity. Here the reality of societal pluralism raises a second challenge that is forming the new mode of social mission since the Council. Just as the acknowledgement of the irreducible pluralism of contemporary society has caused a reexamination of social mission in theological terms, this same pluralism raises the question of how to distinguish social mission from religious imperialism or theological triumphalism.

The facts that the world is religiously diverse and that the Christian Church is itself internally divided are obvious. How, then, is the Catholic community to seek to influence the public life of a local community, a nation, or the global economic and political order without imposing its theological vision through brute power? The tension between a theologically rooted social mission and the respect due to the religious freedom of one's fellow citizens has moved front and center since the Council, sometimes in very concrete and painful conflicts.

There are two ways to avoid this tension, both of which would be unfaithful to the Council itself. The first is to give in to the pressure to keep religion a private matter having little or nothing to do with the affairs of the commonwealth. Though one need not accept the thesis that modern history has been a one-way movement toward an increasingly secularized society, it is undeniable that modern social conditions tend to privatize religion.[17] The Council called this tendency one of "the gravest errors of our time."[18] Belief that God is both Creator and Lord of all the universe is a direct challenge to such a domesticated or privatized definition of the Church's task.

A second, opposite, approach was also judged unacceptable by the Council, namely that which seeks to secure a privileged position for the Church in the public and political life of society. During the 1950s an intense debate took place among Catholic theologians about the Church-state question. In the nineteenth and first half of the twentieth century the papal approach to the Church-state issue was to advocate the establishment of Catholicism as the official religion of the realm wherever this was made practically possible through the presence of a Catholic majority. The Council rejected this approach, bringing about a major development of doctrine within the Catholic tradition. The way this development was effected is of continuing relevance for the effort to understand the Church's social mission. For though the Church-state issue was resolved at the Council in favor of religious liberty, the relation of the Church to a religiously pluralistic society continues to need clarification.

The participants in the 1950s' debate who continued to advocate a privileged political position for the Church had a rationale for their position. They argued that since Roman Catholicism in fact possesses the true vision of the nature and destiny of humanity and the cosmos, this vision ought to form the basis for the whole of social and cultural existence. On the theological level this approach is known as "integralism." It stresses the *unity* of religion, daily life, politics, the sciences, the economy, and the whole gamut of human endeavor. It manifests the deep Catholic instinct to see all things human as potential mediators of the divine presence and grace. On this level its argument is similar to the post-conciliar argument that the shaping of the social order in accord with the vision of the kingdom of God is "integral" to the preaching of the Gospel.[19]

This is a theologically healthy instinct. It can, however, become perverse when interpreted to mean that all knowledge can be reduced to theology or that all social institutions ought to be extensions of the Church. In the words of Karl Rahner, it can lead to a way of thinking that simply assumes that "human life can be unambiguously mapped out and manipulated in accord with certain universal principles proclaimed by the Church and watched over by her in the manner in which they are developed and applied."[20] The temptation to this way of thinking has not disappeared since the Council. It is as likely to be found among those on the political left as among those on the right. Indeed the fact that the Church's social mission has become more immediately grounded in biblical and theological perspectives since the Council may in fact intensify the temptation to move in this direction. In order to avoid this danger it is important to note how the Council sought to counter the privatization of Christian faith without falling into the ecclesiastical triumphalism of the integralist theology.

The Declaration on Religious Liberty unambiguously affirmed the right to religious freedom as a human and civil right. It defined the right this way: "Freedom of this kind means that all men should be immune from coercion on the part of individuals, social groups and every human power so that, within due limits, nobody is forced to act against his convictions nor is anyone to be restrained from acting in accordance with his convictions in religious matters in private or in public, alone or in association with others."[21] The two aspects of the right (non-coercion of religious belief and non-restraint of the exercise of belief) are analogous to the two religious clauses of the first amendment of the U.S. Constitution: non-establishment and free exercise.

The relative weight of the two clauses of the First Amendment has been and remains one of the most contentious points in U.S. jurisprudence. Broadly, the question is this: When does the free exercise of one person's religious freedom begin to restrict such freedom for others? A similar tension exists in the conciliar Declaration. For along with its strong defense of immunity from coercion in religious matters, the Council insisted that churches and other religious communities have a right to seek to influence public policy in ways that reflect their deepest convictions. In its words: "It comes within the meaning of religious freedom that religious bodies should not be prohibited from freely undertaking to show the special value of their doctrine in what concerns the organization of society and the inspiration of the whole of human activity."[22] In other words, the Council includes the right of the Church to engage in an active social mission and social ministry within its definition of religious freedom. This mission includes the effort to shape public policies, and these policies will necessarily affect the freedom and behavior of non-Catholics. Here the tension between social mission and religious freedom again comes into view.

If both privatism and integrism are to be avoided, this tension must be understood at a deeper level than either of these unacceptable alternatives attained. John Courtney Murray's extensive writings on the subject, which prepared the way for the conciliar Declaration, provide a route to such deeper understanding. Murray argued that affirmation of the right to religious liberty rests on a *complex* insight, an insight that has theological, political, moral and juridical dimensions.[23]

Theologically, religious liberty is necessary to protect and secure the freedom of the Church to pursue its mission. The response of human beings to God transcends the order of the political and cannot legitimately be brought under the control of the coercive powers of government. To do so would be to *subordinate* the Church to the state. This theological principle correlates with the *political* principle of the essentially limited nature of governmental power. Government is not omnicompetent, and least of all is it competent in matters religious. The denial of such limits on governmental power is the seed from which all totalitarianisms spring. Governmental power is *limited* by its obligation to protect and support the transcendent dignity of the human person. One aspect of this dignity is freedom in matters religious. *Juridically and ethically,* religious freedom rests on the insight that law has a moral function but does not have the task of enforcing *every* humanly beneficial activity or of coercively forbidding *every* moral evil. Its role is the more limited but nonetheless crucial one of ensuring the basic conditions of social existence: public peace, justice, and those aspects of public morality on which social consensus exists. These are moral tasks, but they are not the whole of morality. The pursuit of the *full* moral good belongs to other communities within society such as families, voluntary associations and churches. Their freedom to do so must be protected. The function of law, properly understood in its relation to morality, therefore, also supports the right to religious freedom.

In short, Murray argued that neither a purely theological, purely political, purely juridical, nor purely ethical form of reasoning would yield an adequate understanding of religious freedom. The same can be said of an adequate understanding of the Church's social mission.

Murray further maintained that the Council's approach to religious freedom was a synthesis of the four levels of analysis made possible by the historical experience of the Church in its engagement with the world. Synthesis by definition is not a deductive form of reasoning modeled after Euclidian geometry with its linear movement from axioms to corollaries to theorems, all summed up with a resounding *quod erat demonstrandum*. Synthetic reasoning proceeds by way of dialectic and analogy. It discovers correlations and similarities between different spheres of thinking and action. It depends on imagination, not simply the logic of ratiocination. It is therefore a persuasive rather than deductive enterprise, more like the rationality of classical rhetoric than logic or mathematics. And to be persuasive it must be rooted in experience, history, and culture. It is in fact a form of prudence or practical wisdom—a sense of the fitting.

This complex argument for the right to religious freedom can greatly illuminate the question of the way that the Church should pursue its social mission in a pluralistic world. Just as the affirmation of religious freedom depended on establishing a *correlation* between theological, moral, political and juridical concepts, the goals of social mission emerge from the discovery of such correlations between the vision of the kingdom of God and the shape of social-political existence. The movement from theology to social policy is one of reciprocal mediation of meaning between several different modes of understanding. Though the *ground* of the Church's social mission is theological and moral, its actual practical objectives must also be shaped by social, political, economic and legal analysis. If the distinctive contributions of these other modes of thought are not acknowledged, the relevance of the Christian vision to public life will remain obscure. At the same time, precisely because there are many different social and political analyses competing for adherents in a pluralistic society, fundamental theological perspectives must serve as criteria of discernment among them.

In other words, the virtues of prudence and Christian discernment are essential in the task of discovering the basic contours of the Church's relation to the world. Murray maintained that the affirmation of the right to religious freedom was not a conclusion of theoretical reason and pure logic, but of practical wisdom schooled by historical experience. This practical-historical synthesis mediated secular wisdom to the Church and theological insight to the spheres of politics and law. The Church and the world both learned from each other.

The chief implication of this for the social mission of the Church today is that the Church's participation in public affairs must proceed according to a mode of dialogue and persuasion. Religious vision and theology have crucial roles to play in shaping a just and peaceful society. This role can be played, however, only to the extent that faith and theology are seen as participants in a drama that involves numerous other actors. The Church is not the producer or director of this drama. God is—the God who created the politics, law, science, the economy, and culture just as surely as God created the Church and gave it a mission.

The new importance given to the theological basis of social ministry by the Council means that theology has a new task—that of seeking a Christian interpretation of social reality and proposing concrete directions for Christian social action. In the Council's view, such interpretation and action proposals can only be developed through dialogue with the various interpretations and proposals present in a pluralistic society. The Council was well aware that the interchanges between religion and secular modes of thought had been mutually beneficial to both in the past. The need for increased exchanges of this sort was judged even greater today: "Nowadays when things change so rapidly and thought patterns differ so widely, the Church needs to step up this exchange."[24] The task here is neither defense of the Church against the world nor conquest of the world by the Church, but a mediation of understanding and criteria for action between them.

This task will be most fruitful when based on a relation of mutual respect and when it occurs in an atmosphere of freedom. Though there will surely be times when the Church must take prophetic and uncompromising stands over against cultural tendencies or specific social policies, confrontation is not the ordinary relation between the Church and the world as envisioned by the Council. In fact one can extrapolate from the Council's explicit words and suggest that even when the Church takes vigorous positions on matters of public policy, it is likely to be most effective in securing social change when it presents cogent reasons for its position that are intelligible to those outside the Christian community. Speaking of the social ministry of bishops and pastors, the Council recommended: "Let them prepare themselves by careful study to meet and play their part in dialogue with the world and with men of all shades of opinion."[25] The same words can be applied to the laity as well. Thus the new centrality of the Bible and theology in shaping the Church's social mission should be accompanied by a strong spirit of respectful and rational debate. The complementarity of religious fidelity and public civility is the deeper meaning of the Catholic understanding of the relation of faith and reason that is particularly relevant in a pluralistic and conflicted world.

The two recent pastoral letters of the U.S. bishops exemplify both of the themes traced in this essay. Both the letter on the nuclear weapons question and that on the U.S. economy insist that the Church's involvement in these urgent social questions is not an unjustified meddling in politics. The bishops speak on these issues because it is part of their religious mission to do so. Also, the perspectives on peace and economic justice in the letters are firmly rooted in biblical sources and in the call of the kingdom of God. At the same time both letters seek to mediate these religious themes to a pluralistic society through reasoned reflection on fundamental moral norms.

The Council's call for increased dialogue with the many competing social visions of a pluralist society has been particularly influential in shaping these documents. The process of drafting them involved broad consultation with numerous experts in theology, philosophy, and the social sciences, as well as with persons with rich practical experience in government, business, labor and the military. The issuing of successive drafts with the invitation to all interested parties to submit responses represents a new style of social teaching that places maximum emphasis on dialogue and debate.

Finally, both documents not only propose general moral principles that should shape military and economic activity but also advance a number of more specific recommendations about public policy, such as the call for a policy of "no first use" of nuclear weapons by the United States and the adoption of economic policies that seek full employment. These policy recommendations cannot be deduced from theology or fundamental moral principles. They involve prudential judgments among the competing strategic and economic concepts that form the framework of the contemporary policy debates. The bishops do not propose these recommendations as the only possible moral positions on these issues. They do not, in other words, attempt to close off debate on these policies either within the church or in society at large. Rather they make these recommendations precisely in order to bring the Christian moral perspective into active engagement with this debate.

Karl Rahner has observed that if the teaching office of the Church restricts itself to the enunciation of general moral and religious principles for social existence, these teachings "become remarkably abstract and thus singularly ineffective. They are very often recognized as wholly right and yet seem so inept that we are left helpless when faced with a concrete choice."[26] Therefore Rahner urged that the Church must have the courage to move to a more concrete level in addressing the pressing social issues of the day. Such a step does involve certain risks, such as identifying the official Church too closely with contingent policy options. However, it also has considerable advantages. It exemplifies how Christians should translate their fundamental convictions into concrete decisions. It also provides a key means for engaging the Church in the debates about national priorities, debates that are crucial for the cause of justice and peace. On balance the U.S. bishops have concluded that the advantages outweigh the risks. This judgment is itself rooted in pastoral prudence and discernment. It acknowledges the legitimacy of pluralism on the level of policy but it seeks to engage this pluralism in serious moral argument. It is a prime example of the conciliar commitment to dialogue as the means for mediating the Christian vision to a pluralistic world.

Much work remains to be done to give greater depth and breadth to the new form of social mission that has been developing since the Council. Further reflection is needed on how biblical, theological, philosophical and social scientific modes of analysis are to be related and integrated. The respective roles of clergy and laity both need greater clarification and stronger communal support in the routine life of the Church. The limits on how far legitimate pluralism on social issues extends must be given greater attention. But despite this unfinished agenda, it seems clear that the Council has opened up an important new place for vigorous and innovative forms of social mission as essential to the life of Church today.

NOTES

1. J. Bryan Hehir, "Church-State and Church-World: The Ecclesiological Implications," paper delivered at the Forty-First Annual Convention of the Catholic Theological Society of America, Chicago, Illinois, June 13, 1986, forthcoming in the CTSA *Proceedings* as this essay is written.

2. *Aeterni Patris*, No. 9, in Etienne Gilson, ed., *The Church Speaks to the Modern World: The Social Teachings of Leo XIII* (Garden City, NY: Doubleday Image Books, 1954), 38.

3. Johann Baptist Metz, *Faith in History and Society*, trans. David Smith (New York: Seabury, 1980), 18–19.

4. *Gaudium et Spes*, no. 4.

5. See David Hollenbach, *Claims in Conflict* (New York: Paulist, 1979), 122. For parallel though in some ways quite different views see also Alasdair MacIntyre, *After Virtue: A Study in Moral Theory* (Notre Dame, IN: University of Notre Dame Press, 1981), and Roberto Mangabeira Unger, *Knowledge and Politics* (New York: Free Press, 1975).

6. *Gaudium et Spes*, nos. 10 and 11.

7. For an overview of many of these theological developments see Mark Schoof, *A Survey of Catholic Theology, 1800–1970* (Glen Rock, NJ: Paulist/Newman Press, 1970).

8. Metz, op cit., 19.

9. For discussion of recent debates about the proper way to express the unbreakable link between social mission and the Church's core identity see Charles M. Murphy, "Action for Justice as Constitutive of the Preaching of the Gospel: What Did the 1971 Synod Mean?" *Theological Studies* 44 (1983), 298–311, and Francis Schüssler Fiorenza, *Foundational Theology: Jesus and the Church* (New York: Crossroad, 1985), Part III.

10. *Gaudium et Spes*, no. 42.

11. *Gaudium et Spes*, no. 40.

12. *Gaudium et Spes*, no. 22. See John Paul II, *Redemptor Hominis*, nos. 8, 13, and 14, and passim. Referring to the passage from *Gaudium et Spes* cited here, Joseph (now Cardinal) Ratzinger has written: "We are probably justified in saying that here for the first time in an official document of the magisterium a new type of completely Christocentric theology appears. On the basis of Christ this dares to present theology as anthropology and only becomes radically theological by including man in discourse about God by way of Christ, thus manifesting the deepest unity of theology." "The Dignity of the Human Person," in H. Vorgrimler, ed., *Commentary on the Documents of Vatican II*, Vol. V (New York: Herder and Herder, 1969), 159. This implies, I take it, that any suggestion that the Church's mission to defend the dignity of the human person is not essential to the preaching of the Gospel of Christ would be a threat to this unity of theology.

13. *Gaudium et Spes*, nos. 23–32.

14. *Gaudium et Spes*, no. 42.

15. *Gaudium et Spes*, no. 33.

16. *Gaudium et Spes*, no. 38.

17. See, for example, John A. Coleman, "The Situation for Modern Faith," *Theological Studies* 39 (1978), 601–632.

18. *Gaudium et Spes*, no. 43.

19. See note 9 above.

20. Karl Rahner, "Theological Reflections on the Problem of Secularization," *Theological Investigations* X (New York: Herder and Herder, 1973), 322.

21. *Dignitatis Humanae*, no. 2.

22. *Dignitatis Humanae*, no. 4.

23. John Courtney Murray, *The Problem of Religious Freedom*, Woodstock Papers, No. 7 (Westminster, MD: Newman Press, 1965), 20–22.

24. *Gaudium et Spes*, no. 44.

25. *Gaudium et Spes*, no. 43.

26. Karl Rahner, *The Shape of the Church To Come*, trans. Edward Quinn (New York: Seabury, 1974), 76.

Joseph J. Koury, S.J.

THE REDISCOVERY OF A TRADITION: THE "ENDS" OF MARRIAGE ACCORDING TO VATICAN II

My purpose is to look at the Second Vatican Council's teaching on marriage, and how that doctrine continues to have an expanding influence in the revision of canon law, in the decisions of ecclesiastical tribunals, in marriage preparation and the celebration of marriage, and indeed in contemporary developments in elaborating a theology of Christian marriage.

To do that, after some preliminary comments, I will examine the content of five canons from the 1917 Code of Canon Law, discuss how that Code affected the deliberations and the final document of Vatican II on marriage, look at how Vatican II has affected the 1983 Code of Canon Law, and offer some reflections.

SOME INTRODUCTORY COMMENTS: DISTINCTIONS FURTHER DISTINGUISHED

a. Distinctions

There are several initial factors to consider when discussing the Church's doctrine of marriage and its practices.

Marriage is first of all a human reality. Not only Catholics, not only Christians marry. So the first language of marriage is human language. It is not canonical, theological, sacramental or liturgical language. Those who marry bring with them all their cultural, political, social, psychological and economic characteristics.

They also bring to marriage their belief or unbelief: in a deity, in an afterlife, in certain religious-based ethical or moral values. In Roman Catholic theology, marriage is seen as more than a human reality; it is a saving mystery, a sacrament, and its language is therefore also theological and liturgical. And because marriage has certain social and juridical consequences, the language of marriage is also canonical language. Sometimes our human, theological, and canonical languages overlap; at other times these languages make distinctions, establish categories or view realities in different ways. It is important to know when the differences are operating, and when the similarities. (It is also critically important to know the theological and canonical significance of the different kinds of documents we are reading.) For example, when we speak of the right of people to marry, are we referring to all marriages, or to civil marriages, or to sacramental marriages between the baptized? For theology and canon law assign different meanings and consequences to these different kinds of marriages.

In theology and canon law, there is a primary distinction which must be grasped: the marriage of two baptized persons differs from the marriage of two non-baptized persons or the marriage of a baptized person and a non-baptized person. The marriage of two baptized persons is a sacrament, and marriage which is a sacrament enjoys "a special firmness" not attributed to non-sacramental marriage. Likewise, a consummated marriage is valued differently from a marriage that is not consummated.

What we teach and what we practice is much more complex than at first seems: all marriages are indissoluble, but some marriages are more indissoluble than others. Why? Because only some marriages are sacraments. For a couple's marriage to be sacrament, both persons must be baptized. Therefore, we must first consider the baptismal status of those who marry. Then, a further distinction is introduced: After that marriage was contracted, was it also consummated? Because a non-consummated marriage, whether a natural or sacramental marriage, can be dissolved.

Another consideration is this: there is a level of objectivity in our theological and canonical language, namely, that a sacrament is a thing (*res sacra*), and we perhaps too easily talk of the sacrament apart from the people who enact or receive the sacrament. This level of objectivity sometimes overwhelms that other important level of theological and canonical language, namely, that sacraments are for people, sacraments are relationships, sacraments involve a community of faith. It is the nature of law to deal with the objective: the doing of the thing itself, which yields clarity, certainty, legality. But this need for objectivity sometimes operates at the expense of the subjective aspect: Who is the doer? What internally is happening? What unspoken yet often constitutive values, traits, expectations, faith and ability to respond to grace do the persons who marry bring with them? (In fact, we do carefully consider these subjective aspects.)

Canon law needs easily objectifiable categories, such as date and place of contracts, categories of consent and validity of baptism, required form and delegation to officiate. Also, the law operates using certain assumptions, such as that all who approach marriage do so according to the Church's understanding of marriage as a permanent, exclusive, and procreative reality. There is increasing evidence, however, that this presumption no longer operates as a true description of a number of even post-Christian societies—and in canon law a presumption yields to contrary fact.

We teach that marriage is a permanent, exclusive, and procreative reality for all persons who marry. But not all persons, baptized and non-baptized, esteem marriage in this way. Some positively and intentionally marry otherwise. Some on the other hand may well understand and seek marriage as the Church understands it, but lack either due discretion in decision-making, or due capacity to assume (let alone fulfill) the obligations of marriage. In these later cases, we speak not of dissolution but of nullity.

Human beings are in transit: journeyers and pilgrims; covenanters with God and Church and others; more or less believers; more or less capable of that intimate communion of life and love that is marriage. Lastly, marriage as a human and saving reality is no more static than human nature and human cultures, and is as complex and dynamic as the two persons who marry, and the variety of cultural contexts in which they marry.

The canonical tradition in the Catholic Church has entered a new (or, more accurately, revised) stage: the Code of Canon Law (1983) depends on the doctrine of Vatican II and reflects an attempt to juridicize that doctrine. How successful the revision of the law on marriage is remains to be seen. It will take years of marriage case work and developing jurisprudence from many Tribunals around the world and in the Roman Rota to work out the implications of the changes in doctrine and canon law.

By way of concluding these introductory comments, it seems to me that at this point in the Church's history and its understanding of marriage, what we are experiencing is a symptom of a difficult yet positive attempt to recover the canonical tradition of conjugal affection (*affectio maritalis*). This attempt necessarily introduces what are called personalist (or subjective) elements, which are not so easily legislated for.[1]

b. Elements Borrowed from St. Thomas Aquinas:
The "Primary and Secondary Ends" of Marriage

The 1917 Code of Canon Law referred in canon 1013, §1, to the "primary and secondary" ends of marriage. Where does that language come from? It has roots as ancient as Augustine's discussion of the "goods of marriage" and the "excuses which make sinful sexual intercourse not sinful." But, more directly, the terms derive from Thomas Aquinas, in his discussion of the "ends of marriage" and marriage as a "remedy for concupiscence."[2] In his *Summa Theologica*, Supplement, Question 41, which is entitled "that marriage is of the natural law," art. 1, Thomas wrote:

> [M]atrimony is natural because natural reason inclines thereto in two ways: First, in relation to the *principal* (primary) end of matrimony, namely the good of the offspring. For nature intends not only the begetting of offspring but also its education and development. . . . Secondly, in relation to the *secondary* end of marriage which is the mutual services which married persons render one another in household matters. . . . Wherefore, nature inculcates that society of man and woman which consists in matrimony" [emphases mine].[3]

If one stops reading there one might conclude that there is a primary and a secondary end of marriage. This is often referred to as the "hierarchy of ends," which suggests that one is greater and more important than the other, that one must seek first the greater and then the lesser.

But if one reads on, in the following paragraphs, Thomas replies to certain objections and reveals clues as to the proper meaning of "primary" and "secondary"—clues not surprising to those familiar with the methodology of classical Scholastic theology: namely, one moves from the universal to the particular.

> Man's nature inclines to a thing in two ways. In one way, because that thing is becoming to the *generic* nature, and this is *common to all animals;* in another way, because it is becoming to the nature of the difference whereby the *human species* insofar as it is rational overflows the genus. . . . Accordingly man's nature inclines to matrimony on the part of the [specific] difference as regards the second reason (end, or mutual service) (emphases mine).[4]

In other words, primary and secondary refer not to a hierarchy of ends, but to a distinction according to the more universal (generic) and the more particular (specific). Thomas describes first what humans share with all animals: the generic, having offspring. He describes secondly what is specifically human about matrimony: mutual service.

To put all this quite bluntly: all animals procreate; this has been called the "good of the offspring." But only human animals find human care and satisfaction in it; this has been called the "good of the spouses." Is there not, then, a certain irony that the so-called "traditional" view of marriage subordinates "mutual service" to the procreation of offspring, thus making the generic (that which is common to all animals) the first and primary end of marriage, and relegating the specifically human (mutual care, marital affection) to the lesser or secondary end of marriage?

While Thomas may not have intended his distinction to be so used, neo-Scholastic theology did so use it; so did Cardinal P. Gasparri in the process of forming the first codified canon law in the early twentieth century.[5]

PART I: THE DOCTRINE OF THE CODE OF CANON LAW (1917)

The provisions of the 1917 Code contain the distillation of doctrine and disciplinary law of marriage which governed the Church's theology and canonical practice until the decree of Vatican II. By selecting five canons from that Code, which illustrate the consistency of its view of primary and secondary ends of marriage, we shall be better able to understand the continuing and expanding significance of the doctrine of Vatican II on marriage.

1. C. 1013, §1: The primary end of marriage is the procreation and education of children; its secondary end is mutual help and the allaying of concupiscence.[6]

It is often commented that this canon "defines the ends of marriage as an institution, that is, the purposes which the Creator intends in instituting marriage."[7]

Twice (1944, 1951) the Holy See affirmed the primacy of procreation and education, and condemned the views of some writers (presumably H. Doms and the school at Tübingen) who "either deny that these constitute the primary end or hold that the secondary ends are 'equally principal and independent.' "[8]

2. C. 1081, §2: Matrimonial consent is an act of the will by which each party gives and accepts a perpetual and exclusive right over the body for acts which are of themselves suitable for the procreation of children.

What is to be noted here is the consistency of the doctrine contained in the 1917 Code. The specific object of the consent of the two parties who marry is directed to the primary end of marriage: both must give and accept "a perpetual and exclusive right over the body" to sexual intercourse which is procreative.

3. C. 1082, §1: In order that matrimonial consent may be possible, it is necessary that the contracting parties be at least not ignorant that marriage is a permanent society between a man and a woman for the procreation of children.

Again, note the internal consistency: even in some minimal fashion, what the two parties must know (not be ignorant about) is that the permanent commitment of marriage is "for the procreation of children."

4. C. 1086, §2: But if either party or both parties by a positive act of the will exclude marriage itself, or all right to the conjugal act, or any essential property of marriage, the marriage contract is invalid.

If, in giving consent, one or both of the parties excludes "the right to the conjugal act" then the contract of marriage is null and void. No one can validly contract marriage while at the same time positively excluding the right to the conjugal act.[9]

5. C. 1111: From the very beginning of the marriage both parties have the same right and duty as regards the acts peculiar to the conjugal life.

Logically and consistently, of course, the act particular to conjugal life was sexual intercourse that was at least potentially procreative.

It is especially noteworthy that none of these five canons, which are so explicit concerning the "primary" end of marriage, make any mention at all of the "secondary" end of marriage. The language of contracts is apparent; what is not so apparent is that a contract is an agreement concerning a thing—and, in the view of the 1917 Code, the "thing" agreed to is the mutual right to sexual intercourse. There is practically no recognition that marriage is a relationship of affection and mutual care.

PART II: THE SIGNIFICANCE OF THE DOCTRINE OF VATICAN II

The 1917 Code is a shorthand, concise way of entering into the theological and canonical world prior to Vatican II. Its doctrine and discipline on marriage was largely repeated in Pius XI's encyclical *Casti Connubii* (1930) and in the proposed text on "Marriage, Family and Chastity" prepared by a preparatory commission of the Council: the first good of marriage is offspring, the second is the mutual right to the body.

The Council participants were expected to approve and decree this unchanged understanding of marriage and its ends. But in acts that were then and remain quite bold, the bishops who convened for the opening of the Council decided to set up their own commissions to prepare documents for discussion. B. Haring, a *peritus* (expert) to the Council, has written:[10]

Before the Council, the bishops had been sent a schema on "Marriage, Family and Chastity." Taken as a whole, it was timeless and unproblematic. It was intended to perpetuate the negative and rigorist casuistry of the standard text-books. . . . How momentous a decision it was to deal with marriage and family in this perspective—that of the world today (and as the first among the "burning questions" of our time) can be seen clearly if comparison is made with *Casti Connubii* and even more with the schema on Marriage, Family and Chastity which emerged from the laboratory of the Preparatory Commission and was sent to all the Council fathers before the first session. That [schema] . . . adopted a hostile attitude to all the questions of our time. [When the first drafts] were laid on the table of the Preparatory Commission, a moderate conservative advised me not to propose any amendments. He was convinced that a text of that kind would give the Council a salutary shock.

Attempts to draft a section on marriage and family moved from the pre-conciliar text to another text prepared by a sub-commission of the commission preparing a document on the Church in the world. Even here there were attempts to keep the pre-conciliar text. Compromise led to a mixed document, which the Central Preparatory Commission rejected. It was back to the drawing boards. Without tracing each of the steps that followed, it is important to note that only in November 1965, one month before the Council was to end, was a text voted upon by the plenary session of the fathers; this was amended somewhat, and received papal promulgation and final Council approval on December 7, 1965. The chapters on marriage and family had indeed been made a part of the "burning questions of our time" in the very last document approved by the Council.

The Second Vatican Council's doctrine on marriage is to be found in Part II: "Questions of Special Urgency" in the Pastoral Constitution on the Church in the Modern World, nn. 47–52.

First of all, marriage is described as an "intimate partnership of life and love . . . established by the Creator and endowed with its own laws; it is rooted in the contract [sic: covenant] of its partners, that is, their irrevocable personal consent. It is an institution confirmed by the divine law and receiving its stability, even in the eyes of society, from the human act by which the partners mutually surrender themselves to each other; for the good of the spouses, of the children, and of society this sacred bond no longer depends on human decision alone" (GS 48).[11]

Several times the Constitution refers to the institution of marriage and married life itself as ordered to the procreation of offspring and the mutual help and service of the spouses, for which total fidelity is demanded. In notably non-juridical terms, the unitive aspect of married love is described: the free and mutual giving of self, the equal personal dignity of the spouses. Married love is "an eminently human love because it is an affection between two persons rooted in the will and it embraces the good of the whole person . . . " (GS 49).

Marriage and married love are then described as procreative: " . . . by nature ordered to the procreation and education of children. Indeed children are the supreme gift of marriage and greatly contribute to the good of the parents themselves. . . . Married couples should regard it as their proper mission to transmit human life and to educate their children." And later: "But marriage is not merely for the procreation of children; its nature as an indissoluble compact between two people and the good of the children demand that the mutual love of the partners be properly shown, that it should grow and mature. Even in cases where despite the intense desire of the spouses there are no children, marriage still retains its character of being a whole manner and communion of life and preserves its value and indissolubility" (GS 50).

On February 25, 1969, a three-judge panel of the Roman Rota headed by Monsignor L. Anné handed down a decision of nullity in a marriage case, and cited for the very first time the doctrine of Vatican II on marriage. Until that time, the apparent attitude of the Rotal judges had been that the conciliar teaching on marriage, located as it is in a "pastoral constitution," had no bearing in canon law.[12] That 1969 Rotal decision has had a considerable effect not only on Tribunal jurisprudence world-wide but on the revision process that gave us the 1983 Code of Canon Law, and in particular, canons 1055 and 1095.

PART III: THE CODE OF CANON LAW (1983)
AS THE JURIDICIZATION OF DOCTRINE

Now it is time to look at the canons of the revised canon law which correspond to the canons cited earlier from the 1917 Code.[13]

1. C. 1055, §1: The matrimonial covenant (*foedus*), by which a man and a woman establish between themselves a partnership of the whole of life, is by its nature ordered toward the good of the spouses and the procreation and education of offspring; this covenant between baptized persons has been raised by Christ the Lord to the dignity of a sacrament.

Note what is not given: the hierarchy of ends. The Code follows the text of Vatican II.

2. C. 1057, §2: Matrimonial consent is an act of the will by which a man and a woman, through an irrevocable covenant (*foedus*), mutually give and accept each other in order to establish marriage.

Note the object of conjugal consent: to establish marriage. This is a change from the 1917 Code which specified the object of consent as "the right to the body."

3. C. 1101, §2: But if either or both parties through a positive act of the will should exclude marriage itself, some essential

element or an essential property of marriage, it is invalidly contracted.

4. C. 1135: Each of the spouses has equal obligations and rights to those things which pertain to the partnership of conjugal life.

5. C. 1095: They are incapable of contracting marriage:

> 2°: who suffer from grave lack of discretion of judgment concerning essential matrimonial rights and duties which are to be mutually given and accepted;

> 3°: who are not capable of assuming the essential obligations of marriage due to causes of a psychic nature.

Note in the latter three canons the inclusivity of the notion of essential obligations and essential elements of the conjugal partnership.

CONCLUSION: SOME REFLECTIONS ON THE SIGNIFICANCE OF THE DOCTRINE OF VATICAN II, AND SOME QUESTIONS

a. The Continuing Significance of the Language of "Contract" and "Covenant"

Despite the four uses of the word covenant (*foedus*) in the revised Code, that same canon law returns to the language of contract some twenty-five times in its one hundred and eleven canons on marriage. Indeed, the outcome of the procedure of nullity in marriage cases has but one final purpose: to answer the question, "Has it been shown that the [contract of] marriage is null and void?"

For all the importance of the text of Vatican II, in which the assembled bishops purposefully avoided using contract language and chose deliberately to use a biblical and theological word, the legal reality has remained unchanged: contract is the content of the Church's law on marriage. But the theological framework for the juridical expression has been enriched: covenant denotes a special relationship, something more than legal contract.

An assessment: The canonical tradition has over the centuries developed jurisprudence concerning the procreative good of marriage and what is required for the completion of the sexual act, such as the juridical notions of rendering the marital debt; the right to the body (*ius ad corpus*); the purpose of acts by their nature procreative—hence the preoccupation with the biologicalism of impotence and consummation which at times seemingly made forceable rape of the woman sufficient for consummation. But we do not yet have an equivalent jurisprudence concerning the essential obligations or characteristics of the good of mutual help. In other words, there has been an almost complete neglect of the canonical tradition of conjugal love (*affectio maritalis*).[14]

b. Faith and Sacrament, and the Canonical Form of Marriage

Similarly, there has been the nearly total neglect of what faith is required for sacramental marriage; and a preoccupation with consent (act of the will) almost to the exclusion of knowledge (act of the intellect), with the result that something could be (presumed to be) willed that was not known.

What we are speaking of here could be summarized in this way: consent is surely constitutive of contract; and impotence/consummation are surely constitutive of procreation; but surely something other, namely, faith—a relationship with God and with one's spouse—is constitutive of covenant.

Neither Vatican II nor the 1983 Code nor several post-conciliar documents have been able to resolve once and for all the question of the faith required for reception of the sacraments. Despite documents urging that the question *is* answered, the question seems not to be going away. The numbers of baptized non-believers and baptized Catholic non-believers in the sacrament of marriage are increasing, not decreasing. The number of marriages begun without Church form or presence, and the number of marriage nullity cases involving lack of form, are increasing, not decreasing. And there are few if any pastoral leaders who have not had to deal with lack of faith in those seeking merely a "church wedding."

The problems are not new, although the context is far different. Defending itself against the reformers, the Council of Trent taught that marriage between the baptized is a sacrament, and required a certain public form for celebrating the marriage. The teaching was summarized in c. 1012 of the 1917 Code:

§1: Christ the Lord raised to the dignity of sacrament the very contract of marriage between baptized persons; §2: for that reason, between the baptized a valid marriage cannot exist which is not from its very nature, a sacrament.

That doctrine is repeated in c. 1055 in the 1983 Code: the matrimonial covenant between baptized persons has been raised by Christ the Lord to the dignity of a sacrament.

On the other hand, an awareness that some faith is required for sacrament is emerging. The Constitution on the Liturgy [SC] states that "sacraments not only presuppose faith, but by words and objects they also nourish, strengthen and express it; that is why they are called sacraments of faith. They do indeed impart grace but, in addition, the very act of celebrating them disposes the faithful most effectively to receive this grace in a fruitful manner, to worship God rightly, and to practice charity" (n. 59).[15] And there are ten canons in the revised Code (cc. 1063-1072) on "pastoral care and what must precede the celebration of marriage," as well as c. 846, which point to the Church's concern that a celebration of the sacrament is a work "which proceeds from faith and is based on it."

Still, the automatic identification of a valid contract of marriage between two baptized persons as a sacrament results in the strange cases of the marriage tribunals of the Roman Catholic Church judging the validity of the marriages of two baptized non-believers in a sacramental marriage (two Lutherans, or two Methodists) or two believers in the sacrament but non-members of the Catholic Church (e.g., two Orthodox), or, ironically, declaring null the marriage of a Catholic begun without canonical form or dispensation from form, i.e., the Catholic who does not do what the Church requires is more easily declared free to marry again than the Catholic who does precisely as the Church asks.

Is it possible that someone receives a sacrament who neither seeks it nor believes in it? And since it is our theology and canon law that the two persons who marry administer the sacrament to each other (and the Church only officially witnesses what they have done), can two non-believers minister what they do not believe in? If sacramentality and nullity are hard enough to explain to cradle Catholics, then how much more the difficulties in explaining these to non-Catholic Christians!

But that is what the Church teaches: what makes a marriage dissoluble or indissoluble is not primarily the understanding and experience of marriage which the two parties bring with them, nor is it the moral or faith values of the two parties, but first (although not only) their baptismal status. And marriage case work becomes detective work on the baptismal status of the two parties to the marriage.[16]

There remains a great deal of work to be done in the area of sacramental theology, but this must be the work of those who are married, those who were married, lay persons and clergy, theologians and teachers. The doctrine of Vatican II has provided the basis for continuing the task of creating for the Church in the modern world a covenant theology of marriage rich enough to overcome the millennium-long hold of contract and consummation language which has predominated in the Western, Roman Catholic Church.

c. For the longest part of the canonical tradition of the Roman Church, the emphasis has been: "How does marriage come into being?" There are other ways of asking the same question: "What is the efficient cause of marriage?" or "What makes or brings about marriage?" Questions such as these reflect the perspective of *matrimonium in fieri*. There is also the legitimate concern with public *form;* there is a societal need to know who is married and who is not married. These concerns can be found in civil and canon law regulations.

In canon law, all marriages are made by the consent of the two persons who marry; this is stated in abstract, general and universally applicable principles in the 1917 Code, c. 1081, and the 1983 Code, c. 1057; in language which has not been changed, we read that "the consent of the parties makes the marriage" (*consensus partium facit matrimonium*), and, further, that matrimonial consent is an act of the will (*consensus matrimonialis est actus voluntatis*).

To this is added another perspective, which also has a long tradition in canon law: "What makes a marriage indissoluble?" And the response is "consummation." But here the canonical tradition also makes a further distinction: while a consummated marriage is intrinsically indissoluble (the parties themselves cannot end it), still in some cases it may be dissolved extrinsically (by a power to dissolve which is variously located as belonging to the Church, or to the Pope).

Hence the patterns of the Church's current practice:
a non-consummated marriage may be dissolved; a consummated marriage of two non-baptized persons, if certain circumstances pertain, may be dissolved ("Pauline privilege" cases); a consummated marriage of a baptized person and a non-baptized person (even one begun with a dispensation of disparity of cult), if certain circumstances pertain, may be dissolved ("favor of the faith" case); however, a valid contract of marriage between two baptized persons which is consummated cannot be dissolved.[17]

d. But there is another perspective on marriage, and it is as ancient as pre-Christian Roman civil law, and as modern as the current discussions of marriage as personal, as relational and as companionate. This has been referred to as *matrimonium in facto esse*. This perspective on marriage emphasizes the on-going state of married life (even though the word "state" may imply something static, here we refer to something dynamic), a permanent society, alliance or partnership (the *consortium omnis vitae*) and a communion (the *communio vitae*).

In this perspective, it is a question of the material cause of marriage: it is not so much consent bringing marriage into being, nor consummation, but the human wherewithal to sustain married life that is considered.[18] Thus, the questions being asked and the issues being debated more and more frequently in tribunals and theological commissions, in schools of theology and in seminaries, reflect all the value-laden personal and religious, psychological and sociological, historical and cultural factors that characterize the abilities and disabilities of the two persons who marry to assume (and if one cannot assume something, by definition one cannot fulfill something) the essential obligations of marriage (c. 1095, 3°).

These human qualities are necessarily subjective and not easily regulated. They reflect the sociological, cultural, and familial environments, and all the psychological categories of personality and emotional disorders which shape one's capacity for intimate interpersonal relationship. Tribunals are going in that direction, sometimes leading but often following the lead of the Roman Rota.

It seems to me that the Church has just begun to explore the meaning for the contemporary world of the canonical tradition of marital affection, and that the influence of the doctrine of Vatican II on marriage will continue to expand.

NOTES

1. This despite the glaring absence in the revised Code of the Vatican II reference to conjugal love (*dilectio conjugalis*). *Dilectio*, from *diligo*, means to esteem highly, prize; affection. The Latin conciliar text does not use the word *amor*, meaning love from inclination, or, in a negative sense, passion, or desire. The richness of the expression should attract our interest; we should not shy away from exploring at least what its minimal sense might mean for canon law!

2. The 1917 Code, in c. 1013, §1, included in the secondary end of marriage the clause "and a remedy for concupiscence." That clause

has been deleted from the corresponding canon in the 1983 Code, and, in fact, is nowhere to be found in the Code nor in the texts on marriage in GS. Perhaps the Roman Catholic Church has finally begun to shed its largely negativistic "excuse" for human sexual intercourse even in marriage! It is the task of moral theologians to probe the long-range significance of the suppression of the notion of "remedy for concupiscence."

It is appropriate here to make this further note: there are parts of Aquinas' *Summa* which are no longer the Church's disciplinary law. For example, he lists "spiritual affinity" which arises from baptism, and consistently enough: if the "less important" blood or marriage affinities were impediments to marriage, then how much more the greater "spiritual affinity." Thomas also gives the then-current minimum ages for marrying (for a boy, fourteen, and a girl, twelve), and "forbidden times" for marrying. But these have been changed: some changed as long ago as Trent (minimum ages), some by post-Vatican II papal legislation (suppression of forbidden times), and some by the 1983 Code (there is no impediment of spiritual affinity).

It is likewise necessary to recognize that some elements of Thomas' theology of marriage are now inappropriate: beside his need to find an "excusing cause" for sexual intercourse even in marriage, there is also his view of "the debt" of marriage which had to be rendered and his opinion that "marriage is an obstacle to contemplative life" (Q. 41, art. 2, in *Supplement*).

3. *The Summa of St. Thomas Aquinas*, v. 3, p. 2711 (in the translation prepared by the Fathers of the English Dominican Province; New York: Benziger Bros., 1948).

4. *Summa*, v. 3, 2711–2712.

5. It is a standard commentary on c. 1013, §1, that what is being referred to are the ends of marriage "as an institution," that is, considered abstractly, independent of persons.

Nowhere in the official footnote references to c. 1013, §1, is there reference to Thomas' *Summa*, or the designations "primary, secondary."

6. Translations of the 1917 Code are taken from T.L. Bouscaren, A.C. Ellis and F. Korth, *Canon Law: A Text and Commentary*, 4th rev. ed. (Milwaukee: Bruce Publishing, 1966; hereafter, Bouscaren).

7. Bouscaren, 466.

8. Bouscaren, 467; for the texts, *Canon Law Digest* 3, 401–404.

9. For a time in the canonical tradition, jurists made a distinction: one could exchange *the right* to the conjugal act while at the same time deny *the exercise of that right,* and the contract would be deemed

valid. Such mental gymnastics in the jurisprudence of the tribunals should long remain an embarrassment.

10. In H. Vorgrimler, *Commentary on the Documents of Vatican II* (New York: Herder, 1969), v. 5, 225–245.

11. Only the Latin version is the official text. While I cite here the translation as given in A. Flannery, *Vatican Council II: The Conciliar and Post-Conciliar Documents* (Costello Press, 1975), 950–958, I prefer the translation given in W. Abbott, *The Documents of Vatican II* (Guild, America, Association Press, 1966), 249–258. The reader is especially alerted to the translation of the Latin term *foedus,* which Flannery wrongly translates as "contract" when it means "covenant." Had the Council wanted to use the word for contract, it would have borrowed the Latin *contractus* from the 1917 Code. That it did not is most significant.

Here is the opening paragraph of n. 48 as given in Abbott: "The intimate partnership of married life and love has been established by the Creator and qualified by his laws. It is rooted in the conjugal *covenant* of irrevocable personal consent. Hence, by that human act whereby spouses mutually bestow and accept each other, a *relationship* arises which by divine will and in the eyes of society too is a lasting one. For the good of the spouses and their offspring as well as of society, the existence of this sacred bond no longer depends on human decisions alone" [emphases mine].

For the purposes of this chapter, I will cite only brief portions of those numbers, but I urge the reader to study the complete text for its richness of expression and its estimation of contemporary marriage.

12. Much has been made of the different weight to be accorded a "pastoral constitution" and a "dogmatic constitution." But much more important is the explicit content of the Pastoral Constitution on the Church in the Modern World (*Gaudium et spes;* GS) in which the doctrine on marriage is to be found. For the text reads: " . . . the Council intends to present certain key points of the Church's *teaching* in a clearer light . . . " (GS 47; emphasis mine). Another translation (Abbott, *The Documents of Vatican II*) reads: " . . . certain key points in the Church's *doctrine* . . . " (emphasis mine). Whether the constitution itself is dogmatic or pastoral, the section on marriage is labeled clearly: doctrine is being presented.

13. *Code of Canon Law: Latin-English Edition.* Translation prepared under the auspices of the Canon Law Society of America, Washington, D.C., 1983. For commentary on the canons, see T. Doyle in *The Code of Canon Law: Text and Commentary,* eds. J. A. Coriden, T. J. Green, and D. E. Heintschel (Paulist, 1985) 737–833, and Ladislas Orsy, *Mar-*

riage in Canon Law: Text and Comments, Reflections and Questions (M. Glazier, 1986).

14. The reader is directed to an address given by Lawrence Wrenn at the October 1986 convention of the Canon Law Society of America. In that address, to be published in the *CLSA Proceedings* 48 (1986), Wrenn offers a definition of the nature and essence (namely, conjugal love) of the marital relationship.

15. This is quoted in part in canon 840 of the 1983 Code, under the title of introductory canons on sacraments. See the pivotal article by E. Kilmartin, "When Is Marriage a Sacrament?" *Theological Studies* 34 (1973) 275–286, and more recent articles by W. Cuenin, "Marriage of Baptized Non-Believers: Questions of Faith, Sacrament, and Law," *CLSA Proceedings* 40 (1978) 38–46, and R. Cunningham, "Marriage and the Nescient Catholic: Questions of Faith and Sacrament," *Studia Canonica* 15 (1980) 263–83. These articles pose a series of questions: Can sacraments occur outside some context of worship? Do not sacraments invite a faith response to God's saving presence?

It is interesting that questions of this sort were discussed by the International Theological Commission, an advisory commission to the Pope, in 1978. See its "Sixteen Theses" in English translation in *Origins* 8 (1978) 321–28 and in *CLSA Proceedings* 40 (1978) 38–48.

16. This will be increasingly complicated now that the revised Code recognizes that in some "formal" way a Catholic baptized person may leave the Catholic Church, and she or he will not be bound to the requirement of canonical form for marriage. There is in the current periodical literature a great deal of discussion on whether the requirement of canonical form should or should not have been retained in the Code.

17. The reader now appreciates why it is most accurate to state that the Roman Catholic Church teaches the relative dissolubility of marriage. In what are commonly referred to as "annulments," but which are more accurately to be called "contract nullity," it is the task of the Tribunals to determine whether the contract of marriage was, from the very beginning, invalid. The two concepts, dissolution and nullity, involve very different procedures.

18. There is increased periodical literature and reports of decisions by the Roman Rota concerning the interpersonal dimension of marriage. For example, see W. Schumacher, "Interpersonal Communication in Marriage," *Studia Canonica* 9 (1975) 5–35, and "The Importance of Interpersonal Relations in Marriage," *Studia Canonica* 10 (1976) 75–112.

Virginia Sullivan Finn

LAITY: MISSION AND MINISTRY

The message from the Second Vatican Council to the people of God who are identified as laity was twofold: empowerment for greater participation in Church and encouragement for vibrant mission in secular world. The voice of the lay pilgrims, in word and in action, is to be heard in the Church. According to the conciliar documents, lay vocation within the Church relates to the building up of the Church. In addition to disclosing with freedom and confidence their needs and desires, lay believers are to undertake works on their own initiative, give prudent advice to pastors, propose suggestions and desires, and manifest their opinion, by reason of their particular knowledge, competence, and pre-eminence, on those things which pertain to the good of the Church (LG IV). Called to cooperation in the apostolate of the hierarchy, lay pilgrims have the capacity of being appointed by the hierarchy to some ecclesiastical offices with a view to a spiritual end. They are to be ready on the invitation of their bishop to make their own contribution to diocesan undertakings and to extend their cooperation to interparochial, interdiocesan, national and international spheres. In addition to originating, with free choice, and running, at their own discretion, apostolic enterprises, the laity is also entrusted with the teaching of Christian doctrine, certain liturgical actions, and the care of souls. Young and old, male and female, lay people within the Church have the right to develop their religious aptitudes in centers of research and documentation dedicated to this purpose (AA).

The voice of the lay adult, in word and in action, is to be heard in the secular world. As adults the vocation of laymen and laywomen, according to the conciliar documents, is to make the Church present and fruitful in those places and circumstances where it is only through them that it can become the salt of the earth. Contributing to that wonderful diversity through which the Church is to be ordered and governed, the laity are empowered to be heralds within the secular world, to evangelize, to act directly and in their own specific manner in the secular domain, to read the new signs of the times, to help form a new humanity and a new society, to be the people of the Church in the midst of the world and people of the world in the midst of the Church.

Today, twenty-five years into the post-conciliar age, what is said about the twofold call to laywomen and laymen that emerged at the Second Vatican Council? The Lineamenta for the 1987 Synod on the Laity continues a stress on both participation in Church and participation in the mission of the Church in the secular world. Few commentators on progress in post-conciliar reform, however, declare that the promises of Vatican II regarding lay people have come to fruition. For example, the preparatory statement for the National Consultation on the Vocation of the Laity in the World, held in Chicago in September 1986, declares: "The hope that Vatican II would herald a new age of the laity has not yet been fulfilled despite the great growth of lay ministries. . . . We have been accustomed to keeping our religion in church, but we know from our faith and experience that God's grace and love are present in our world—in our work and our intimacies. . . . Our Church has paid too little attention to the religious nature and needs of our worldly vocation."[1]

The slow progress regarding lay leadership and participation within the Church also is brought to light. At the Future of Ministry in the Church of New England Symposium held in Holyoke, Massachusetts in October 1984, descriptive reports on each New England diocese ranged from a diocese moving to establish an Office of the Laity and a diocese where lay involvement is still confined to religious education and marriage preparation. Cardinal Eduardo Pironio of the Pontifical Council for the Laity, commenting on the conciliar Decree on the Apostolate of the Laity, reminded readers that, within the Church, a requirement of ecclesiology of communion is that "the laity should participate in the formulation, implementation and evaluation of pastoral projects. . . . "[2] Referring to lay mission in the world, Cardinal Pironio said, "The laity should be the way of the world in the midst of the Church, and this presupposes that they have the responsibility to discern temporal realities and the right and duty to transmit the results of their discernment to the ecclesial community with sincerity and courage."[3]

In the United States the National Conference of Catholic Bishops' Committee on the Laity has worked strenuously in its attempt to foster conciliar reform. For example, since it was established in 1977, the committee has held many regional "conversations" and five major national conferences: The Manresa Conference, a gathering of the leadership of forty national organizations and movements; the Diocesan Councils of Catholic Laity Consultation; the Learning To Share Ministry Responsibly Conference; the Consultation on Lay Spirituality in America; the Work and Faith in Society: Catholic Perspectives Conference. Further, the Bishops' Committee on the Laity with lay advisors developed the pastoral statement *Called and Gifted: The American Catholic Laity*, unanimously approved by the NCCB at their meeting in November 1980. Summarized recently, the pastoral statement identified four "calls to the laity: (1) the call to adulthood; (2) the call to holiness; (3) the call to ministry (both in the world and in the Church); (4) the call to community."[4] This framework is handy for a reflection on the laity in the post-conciliar age. For example, the call to adulthood reveals a decided shift in the identity of the layperson from the preconciliar to the post-conciliar church. The call to holiness implies that resources would be available within the Church for nourishing and encouraging spiritual growth and development. The call to ministry, perhaps the most conflictual area to emerge since Vatican II, challenges the Church regarding theological clarity concerning valuation of lay roles within the Church and the secular world. Finally, the call to community, in the words of *Called and Gifted*, leads to "a review of parish size, organization, priorities, and identity. It has already led to intentional communities, basic Christian communities, and some revitalized parish communities." This "review" is necessary because laywomen and laymen seek "intimacy, support, acceptance" not only in family life but also in their Christian communities.[5]

In considering the above, we will begin with a reflection on the overall management of the implementation of the Second Vatican Council. Each ordinary was in charge of the management of conciliar change within his diocese. Of necessity oversimplifying, I will present two common models of implementation. In some dioceses the bishop returned from Rome with a contemplative sense that the central thrust of the Council was collegiality, updating and mission. In these dioceses mechanisms were set up for taking strong and systemic management responsibility for the application of thorough renewal related to the *meaning* of the Council. For example in Diocese Z, the ordinary mandated a year of sermons preached on all aspects of the Council with an emphasis on collegiality and mission; parishes were encouraged to sponsor a conciliar lecture series that included the peritus; in some areas inter-parish workshops on the Council led to on-going committees that offered an outreach to the civic community to enhance ecumenism and social justice. Later a diocesan synod with many lay representatives was held. All of these together provided a context for the more sensitive liturgical changes as well as for the enablement of lay voice within Church and secular worlds.

In the city where I met the Council first-hand, exchanging the kiss of peace at Mass went hand in hand with exchanging a new and initial gesture of reconciliation with our Protestant neighbors which went hand in hand with extending concern to those who were poor and/or disabled. The Council was not perceived as an entity with innumerable separate components to pick apart subjectively; Vatican II was a new way of doing faith, of being God's people, of living Church in the world. The ordinary established management dynamics that carefully integrated insights from the documents into a process that revealed both the meaning and practice integral to this event of the universal Church.

In other dioceses management implemented conciliar development, liturgical changes in particular, without providing a framework of theological substance on the meaning that had evoked the changes. In other words the changes were not introduced within a *context of mission and collegiality*. The latter may have been mentioned from the pulpit but what the people *experienced* was a Sunday event in the parish, unrelated to the identity of the lay adult believer as posited in LG IV, 31:

> They live in the world, that is, they are engaged in each and every work and business of the earth and in the ordinary circumstances of social and family life which, as it were, constitute their very existence. There they are called by God that, being led by the spirit to the Gospel, they may contribute to the sanctification of the world, as from within like leaven.

(In Walter Abbott's translation the phrasing for "constitute" is "from which the very web of their existence is woven.")

This fragmented rather than inclusive approach, this undermanagement of a local application of the Council on the part of a diocese, this lack of a theological synthesis and diocesan involvement encouraged the lay believer to experience the Council as a liturgical activity limited to an isolated parish setting. The fruit of this over the past twenty-five years and even today is Church-centered renewal, not mission-centered renewal.

The initial years of discovery about the Council provided an unrepeatable opportunity linked to the power of first impressions. In dioceses where management encouraged an introduction of the changes in piecemeal fashion, lay voice in word and action was seldom heard and the steam went out of the process as time went on.

To review—what came to shape North American Church and *lay perceptions of mission and ministry* originated often in the attitude the ordinary brought from the Council and in his response to section 26 of AA, the call for diocesan councils as well as councils that are parochial, inter-parochial, and inter-diocesan. Like a pebble tossed into a pond, uneven implementation of the Council has evoked widening circles of reaction in the Church—from the varying perceptions of post-conciliar leadership within the NCCB to parochialism and timidity within laity in isolated local parishes where leadership clings to pre-conciliar motifs.

To return to the four calls to the laity posited by the American bishops in their pastoral statement *Called and Gifted:* (1) the call to adulthood; (2) the call to holiness; (3) the call to ministry; (4) the call to community.

THE CALL TO ADULTHOOD

"The call to adulthood is the first of the bishops' calls to the laity and they state, 'One of the chief characteristics of lay men and women today is their growing sense of being adult members of the Church. Adulthood implies knowledge, experience and awareness, freedom and responsibility, and mutuality in relationships.' "[6] That a sense of being adult members is a *growing* phenomenon indicates that a shift in lay identity did not happen overnight. Only after the first flush of enthusiasm for conciliar change had ebbed did a quiet realization take hold that a dependent passive flock would not become the heralds, the evangelizers, the missioners, the leaven through the "vigor of their Christian spirit" (AA I) the Council envisioned them to be.

If grappling for an adult identity has been a significant, on-going process since the Council, valuation of self as adult in spiritual and Church identity and valuation of lay life setting appear to be at the heart of the issue. Although most laymen and laywomen possess an internalized sense of adulthood within family, at work, in avocations and civic pursuits, an internalized sense of adulthood within the Church and within the mission of the Church in the world continues to elude many lay believers. Jay Dolan points out that by the 1960s "the descendants of Catholic immigrants had become fully American. . . . Educationally and economically, they no longer stood apart as inferior or below par."[7] Yet a participant at the 1985 Word and Faith in Society

Consultation at Notre Dame could say, "Lay people need to be told that they are good, that as God has forgiven them, they should forgive themselves, that they need not be afraid, neither for now nor eternity."[8]

A reason for a less than adult assessment of Church identity on the part of some laity may lie in a reactive definition of self that has been internalized, i.e., who I am *not* rather than who I am. Although many lay believers embraced readily the concept of belonging to the people of God, the *contrast among Church identities,* voiced forcefully at the Council, lingers on.

Chapter IV of the Dogmatic Constitution on the Church (LG) initiates this contrast by declaring that "the term [laity] . . . is here understood to mean all the faithful except those in holy orders and those who belong to a religious state approved by the Church." In the statements that unfold from this, two dynamics are manifest—setting as the distinguishing characteristic of lay identity and a contrast between priests and lay people: "Their secular character is proper and peculiar to the laity. Although those in holy orders may sometimes be engaged in secular activities . . . yet by reason of their particular vocation, they are principally and expressly ordained to the sacramental ministry. At the same time, religious give outstanding and striking testimony that the world cannot be transfigured and offered to God without the spirit of the beatitudes" (LG 31). The contrast continues as introductory matter for statements about the laity: "Although by Christ's will some are established as teachers, dispensers of the mysteries, and pastors for others . . . the distinction which the Lord has made between the sacred ministers and the rest of the people of God . . . the laity have as brothers those in the sacred ministries" (LG 32).

The great diversity of the laity made it challenging to specify what, besides setting, was unique about lay witness and engagement in mission. Nonetheless, the preponderance of generalizations about lay adulthood and call ("every lay person . . . is at once the witness and the living instrument of the mission of the Church itself . . . all the laity, then, have the exalted duty of working for the ever greater spread of the divine plan of salvation"— LG 33) lent credence to the belief that what typified laity was what they were not and what pertained to their setting—"they live in the world."

Within the conciliar documents there are, of course, affirmations. One example is the radical equality of belonging to the people of God: "one Lord, one faith, one baptism," sharing "a common dignity . . . a common grace . . . a common vocation." A direct relationship with Christ regarding mission is affirmed, for it is Christ who sends the lay pilgrims "on the Church's apostolate—an apostolate that must at all times be adapting itself to the needs of the moment" (AA IV 33). The needs of the moment erupt in the secular milieu, and the formative power of this setting where the lay believer works, develops intimacies, and socializes is acknowledged by pointing to the fact that these "constitute [the] very existence" of laywomen and laymen. That this web of existence forms identity the documents affirm.

On the other hand, the value of this secular setting is not so apparent, i.e., the Pastoral Constitution on the Church in the Modern World, Chapter I. Suspicion of the "web" can sometimes spawn suspicion of those formed by this web. While a lack of exactness within the documents about *how* the lay pilgrim is to accomplish his or her role in the mission may enhance the freedom, autonomy and adulthood of the lay pilgrim, the ambivalence about the valuation of the world, the lack of opportunity to articulate honestly within the Church the secular orientation so strongly pronounced in the documents as inherent in being a lay believer, compromises adult identity, evoking a quasi-dependency that counters mature adulthood. Although we find in AA the call to priests to "work as brothers with the laity" (AA V 25), authority continued to rest in local pastors who "pass judgment on the authenticity and good use" of gifts given to laity (AA I). The laity are told to "promptly accept in Christian obedience what is decided by pastors who, as teachers and rulers of the Church, represent Christ" (LG IV 37).

THE CALL TO HOLINESS—THE CALL TO COMMUNITY

Although the need for holiness on the part of the laity as well as the clergy is stressed in the documents, spiritual development is dealt with rather indirectly (AA I 4). Considering the current importance given to spiritual formation, this is unfortunate. With few clear guidelines for personal spiritual development other than liturgical participation, it is perhaps not surprising that original responses have emerged regarding spirituality and laity.

Although *Called and Gifted,* reiterating Vatican II, points out that "the spiritual needs of lay people need to be met in the parish," innumerable American Catholic lay people, not finding the parish to be a resource for spiritual depth, have challenged the American Church because their desire for "spiritual formation and direction in deep ways of prayer" has "helped to spur several renewal movements."[9] These associations and movements evoke considerable dynamism and characteristics common to our American culture. For example, the charismatic movement, non-territorial parishes, Marriage Encounter, the Cursillo Ultrayeas, the ministry to the divorced and separated movement, Pax Christi, and other social justice movements all utilize small-group sharing and participation, all integrate men and women together, all focus on the actuality of current, pragmatic phenomena, and all function, for the most part, independent of parish clerical leadership. Most importantly, all evoke a sense of community.

Ministry, both voluntary and profession, evokes a similar bonding. Parishes that develop strong communal dynamics and cadres of lay ministerial leadership tend to reflect vitality and a sense of spiritual unity. The American bishops in *Called and Gifted* affirm this bond between ministry and community, declaring that "we acknowledge gratefully the continuing and increasing contributions of volunteers and part-time workers. . . . Ecclesial ministers, i.e., lay persons who have prepared for professional ministry in the Church, represent a new development. We welcome this gift to the Church. . . . The combination of all these responses to the challenges of our time proclaims the interrelated oneness of ministry as a gift of the Spirit and we rejoice in this."[10] What the Church in North America reveals in many places is that spirituality and ministry and community form a seamless cloak.

THE CALL TO MINISTRY

Today, however, a conflict stance between mission and ministry may be in danger of erupting in the North American Church. For example, in the preparatory paper for the National Consultation on the Vocation of the Laity in the World, the "great growth of lay ministries" is acknowledged and these are perceived as "valuable contributions," but the focus of the paper is the disinterest within the Church related to the vast majority of Catholics who are primarily engaged in mission in and to the secular world, i.e., "the tendency among many members of our Church, both clerical and lay, to legitimize as religious only the work of Church professionals and to ignore or downgrade the work that Catholics do in the world."[11]

An unfortunate inference in the paper is that the valuation of lay ministry within the Church is somehow to blame for the lack of valuation for the mission efforts of lay Catholics. This is far too facile. The resolution of the dilemma rests with a realization that the Church has yet to determine with clarity the valuation of involvement in the secular world as posed in The Church in the Modern World and to implement the training centers urged in this document and the centers for research and documentation urged for laity in other documents.

But why is specifying the valuation of involvement in the secular world crucial to laity and mission? 1. Without such specification there is no depth of understanding regarding mission, no insight into the relationship between mission and kingdom, and no appreciation or recognition for laity as the primary agents of mission. 2. If the web of work, intimacies, socialization and civic activity forms adult lay identity and is the nub of the evocation lay spirituality, yet valuation of this setting is still questioned or denied and left outside Church settings, lay identity and spirituality remain under suspicion and continue to be perceived as second rate. 3. The documents stress cultural and international mission settings for the laity, yet lay efforts in that direction are seldom articulated in church or broadcast within church to enhance adequate recognition. John F. Kennedy, Lech Walesa, Corazon Aquino, and other political leaders model mission for laity yet are seldom acknowledged by Church in a way comparable to the secular press.

We seem caught in limbo, not knowing which of the following options to respond to affirmatively: (a) It makes no difference what the particularities of "earthly realities" are. There is one Christian response to fit all, i.e., love or justice or ministry. (b) Each significant "earthly reality" differs from other "earthly realities." Each has its own God-intended end that must be discovered.

In countless ways The Church in the Modern World, the least implemented document of the Council, affirms the latter option for mission. M. D. Chenu had the foresight in 1965 to recognize the momentous change happening in the Church regarding its view of the world and the impact this might have on the lay pilgrim.

A Christendom that "belittled the specific truthfulness of natural realities," that viewed the building of the world and the occupations and professions of lay men and women as "no more than the occasion . . . for the sanctification of the Christian in the world, the dull locale of a provisional existence," has been left behind according to Chenu along with "the simply negative role of the faithful lay person, busy with his own toil."[12]

Chenu believed that the "common good of human groups on all levels . . . possesses value as an end . . . and not just as a means."[13] In a postscript to his article (written during the Council), Chenu deplored the generalized meaning given Consecratio Mundi by the Council fathers: "And so, worshiping everywhere by their holy actions, the laity consecrate the world itself to God" (LG IV, 34). The locus of the difficulty, according to Chenu, is in a narrowly technical application of *consecratio* as "set apart," "separate." Seeing a close connection between consecratio and sacred, Chenu apprehends the danger of a *sacralization* in which the natural realities of world would cease to be valued for their very realities.[14]

The Church is only missionary if "she goes out of herself," Christianizing the world "exactly as it is being built" and not constructing "a 'Christian world' at her own expense and on her own initiative."[15] Within lay pilgrims, through their union with God in Christ, "the movements of faith, hope, and charity, nourished through worship, enliven and sanctify the *believer and his or her works and actions* which become evangelical leaven."[16]

Chenu presented seminal propositions related to the valuation of the world and the world-constitutive identity of the lay adult person as posited in LG IV, 31 and affirmed in The Church in the Modern World. In the past, Christianity, by its one-sided exaggeration of the absoluteness of God (evoking separation), became a catalyst for the tendency of certain cultures within the world to become secularized in a militant way.[17] Not losing sight of the "communal destiny of humanity and the cosmos"[18] while also not equating secularity and salvation history[19] is the challenge confronting the Church regarding mission and lay people.

The emphasis within the documents on the significance of the mission effort of the laity has yet to unfold adequately on the local, diocesan and national level. An abyss between Church as world and world as world still exists inhibiting mission on the part of grassroots laity. Consequently, something very different from what the documents led us to expect has come to pass.

A groundswell of lay ecclesial ministry was by 1977 filling the horizon. That trend, however, should not have come as a surprise, considering

. . . that prior to the Council lay voice and activity *within* the Church had a forbidden aura to it in many settings.

. . . that North Americans regarding organizations are characterized by a voluntaristic, participatory disposition.

. . . in many dioceses conciliar emphasis was on liturgical change (not on The Church in the Modern World), consequently, forming a perception within the people that valued ministry over mission.

... that internal Church functioning, not external mission, is
what a Church that had kept itself aloof from secularity knew
best.

To be other than what the post-conciliar Church became would
have necessitated a massive unfolding of earthly realities and the discovery of the appropriate ends integral to each. If we still treat the
world, to use Chenu's words, as a "makeshift scaffolding for the heav-
ens,"[20] we need to remind ourselves that to do other than that demands a bringing of the "world" into the Church by the laity who
experience that world, to do it not to anoint it but to discern in mutuality as the people of God the vital, God-intended goals of its earthly
reality. Ironically it may be lay ministers who eventually will accomplish that task, for they are, in increasing numbers, the lay voice, in
word and in action, that is heard in the Church and the lay pilgrims
who have the broad experience of both secular culture and Church
culture.

In light of these trends it is interesting to read Donald Goergen
and Robert Kinast who in a sense collapse mission into *ministries*. Goergen, rather than positing mission in relation to kingdom, states that
ministry is the purpose of mission: "Ministry is what one is called and
sent for." The elements of ministry ("love overflowing in praxis") exercised by lay people are: "response to need," "reverence for others,"
"presence to people."[21]

In Kinast there is a similar ministerial tone in his designation of
lay adults as the "carers" of society. Perceiving Congar's modes of service as synonymous with ministries, Kinast encourages lay women and
men to take on a shepherding role in society, one he identifies as "pastoral activity."[22]

Sacralizing the lay believer's *role* in secular society (what Chenu
feared) seems somewhat antithetical to what the documents claim as
the formative milieu of lay life and the call to bring it, with its own God-
intended purposes, to fulfillment.

Mission to the world was in many dioceses and parishes not only
a weak "third wave," it was also a wave intended for a locale beyond
the church buildings. For some laity, riding this wave would take place
on what was perceived as "lay turf," or what many call the "real" world.
Who has the expertise here?

The greatest lacuna of the Second Vatican Council emerged because without substantial and rigorous lay input and expertise how to
do mission remains an unanswered question. What was at the heart of
the message proclaimed by the Council was not implemented because

the institution suggested a vision without knowing the path toward actualizing the vision.

What the Church knows how to do, whether one approves of the approaches utilized in a given setting or not, is *manage ministry*, and in the post-conciliar Church in the United States the inventory of ministers and ministries has increased beyond all expectation. To approach the lacuna regarding laity and mission with what the Church knows well—ministry—is one option for the future. Another option would be to bring into institutional discernment and governance a mission focus and formation process for lay women and men, enabled by lay ministers and lay secular leaders. We would be wise not to dismiss Chenu's suggestion to discover the God-intended ends for the glittering variety of earthly realities humankind confronts in the short-term and the long-term and acknowledged in The Church in the Modern World. Will this be accomplished by imaging the earth as a vast church where lay Catholics minister? Or will it be accomplished by developing a greater urgency about mission and a greater involvement in the management and governance of mission by lay Catholics, often animated by professional lay ministers, who know secularity by first-hand experience yet who are committed to spiritual depth and to the social justice dimension that is constitutive to Christian faith? A mission ambiance in our culture calls for less reflection on the crisis of no-power, and more reflection on the crisis of the misuse and the under-utilization of powers for justice by large numbers of citizens who *are* empowered. Other crises of meaning that provide the potential for fertile and fruitful mission by lay adults are:

(1)   The crisis of failure of commitment in personal relationships and in generative regard for the young, the aged, the handicapped, the poor.

(2)   The crisis of economic hedonism which causes suffering to the poor and a diminishment of the middle class in favor of an upper class.

(3)   The crisis of denial of its formational power by those responsible for popular media.

(4)   The crisis of global survival and a viable environment exacerbated by linkages among the defense establishment, corporate life, and scientific-technologically biased education.

The history of the post-conciliar Church in the practical and pragmatic culture of the United States reveals that laity respond to the call
to mission to global and national earthly realities when these mesh with
the earthly realities of life in their lay web of existence. This challenge
will be addressed only by laology—a theology and a spirituality of the
laity that eschews any instrumental "use" of the laity and instead has a
depth and rigor based on the reality of who lay adults are as believers
within twentieth century North American culture. This will happen
when the Institution and the communities that are the Church clarify
and embrace more vigorously insights from The Church in the Modern World and what Leonard Doohan calls "a preferential option for
the laity,"[23] the people of the Church empowered for mission in this
world.

NOTES

1. "The New American Catholic: The Challenge of Power and
Responsibility—A Call for Lay Initiatives," National Center for the Laity, 1986, Chicago.
2. Cardinal Eduardo Pironio, "The Decree on the Apostolate of
the Laity: Significance and New Perspectives", Pontifical Council for
the Laity Information Service, 5/1986, Vatican City.
3. Ibid.
4. Secretariat, Bishops' Committee on the Laity, National Conference of Catholic Bishops, *Consulting the American Catholic Laity*,
Moira Mathieson, Editor; United States Catholic Conference Publications, Washington, D.C., 1986, p. 5.
5. National Conference of Catholic Bishops, *Called and Gifted:
The American Catholic Laity*, Washington, D.C., 1980.
6. Op. cit. *Consulting the American Catholic Laity*.
7. Jay Dolan, *The American Catholic Experience: A History from Co-
lonial Times to the Present*, Doubleday, Garden City, 1985, p. 427.
8. Op. cit. *Consulting the American Catholic Laity*.
9. Op. cit. *Called and Gifted*.
10. Ibid.
11. Op. cit. *The New American Catholic*.
12. M. D. Chenu, "Consecratio Mundi" in *The Christian and the
World*, A. Amer et al., P. J. Kenedy & Sons, New York, 1965, pp. 161–
177.
13. Ibid.
14. Ibid.

15. Ibid.

16. Ibid.

17. Ibid., J. Metz, "A Believer's Look at the World," pp. 68–100, and A. Auer, "The Changing Character of the Christian Understanding of the World," pp. 3–44.

18. Ibid., L. Scheffczyk, "The Meaning of Christ's Parousia for the Salvation of Man and the Cosmos," pp. 130–157.

19. Ibid., K. Rahner, "World History and Salvation History," pp. 45–67.

20. Ibid., Chenu, p. 175.

21. Donald Goergen, "The Call to the Laity," *Spirituality Today* (Fall 1983).

22. Robert Kinast, *Caring for Society*, Thomas More Press, Chicago, 1985.

23. Leonard Doohan, "The Radical Equality of All Ministries, National Association for Lay Ministry Convention, 1986, St. Catherine's College, St. Paul, Minn.

Judith A. Dwyer, S.S.J.

VATICAN II AND THE DIGNITY OF CONSCIENCE

The recent decision by Cardinal Joseph Ratzinger, Prefect of the Congregation for the Doctrine of the Faith, to strip Professor Charles E. Curran of his license to teach theology at the Catholic University of America is a remarkably clear, if not exceptionally sobering, example of the tension which has surrounded moral theology generally and sexual ethics specifically since the close of the Second Vatican Council. Arguments in favor of the right to dissent from official Church teaching in morality frequently cite the "claim of conscience" as the key rationale supporting such a decision. This chapter assesses the legitimacy of such a claim by investigating both the contribution of Vatican II to the topic of conscience and the unresolved questions left in the Council's wake.

THE TEACHING OF VATICAN II ON CONSCIENCE

The two key documents in which the Council develops its teaching on the dignity of conscience are *The Church in the Modern World, Gaudium et Spes* (hereafter cited as GS) and *The Declaration on Religious Liberty, Dignitatis Humanae* (hereafter cited as DH).[1] Taken together, the documents provide a rich, Christian anthropological context for our topic.

GS and DH celebrate the dignity of the human person, a dignity about which the contemporary world is becoming increasingly conscious.[2] While DH acknowledges that human reason itself can grasp this dignity, the emphasis in both DH and GS is to root human dignity in revelation, which "shows forth the dignity of the human person in all its fullness" (DH 9). The ultimate dignity of the human being, who is made "in the image of God" (Gen 1:26), rests above all on the fact that she/he is called to communion with God. This dignified human being, whose nature is dynamic and evolving, is a totality, an embodied soul, endowed with intellect and free will and the responsibility to seek truth and acquire wisdom. Truth, however, can impose itself on the human mind only in virtue of its own truth, which wins over the mind with both gentleness and power; wisdom, the perfection of the intellectual nature, gently draws the human mind to look for and love what is true and good. It is imperative, therefore, that the search for truth be carried out in a manner that is appropriate to the dignity of the human person; a spirit of open inquiry, free from all coercion, must prevail.

Conscience is integral to this process of seeking the truth and adhering to its demands, once that truth is known. The most extended conciliar teaching on conscience occurs in paragraph sixteen of GS:

> Deep within his conscience man discovers a law which he has not laid upon himself but which he must obey. Its voice, ever calling him to love and to do what is good and to avoid evil, tells him inwardly at the right moment: do this, shun that. For man has in his heart a law inscribed by God. His dignity lies in observing this law, and by it he will be judged. His conscience is man's most secret core and his sanctuary. There he is alone with God whose voice echoes in his depths. By conscience, in a wonderful way, that law is made known which is fulfilled in the love for God and of one's neighbor. Through loyalty to conscience Christians are joined to other men in the search for truth and for the right solution to so many moral problems which arise both in the life of individuals and from social relationships. Hence, the more a correct conscience prevails, the more do persons and groups turn aside from blind choice and try to be guided by the objective standards of moral conduct. Yet it often happens that conscience goes astray through ignorance which it is unable to avoid, without thereby losing its dignity. This cannot be said of the man who takes little trouble to find out what is true and good, or when conscience is by degrees almost blinded through the habit of committing sin.

Similar teaching occurs in DH when that document notes that the human person is bound to follow conscience faithfully in all activity, in order to come to God, who is the human being's last end. Therefore, "he must not be forced to act contrary to his conscience. Nor must he

be prevented from acting according to his conscience, especially in religious matters" (DH 3). Elsewhere, the conciliar documents stress the
need for education and a properly formed conscience (GS 31, 43, 87),
the obligation of citizens to obey political authority, provided that it
exercises its role within the limits of the moral order and for the common good (GS 74), the recognition of conscientious objectors to warfare (GS 79), and the fact that the "conscience of mankind" firmly and
emphatically proclaims the natural law of peoples and its binding universal principles, so that an atrocity such as genocide is a frightful
crime which "blind conscience" cannot excuse (GS 79). The Council
reminds us that the Gospel scrupulously respects the dignity of conscience and its freedom of choice (GS 41) and that Catholics must pay
careful attention to the teaching of the Church when forming their
conscience (DH 14).

ANALYSIS AND CRITIQUE OF CONCILIAR TEACHING

Vatican II's teaching on conscience, and the situation of that topic
within the broader context of Christian anthropology, is a substantial
improvement on the earlier manual tradition in moral theology.[3] The
moral manuals, intended primarily to train future priests for their
ministry as confessors, divided their consideration of fundamental
moral theology into the following topics: the ultimate end, human acts,
conscience, law, sin and virtue. After a brief examination of the human
person's ultimate end (God) and a more extended discussion of human
acts, the manuals presented the two norms which should direct human
acts—the proximate, subjective, and intrinsic norm (conscience) and
the remote, objective, extrinsic norm (law).

The manual tradition defined conscience as a dictate of practical
reason which tells us that an action which appears to us to be morally
bad must be omitted, that an action which is here and now commanded
must, if possible, be performed. The manuals clearly distinguished
conscience from synderesis, which is the innate habit of the universal
principles of the moral order; they also enumerated various types and
kinds of conscience, discussed the need for moral certitude before
making a judgment, examined the question of the erroneous conscience and vincible (blameworthy) and invincible ignorance, and suggested certain moral systems for resolving doubt regarding one's
obligations.

The tone of the moral manuals, however, remained basically ra-
tionalistic, legalistic, and minimalistic. When the manuals quoted

Scripture, they did so in proof-text fashion and, as a result, biblical teaching remained unintegrated with moral theology. Similarly, the manuals lacked a sense of historical consciousness; the human being which they described seemed abstract and changeless.

Vatican II introduced a more dynamic and wholistic concept of the human person and, within that context, rearticulated the Catholic tradition that conscience, the judgment about the moral licitness or illicitness of an individual's concrete action, is the subjective norm of morality. The Council also echoed the tradition's emphasis on the obligation to enlighten the mind before making a decision of conscience, the possibility of error, and an ignorance which can be blameworthy or not.

The Council's willingness to articulate some conclusions derived from its teaching on conscience remains especially significant. For instance, if conscience is indeed the highest norm of subjective morality, then the Catholic Church must acknowledge conscientious objection to warfare as a legitimate Catholic stance. By opening up the "pacifist option" for the Catholic, and thereby refuting Pius XII's teaching,[4] the hierarchy came to a conclusion reached much earlier by such pacifists as Dorothy Day and Gordon Zahn, namely, the obligation to follow one's conscience regarding the legitimacy of the Christian using deadly force.[5]

The conciliar teaching on religious liberty is a similar example. If the human person is bound to follow conscience faithfully in *all* activity, and must not be prevented from so doing, then certainly in matters of religious belief this respect must be diligently protected. Karl Rahner articulates the significance of this teaching:

> The Council said that anyone who follows his conscience is
> bound to Christ's paschal mystery and that all—in a way that
> God alone knows—come into contact with divine revelation
> and so can come to faith. Even those who seek an unknown
> God in shadows and images are not far from the true God.
> God wants all to be saved who strive to live righteously.[6]

In an address at Weston School of Theology several years later, Rahner again highlighted the significance of the conciliar teaching: "The documents . . . proclaim a universal and effective salvific will of God which is limited only by the evil decision of the human conscience and nothing else."[7]

While the Council made important contributions to the topic of conscience, it nevertheless left certain key questions unresolved. Generally, the Council failed to delineate clearly the various ways in which the term "conscience" is used theologically. Conscience is judgment about the moral licitness or illicitness of an individual's concrete action. But the roots of conscience are in the depths of the person, where one is innately inclined to the good, to the love of God and neighbor. This inclination to do good and avoid evil nevertheless forces the individual to search out the objective moral values of her/his situation by seeking guidance, direction, and illumination. Ultimately, one must arrive at a concrete judgment about the moral quality of one's own action, that is, that *this* particular action in the here and now is loving or unloving, unselfish or selfish and therefore to be done or avoided. This judgment is conscience in the most precise sense. While all these components of "conscience" are in the conciliar documents, it would have been helpful to have the sequence of development, from the roots of conscience to the concrete judgment, more clearly developed.

The weakest conciliar treatment of conscience occurs in the area of "formation of conscience." While noting that a Catholic must pay careful attention to the teachings of the Church in the formation of her/his conscience, the Council neglected to link the role of Scripture, the practice of virtue, prayer, sensitivity to the Spirit, and consultation with this process.

Specifically, the Council failed to provide a thorough and consistent teaching on the question of conscience and Church authority. Avery Dulles captures this dilemma:

In its teachings about authority and obedience, Vatican II has been variously interpreted. No other council in history—not even Vatican I—so exalted the role of the hierarchy: Vatican II devoted great attention to the powers of the bishops to teach, govern, and conduct official worship in the name of Christ. And yet no previous council gave comparable emphasis to religious freedom and to active participation of the laity in the concerns of the Church. Did Vatican II, then, increase or diminish the functions of authority and obedience in the lives of Catholics? No simple answer is possible.[8]

One need only contrast the teaching found in GS 43 with *The Dogmatic Constitution on the Church, Lumen Gentium,* (hereafter cited as LG) paragraph 25, to see certain unresolved tensions between conciliar documents:

It is their [the laity's] task to cultivate a properly informed conscience and to impress the divine law on the affairs of the earthly city. For guidance and spiritual strength, let them turn to the clergy, but let them realize that their pastors will not always be so expert as to have a ready answer to every problem (even every grave problem) that arises: this is not the role of the clergy; it is rather up to the laymen to shoulder their responsibilities under the guidance of Christian wisdom and with eager attention to the teaching authority of the Church (GS 43).

Bishops who teach in communion with the Roman Pontiff are to be revered by all as witnesses of divine and Catholic truth; the faithful, for their part, are obliged to submit to their bishops' decision, made in the name of Christ, in matters of faith and morals, and to adhere to it with a ready and respectful allegiance of mind. This loyal submission of the will and intellect must be given, in a special way, to the authentic teaching authority of the Roman Pontiff even when he does not speak *ex cathedra* in such wise (LG 25).

The quote from GS explicitly rejects paternalism in moral pedagogy and opts for a pedagogy of personal responsibility.[9] The final document of LG, however, demands loyal submission of mind to non-infallible authentic teaching. Completely missing from the final version are topics which had surfaced in earlier drafts of LG, such as the authority of Roman congregations *and* of Catholic theologians and some helpful principles regarding dissent.[10]

This failure to reconcile what one might call the "spirit of DH and GS" regarding human dignity and conscience with certain sections of LG set the stage for subsequent post-conciliar polarization among Catholics. As John Courtney Murray clearly foresaw, the Council, having defended one's freedom to religious liberty and having situated the relationship of the Church to the modern world in the context of freedom, would force the inevitable next question: "Is not the Christian life within the Christian community to be lived in freedom?"[11] It is not surprising, therefore, that moral theology since the Council, from reaction to the 1968 encyclical by Paul VI on the regulation of birth, *Humanae Vitae*[12] to the present controversy regarding Charles E. Curran's teaching of moral theology at The Catholic University of America, has been marked by tension, and a "deepening crisis."[13]

POST-CONCILIAR DEVELOPMENTS: CONSCIENCE AND
CHURCH AUTHORITY

Before examining the question of conscience and Church authority, it is important to note that post-conciliar developments on
other aspects of conscience have occurred. Space permits citing only a
few suggested resources for the interested reader.

Several anthologies on the topic of conscience now exist; especially informative are William C. Bier's *Conscience: Its Freedom and Limitations*, C. Ellis Nelson's *Conscience: Theological and Psychological
Perspectives*, and the Curatorium of the C. G. Jung Institute's *Conscience*.[14]

In addition to the above volumes, Timothy O'Connell's *Principles
for a Catholic Morality* provides a tidy summary of the three different
meanings which the word "conscience" has traditionally held: one's
general sense of value, an awareness of personal responsibility to do
good and avoid evil (conscience/1), the exercise of moral reasoning
which includes on-going reflection, discussion, and analysis (con-
science/2), and the concrete judgment of specific persons pertaining
to their own immediate action (conscience/3). O'Connell highlights the
importance of the formation of conscience at conscience/2 level; here
the conscience needs guidance, direction, and illumination in its
search for truth, with the Church assisting as a source of wisdom.[15]

Charles E. Curran's *Themes in Fundamental Moral Theology,* after
tracing the scriptural and historical developments of conscience, suggests a more adequate contemporary theory which employs relationality-responsibility as the basic ethical model.[16] Curran also sees the
need to give greater emphasis to the subject or person as moral agent,
to develop an affective dimension to theories of conscience, and to
deepen our understanding as to how the subject arrives at its judgments and decisions. Curran concludes with some practical suggestions: reaffirm the traditionally accepted teaching that conscience is
the norm of personal action, heighten our awareness of the dangers
involved in decisions of conscience, strive to overcome these dangers
through critical self-transcendence, and reemphasize the role of community, especially Christian community, in the formation of conscience.

Finally, Walter E. Conn's *Conscience: Development and Self-Transcendence* interprets conscience as the drive of the personal subject
toward the authenticity of self-transcendence that is realized in every
instance of creative understanding, critical judgment, responsible decision, and genuine love.[17] Conn's work critically grounds the meaning

of authenticity in psychological theories (Erikson, Piaget, Kohlberg) and the philosophical reflection of transcendental method (Lonergan) as he shows how authentic self-realization is found only in genuine self-transcendence.

Despite these recent contributions to a contemporary theology of conscience, the question of conscience and Church authority continues to dominate the discussion. Until the recent controversy involving Professor Charles E. Curran and Cardinal Joseph Ratzinger, two key presuppositions were held. The first presupposition was that Catholic teaching in moral matters fell into the category of authentic, but noninfallible teaching. Such a categorization provided for private dissent on the part of Catholics who believed, in conscience, that certain Church teachings were either inadequately formulated or erroneous. It must be admitted, however, that this provision for private dissent was not often emphasized in Catholic tradition.

Cardinal Joseph Ratzinger's letter of July 25, 1986, to Curran, however, deemphasizes the distinction between infallible teaching, which demands an assent of faith since it comprises the core of faith, and noninfallible teaching, to which submission of intellect and will is due (LG 25). Ratzinger's letter refers to the indissolubility of marriage, defined by the Council of Trent, as belonging to the patrimony of faith.[18] Yet Catholic theologians recognize that the teaching of Trent does not exclude as contrary to faith the practice of *economia* in the Greek Church.[19]

I would maintain that Catholic teaching in moral matters continues to fall into the category of authentic, but noninfallible teaching. This categorization provides for the possibility of private dissent on the part of a competent individual, who, after arduous study, prayer, and consultation, arrives at genuinely persuasive reasons and arguments against a particular noninfallible teaching.

The second key presupposition held prior to Ratzinger's decision regarding Curran was the validity of the norms of *public* theological dissent from some noninfallible hierarchical Church teaching, as developed by the National Conference of Catholic Bishops (U.S.A.) in their 1968 pastoral letter, *Human Life in Our Day*.[20] These norms call for careful respect for the consciences of those who lack the theologian's special competence of opportunity for judicious investigation and require a setting forth of dissent with propriety and with regard for the gravity of the matter and the deference due to the authority which has pronounced it. The bishops emphasized that dissent from the magisterium is in order only if the reasons are serious and well-founded, if the manner of dissent does not question or impugn the teaching authority of the Church, and if dissent does not give scandal. Archbishop James A. Hickey, Chancellor of the University, however, repudiated the 1968 norms in a press conference regarding Cardinal Ratzinger's decision on Curran. "I think we have seen these norms, as applied to public dissent, are simply unworkable," claimed Hickey.[21]

I would certainly hope that Hickey's claim that the bishops' 1968 norms are "unworkable" would not immediately eradicate what I think to be very sound principles against which a theologian can test her or his public dissent. The theologian, in order to serve the Church by examining the moral dimensions of complex contemporary issues, must be free to engage in academic research in an environment where historical-critical investigation and academic freedom are presupposed. My perspective, therefore, understands respectful and reverential public dissent in a more realistic and positive way—as the ordinary path to growth and development in the teaching of the Church, a community of faith which is on pilgrimage in the modern world. I also believe that when there is widespread and responsible theological dissent in the Church on a certain point, the Catholic may legitimately take such dissent into account when forming her/his conscience.

CONCLUSION

The recent developments surrounding the Ratzinger/Curran situation provoke many serious questions for the discipline of moral theology. Do the Catholic faithful have the right to dissent in practice from noninfallible teachings? What is the ecclesial status of those who exercise this right? What does their practice say about the present teaching of the Church? What is the proper role of the Catholic theologian? Are there limits to legitimate dissent? Are the 1968 norms for responsible theological dissent no longer valid, as Hickey contends? What of the need for due process when the Church exercises its corrective function? These questions, which deeply affect the life of the Church, warrant serious and sustained theological analysis in the coming years.

The Council recognized the presence of the Holy Spirit in all members of the community and the need for theological reflection to develop in dialogue with the entire Church and with others. Such conciliar teaching led John Courtney Murray to describe the "vertical relationship" of command-obedience as being completed by the "horizontal relationship" of dialogue between authority and the free Christian community. The two relationships "do not cancel, but reciprocally support each other," continued Murray.[22] How can this reciprocity about which Murray spoke be infused into the life of the ecclesial community today? Is it too much to hope that formulation of all future moral teaching by the Church might employ a process similar to the one used by the United States Catholic bishops in the development of their letters on peace and the economy?[23] Such a process enhances the credibility of the authority of the hierarchy; the product also constitutes an invaluable resource to the Catholic faithful in the formation of a Christian conscience.

In summary, this chapter has investigated the impact of conciliar teaching on the dignity of conscience. The Council, marking a substantial improvement over the earlier manual tradition, nevertheless left certain unresolved tensions regarding the question of conscience and Church authority. This conciliar reserve to address directly the question of dissent inevitably set the Catholic Church on the course we have witnessed since *Humanae Vitae*. While scholars continue to develop a more dynamic concept of conscience by using the insights of developmental psychology and transcendental method, the question of conscience and Church authority remains prominent on the ecclesial agenda. This topic, as well as the roles of Scripture, virtue, prayer and discernment of the Spirit in the moral life, continue to warrant serious scholarly and communal reflection.

Karl Rahner described the theology of Vatican II as "transitional."[24] The Church continues to grapple with the theological direction set by the Council by probing more deeply into the mystery of what it means to be human. At the heart of this mystery remains the secret core of the person, where one is alone with God in the sanctuary of the human conscience.

NOTES

1. All conciliar documentation is taken from Austin Flannery, O.P. (gen. ed.), *Vatican II: The Conciliar and Post-Conciliar Documents* (Northport, NY: Costello Publishing Company, 1975). I retain the exclusive language used in the original English translations in my quotations from the conciliar documents. It is to be hoped that future Church documents will use inclusive language.

2. For documentation of this section, see GS 3, 5, 12, 14, 15, 17, 19, 20, 29, 34, 41, 61, 64, 68 and DH 1, 2, 3, 9, 12.

3. For an example of a moral manual which was used widely in this country prior to Vatican II, see Henry Davis, S.J., *Moral and Pas-*

toral Theology, 4 vols. (London: Sheed and Ward, 1st edition 1935, 8th edition, 1959).

4. Pius XII, "The Contradiction of Our Age: The Christmas Message of Pope Pius XII to the Whole World," December 23, 1956 in *The Pope Speaks* 3 (Spring 1957) 331–46, with the specific reference at 343.

5. See, for instance, William D. Miller, *A Harsh and Dreadful Love: Dorothy Day and the Catholic Worker Movement* (New York: Liveright, 1973), and Gordon C. Zahn, *An Alternative to War* (New York: Council on Religion and International Affairs, 1963).

6. Karl Rahner, "The Lasting Significance of Vatican II," *Theology Digest* 28 no. 3 (Fall 1980) 224.

7. Karl Rahner, "Towards a Fundamental Theological Interpretation of Vatican II," *Theological Studies* 40 no. 4 (December 1979) 720.

8. Avery Dulles, "Authority and Obedience," *The Tablet* 236 (18 December 1982) 1264.

9. For development of this point, see Richard A. McCormick, "Moral Theology since Vatican II: Clarity or Chaos?" *Cross Currents* 29 (1979–1980) 26–27.

10. For discussion of *obsequium religiosum*, which the Flannery edition translates as "loyal submission," see Charles E. Curran, *Faithful Dissent*, (Kansas City, Mo.: Sheed and Ward, 1986), pp. 57–62 where Curran argues that scholars generally translate *obsequium* as "submission," but also recognize that the term does not eliminate the possibility of legitimate, public theological dissent from noninfallible Church teaching. Dulles, "Authority and Obedience," p. 1264 where he notes, "On the precise issue of authority and obedience, the council spoke much less fully that the preconciliar drafts. That on the Church, *Aeternus Unigeniti Pater,* had discussed not only the authority of popes and bishops, but also that of the Roman congregations and of Catholic theologians. It had outlined a theology of obedience resembling that of St. Ignatius of Loyola. The same draft proposed some helpful, though undeniably cautious, principles regarding dissent. It stated that subjects, according to their competence, have the right, and sometimes the duty, to declare their views about what affects the good of the Church (AUP 38), but then added that anyone who denounced evils in the Church must take care to avoid giving scandal and must observe the order of admonitions set forth by Christ in the Gospel (see Mt 18:15–17)."

11. John Courtney Murray, "Freedom, Authority, Community," *America* 115 (3 December 1966) 734.

12. Literature on the reaction to *Humanae Vitae* is vast. I cite only a few works here in order to provide the reader with some sense of the shape which the debate took. For an account of the dissenting theologians, see Charles E. Curran, Robert E. Hunt, and the "Subject Professors," *Dissent In and For the Church* (New York: Sheed and Ward, 1969); for a collection of essays supporting dissent, see Charles E. Curran (ed.), *Contraception: Authority and Dissent* (New York: Herder and Herder, 1969); for a work affirming the teaching of *Humanae Vitae*, see John F. Kippley, *Covenant, Christ, and Contraception* (New York: Alba House, 1970); an excellent way in which to trace this debate is through Richard A. McCormick's insightful *Notes on Moral Theology: 1964–1980* (New York: University Press of America, 1981) and *Notes on Moral Theology 1981–1984* (Lanham, MD: University Press of America, Inc., 1984).

13. Significantly, Lisa Sowle Cahill's recent assessment of the state of moral theology is entitled, "Morality: The Deepening Crisis," *Commonweal* 112 (20 September 1985) 496–99, where she cites deeper crises in two categories: (1) the Church's basic approach to understanding morality and moral obligation and (2) establishing what moral problems should count as "most serious" and therefore deserving of a significant amount of attention by the Church at large generally and by moral theologians specifically.

14. William C. Bier (ed.), *Conscience: Its Freedom and Limitations* (New York: Fordham University Press, 1971); C. Ellis Nelson (ed.), *Conscience: Theological and Psychological Perspectives* (New York: Newman Press, 1973); Curatorium of the C. G. Jung Institute (ed.) *Conscience* (Evanston, Ill: Northwestern University Press, 1970).

15. Timothy E. O'Connell, *Principles for a Catholic Morality* (New York: Seabury, 1976).

16. Charles E. Curran, *Themes in Fundamental Moral Theology* (Notre Dame: University of Notre Dame Press, 1977).

17. Walter E. Conn, *Conscience: Development and Self-Transcendence* (Birmingham, Alabama: Religious Education Press, 1981).

18. Charles Curran's book, *Faithful Dissent*, contains all the documentation involved in this case. For Ratzinger's July 25, 1986 letter see pages 267–70. For scholarly debate on the question of whether or not some moral teaching fits under the category of an "infallible" pronouncement, see Francis A. Sullivan, *Magisterium: Teaching Authority in the Catholic Church* (New York: Paulist Press, 1983); Garth L. Hallett, "Contraception and Prescriptive Infallibility," *Theological Studies* 43 (1982) 629–50; John C. Ford, S.J. and Germain Grisez, "Contraception and the Infallibility of the Ordinary Magisterium, *Theological Stud-*

ies 39 (1978) 258–312; Germain Grisez, "Infallibility and the Specific Moral Norms: A Reply to Francis A. Sullivan," *The Thomist* 49 (1985) 248–87; Germain Grisez, "Infallibility and Contraception: A Reply to Garth Hallett," *Theological Studies* 47 no. 1 (March, 1986) 134–45.

19. This point is noted in Curran's August 20, 1986 remarks in response to Ratzinger's July 25, 1986 letter. See *Faithful Dissent*, pp. 271–76; also pp. 56–57.

20. National Conference of Catholic Bishops, *Human Life in Our Day* (Washington, D.C.: United States Catholic Conference, 1968).

21. Arthur Jones, "Hickey Repudiates U.S. Guidelines on Dissent," *National Catholic Reporter*, September 5, 1986, p. 25.

22. Murray, "Freedom, Authority, Community," p. 741.

23. National Conference of Catholic Bishops, *The Challenge of Peace: God's Promise and Our Response* (Washington, D.C.: United States Catholic Conference, 1983); *Economic Justice for All: Catholic Social Teaching and the U.S. Economy* (Washington, D.C.: United States Catholic Conference, 1986). The bishops employed a process of dialogue, shared reflection, and wide consultation which involved any Catholic who wished to participate. All Catholics were free to write to their local bishops or to a member of the Bernardin Committee (peace pastoral) or the Weakland Committee (economic pastoral) to express a viewpoint on any one of the drafts which preceded the final versions of the letters. Criticisms of both letters were actively solicited in some dioceses. In addition to inviting participation from the Catholic community, the Bernardin and Weakland Committees heard extensive testimony from various experts from the political/military sectors or the economic sector.

24. Rahner, "The Lasting Significance of Vatican II," 222.

ANNOTATED BIBLIOGRAPHY

Bier, William C. *Conscience: Its Freedom and Limitations.* New York: Fordham University Press, 1971.
    Examines conscience from the theological and psychological perspectives, and investigates such topics as conscience and the civil order, the Church, and, specifically, conscience and the encyclical *Humane Vitae.*

Conn, Walter E. *Conscience: Development and Self-Transcendence*. Birmingham: Religious Education Press, 1981.

Interprets conscience as the drive of the personal subject toward the authenticity of self-transcendence that is realized in every instance of creative understanding, critical judgment, responsible decision, and genuine love. Conn grounds the meaning of authenticity in the theories of Erikson, Piaget, Kohlberg, and the philosophical reflection of transcendental method in the work of Lonergan.

Curatorium of the C.J. Jung Institute. *Conscience*. Evanston: Northwestern University Press, 1970.

Inspects the topic of conscience from the Jewish, Protestant, and Catholic perspectives, as well from the economic and psychological.

Curran, Charles E. *Themes in Fundamental Moral Theology*. Notre Dame: University of Notre Dame Press, 1977.

Traces the scriptural and historical development of conscience and suggests a more adequate contemporary theory which employs relationality-responsibility as the basic ethical model.

Nelson, C. Ellis. *Conscience: Theological and Psychological Perspectives*. New York: Newman Press, 1973.

Contains thirteen essays on the theological perspectives, including Anglican, Protestant, and Catholic understandings of conscience, and nine essays which examine psychological insights on the topic.

O'Connell, Timothy. *Principles for a Catholic Morality*. New York: Seabury, 1976.

Provides a helpful summary of the three different meanings which the word "conscience" has traditionally held: one's general sense of value, the exercise of moral reasoning, and the concrete judgment.

Francine Cardman

ONE TREASURE ONLY: VATICAN II AND THE ECUMENICAL NATURE OF THE CHURCH

Vatican II was an ecumenical council, not in the sense of the seven great councils of the so-called undivided Church of the first eight centuries, nor even in the sense in which the Roman Catholic Church persisted in calling its own Western, general councils "ecumenical" after the separation from the Eastern churches in the eleventh century and the great sundering of Western Christendom in the sixteenth. Nor was it ecumenical in the sense evoked by some early reactions to Pope John XXIII's announcement that he would convoke an ecumenical council: the hope (or fear) had been that he meant to gather Protestant and Orthodox as well as Roman Catholic Christians together in some sort of "reunion" council. Rather, Vatican II was ecumenical in a more basic and more surprising sense. It was indeed a council of the Roman Catholic Church, but open to the world (the *oikumene*) and to the churches in a manner unprecedented in the history of Christianity.[1]

TOWARD THE COUNCIL

It was the feast of the Conversion of St. Paul, January 25, 1959 that provided the occasion for Pope John's announcement of a "twofold celebration: a diocesan synod for the city, and an ecumenical council for the universal Church." In linking *urbs* and *orbis*, city and world, as the spheres of his pastoral concern, John gave a preliminary indication of the nature of the undertaking whose design and purpose were only beginning to unfold in his own mind. During the nearly four years between this first glimmer and the splendid opening of the Council on October 11, 1962 the Pope would clarify his hopes and intentions for this extraordinary gathering whose beginnings were, he

174

admitted, to be found in "the intimate voice of our spirit." Addressing those assembled at that solemn opening, John recounted the origins of the Council:

> As regards the initiative for the great event which gathers us here, it will suffice to repeat as historical documentation our personal account of the first sudden bringing up in our heart and lips of the simple words "ecumenical council." We uttered those words in the presence of the Sacred College of Cardinals on that memorable January 25, 1959, the Feast of the Conversion of St. Paul, in the basilica dedicated to him. It was completely unexpected, like a flash of heavenly light, shedding sweetness in eyes and hearts. At the same time it gave rise to a great fervor throughout the world in expectation of the holding of the Council.[2]

The meaning of those "simple words" had already undergone considerable elaboration by the time the Council began; it would be even further refined during the course of the Council's debates, in the processes by which various documents came to be written, and especially in the final form of the Decree on Ecumenism (*Unitatis Redintegratio*).[3]

Already in his address at St. Paul's-Outside-the-Walls, Pope John had sounded the theme of unity and renewal that would give Vatican II its distinctive mark. In recalling "certain ancient forms of doctrinal affirmation and of wise provision of ecclesiastical discipline"—i.e., councils and synods—the Pope had remarked how they had, "in the history of the Church, in an epoch of renewal yielded fruits of extraordinary efficaciousness, through clarity of thought, through the solidarity of religious unity, through the living flame of Christian fervor. . . . " Among the results hoped for from the Council was a "renewed invitation to the faithful of the separated communities that they may follow us amiably in this search for unity and grace."[4] In convoking the Council John noted the "generous and growing efforts for the purpose of rebuilding that visible unity of all Christians which corresponds to the wishes of the Divine Redeemer," which made it natural for the Council to "provide premises of doctrinal clarity and of mutual charity" that would further kindle the "hoped for return to unity." At the conclusion of the bull of convocation, the Pope invited prayers from "all Christians of churches separated from Rome, that the Council may be also to their advantage."[5] Similarly, in an address to the world a month before the Council convened, he commented on "the new breath which the project of the Council has aroused here and there, in anxious desire of fraternal reunion in the embrace of the ancient common mother, sancta et universalis mater ecclesia."[6] Finally, at the opening of the Council itself, Pope John spoke at length about the unity of the Christian and human family that he sought to promote through the Council, and he specified the threefold nature of unity in the Church:

> ... the unity of Catholics among themselves, which must always be kept exemplary and most firm; the unity of prayers and ardent desires with which those Christians, separated from this Apostolic See, aspire to be united with us; and the unity in esteem and mutual respect for the Catholic Church which animates those who follow non-Christian religions.[7]

These preliminary statements are significant, not only for the evolution of the Pope's understanding of the nature and purpose of the Council, but also because they represent a departure from previous Roman Catholic attitudes and policy toward the ecumenical movement. They also contain within themselves, as do so many documents of the Council, the seeds of future difficulties—in this case, disagreement about the ecumenical nature of the Church and the shape of the unity to which it is called.

Prior to the Council, ecumenical activity on the part of Roman Catholics had been very nearly anathema. Repeatedly, Rome had refused invitations and forbidden participation in the early conferences of both the Faith and Order and Life and Work movements that were eventually to lead to the formation of the World Council of Churches in 1948. Indeed, in 1928 Pius XI issued the encyclical *Mortalium Animos* forbidding participation at such assemblies, since that would be tantamount to condoning a false Christianity, and declaring instead that the only way of fostering Christian unity was by return to Rome. Later papal statements reiterated this basic position. Pius XII's 1943 encyclical, *Mystici Corporis*, identified the Roman Catholic Church as the true Church of Christ, in which the Mystical Body exists, to which body other Christians are, at best, only unsuspectingly and tenuously connected. In 1948 the same Pope issued a *monitum* forbidding Roman Catholics to attend the Amsterdam Assembly of the newly-formed World Council of Churches; the warning was repeated before the 1954 Evanston Assembly. And in 1950 Pius XII issued the encyclical *Humani Generis*, primarily concerned with defending the purity of Catholic doctrine against dangerous modern views, among which were an "imprudent irenicism" which might lead toward the resolution of dogmatic oppositions.[8]

John XXIII's decision to call a Council and his hopes for its beneficent effect on the pursuit of Christian unity were thus an inspired departure from the dominant tone of previous papal declarations. Nevertheless, there were echoes of earlier positions in his apparently un-self-conscious use of terminology that tended to connote "return to Rome" as at least the implicit premise of these new overtures toward unity. Phrases such as "separated communities," "churches separated from Rome," "return to unity," and "fraternal reunion in the embrace of the ancient common mother" all suggested that the Roman Church remained the point of reference in any movement toward Christian unity. At the same time, however, the nomenclature of "separated *communities*" and "*churches* separated from Rome" represented an important evaluative as well as emotional shift and presaged the language and approach of the Decree on Ecumenism.

That such a shift could occur is due not only to the personal inspiration of Pope John, but also in good measure to the efforts of Catholic ecumenists during the 1950s. The cautious consent of Pius XII to these and certain other carefully defined ecumenical activities was another necessary pre-condition for John's dramatic gesture in calling the Council. In 1950, several months before his observations in *Humani generis* on false irenicism, Pius issued an *instructio* allowing for dialogues between Catholics and non-Catholics and encouraging all Catholics to grow in ecumenical awareness and desire for unity. In 1952, with Pius' quiet approval, the Catholic Conference for Ecumenical Questions held the first of its annual meetings. The secretary of the conference, Jan Willebrands, would become one of the leading Catholic ecumenists of the day, and Augustin Bea, a Jesuit who served as the Pope's liaison to this group, would in 1960 become the president of the newly founded Secretariat for the Promotion of Christian Unity (SPCU).[9] John XXIII's way was thus paved by these early efforts. The European network of Catholic ecumenical scholars would assist him in translating and refining the meaning of the two simple words, "ecumenical council," as well as in creating the secretariat which was to be so influential in shaping foundational Council documents such as the Dogmatic Constitution on the Church (*Lumen Gentium*) and the Decree on Ecumenism.

The evolution of these two documents, beginning with the dramatic rejection of the Theological Commission's preparatory schema on the Church, is a story that has been told numerous times and need not be repeated here. It is sufficient simply to note the significance of

two decisions: Pope John's announcement on October 22, 1962, ele-
vating the secretariat to the status of a Council commission, thereby
granting it drafting rights; and the Council's December 1 vote to combine into one document the preparatory schema on the Eastern
churches, chapter XI of the schema on the Church, and the secretariat's as yet unwritten schema on ecumenism. Responsibility for the major conciliar statement on ecumenism was thus placed squarely in the
hands of the SPCU, a move that proved crucial not only for the final
form of the decree, but also for the ecumenical outlook of the Council
as a whole.[10]

THE DECREE ON ECUMENISM

It is a tribute to the efficaciousness of the decree to note how un-
remarkable this once surprising document now appears, at least on a
casual or uncontextual reading.[11] Those encountering it for the first
time in the 1980s often find it disappointing, even inadequate. But
that, I think, is a measure of how far we have come from the days of
the Council and the initial, heady ventures of Roman Catholics into the
ecumenical arena. One way to gauge that distance is to look more
closely at some of the principal points of the decree and to inquire into
their application or consequences in the years since the Council.

Among the many important points of the decree, at least four require comment here: the linking of renewal and unity, with the concomitant emphasis on spiritual ecumenism; the admission of guilt on
the part of the Roman Church for historical Christian divisions; the
description of Orthodox and Protestant churches as "churches and ecclesial communities separated from the Roman see"; and the concept
of a hierarchy of truths in regard to Catholic teaching. The theme of
unity and renewal is sounded in the introduction (1) and repeated at
intervals throughout the document. The "primary duty" of Catholics
is to "make a careful and honest appraisal of whatever needs to be renewed and done in the Catholic household itself, in order that its life
may bear witness more clearly and faithfully to the teachings and institutions which have been handed down from the apostles" (4). The
dynamism of unity comes from the increased fidelity to the Church's
calling which results from renewal (6), and the "spiritual ecumenism"
which is the soul of the ecumenical movement calls for a change of
heart, holiness of life, and public and private prayer for the unity of
Christians (8). Indeed, "there can be no ecumenism worthy of the
name without interior conversion" (7).

Vatican II was itself evidence of the renewal and change of heart called for by the decree: renewal of the liturgy, commitment to the central importance of Scripture in both public and private prayer and in theological study, renewal of religious life and the structures of episcopal office and collegiality, a new emphasis on the pilgrim nature of the Church, as well as the reaffirmation of the dignity of the human person and the primary importance of religious liberty together presented a picture of a Church humbly renewing itself in order to make its evangelical witness and its pastoral presence more credible both to the modern world and to its sisters and brothers in Christ. Probably the most enduring image of this new outlook is the ecumenical prayer service for promoting Christian unity held at St. Paul's Outside-the-Walls several days before the close of the Council, in which the observers and delegated guests participated. Although the matter of shared worship has today gone considerably beyond the issues of praying together and now reaches to questions of eucharistic sharing, the dramatic significance of that gathering for prayer at the place where John XXIII had first announced the Council should not be underestimated.[12]

The shadow side of the need for renewal is the acknowledgement that the divisions of Christians are a scandal and a result of sin. The fruits of this admission are a longing for unity and remorse for divisions (1), blame for which rests on both sides (3). In the separation of the Eastern churches from the West, "lack of charity and mutual understanding left the way open to divisions" (14). Although the decree falls short of an outright admission of Roman Catholic guilt for the divisions of the Church, its circumspect quotation of 1 John 1:10 ("If we say we have not sinned, we make him a liar, and his word is not in us") is nevertheless noteworthy, as is the conclusion: "This holds good for sins against unity. Thus, in humble prayer we beg pardon of God and of our separated brethren, just as we forgive them that offend us" (7). After the Council, mutual responsibility and mutual forgiveness for the offense of division was graphically illustrated in the embrace of Paul VI and Athenagoras, Ecumenical Patriarch of Constantinople, in Jerusalem in 1964, followed in 1965 by the mutual lifting of the excommunications of 1054. As ecumenical dialogues and other interchanges between and among the churches have progressed, the question of guilt has been gradually receding into the background, to be replaced by growing doctrinal consensus and concern for appropriate next steps toward unity. It seems unlikely that any of this would have been possible without the reconciliation engendered by a change of heart and an admission of sinfulness.

Perhaps the most significant breakthrough of the decree is the application of the phrase "churches and ecclesial communities" to Protestant and Orthodox churches (chap. III, title, and throughout, especially 14, on the churches of the East, and 19, on the churches and ecclesial communities separated during the Reformation). Despite the language of "separation" and the presumption of Roman priority, this terminology represents a major advance in Roman Catholic thought about ecumenism and the nature of the Church. Although its application is clearer in the case of the Eastern churches than for the Protestant churches of the West, the decree recognizes that baptism "constitutes the sacramental bond of unity among all those who through it are reborn" (22), and it attributes an "imperfect communion" with the Catholic Church to all who have been rightly baptized, so that they "have a right to be called Christians, and with good reason are accepted as brothers by the children of the Catholic Church" (3). Further, the sacred actions of these communities can give access to the communion of salvation (3), even though the "ecclesial communities [Protestant] separated from us lack the fullness of unity with us which flows from baptism" (22). There is thus a certain amount of ambivalence in the evaluation of Protestant sacraments. Despite the admission that the liturgical action of these churches can be a means of salvation, the decree insists that, because they lack the sacrament of orders, Protestant churches "have not preserved the proper reality of the eucharistic mystery in its fullness" (22). Questions about orders and sacramentality remain a sticking point in ecumenical discussion today, though there have been recent hints from Rome about the possibility of resolving the problem of Anglican orders.[13]

In order to get a fuller picture of the Council's understanding of the reality of other churches and ecclesial communities, their sacraments, and the nature of the Church's unity, it is necessary to read the decree along with the related passages of *Lumen Gentium*. There it is asserted that the one Church of Christ "subsists in the Catholic Church," although "many elements of sanctification and truth are found outside its visible confines" (LG 8). Similarly, the ecumenism decree maintains that "the unity of the one and only Church . . . subsists in the Catholic Church as something she can never lose" (4). Although the word "subsists" can bear a range of interpretations, it allows, as one commentator has argued, a "certain nuance of meaning: the first reality spoken of [the Church] is truly present in the second reality [the Catholic Church], but it is not necessarily totally identical or co-extensive with it."[14] Because of this it is possible to affirm that other Christians are joined to the Catholic Church in many ways by means of their baptism and that they "recognize and receive other sacraments within their churches and ecclesial communities" (LG 15).

In contrast, there is considerably less ambivalence in regard to the Eastern Christian churches. The decree acknowledges that they possess true sacraments and, especially, by virtue of apostolic succession, the priesthood and Eucharist (15). Because the Eastern churches and the Roman Church already share in so many ecclesial realities, there are few additional requirements for unity between them: "in order to restore communion and unity or preserve them, one must 'impose no burden beyond what is indispensable' (Acts 15:28)" (18). Taken together with the decree's earlier exhortation to Roman Catholics to maintain "a proper freedom" while "preserving unity in essentials" (4), this principle offers the basis for genuine pluralism within the Roman Church and in its relations with other churches of the East and the West.

The potential for realizing both unity and diversity within the Church is greatly enhanced by the concept of a hierarchy of truth. Despite the standard warning against "false irenicism" which accompanied its presentation, the idea represented a marked advance on earlier notions of doctrinal unity based on the necessity of accepting all points of Catholic teaching. As a principle of ecumenical dialogue, therefore, the decree urges:

> When comparing doctrines with one another, they [Catholic theologians] should remember that in Catholic doctrine there exists an order or "hierarchy" of truths, since they vary in their relation to the foundation of Christian faith. Thus the way will be opened whereby this kind of "fraternal rivalry" will incite all to a deeper realization and clearer expression of the unfathomable riches of Christ (11).

It is perhaps fortunate that there was no attempt in the document itself to specify this order of truths, though a sense of the Council's intent can be gleaned from the debate on the schema. Since the Council there has been growing theological agreement that those doctrines having to do with the mystery of Christ, including the trinitarian mystery and the history of salvation, are at the center or foundation of the hierarchy of truths. It follows, therefore, that many Christian churches share, to a greater or lesser extent, in the foundations of the "unfathomable riches of Christ." The question thus arises whether agreement on such fundamentals might constitute a sufficient basis for the unity and communion of the churches.[15]

ADVANCES AND HESITATIONS

Since Vatican II, questions inherent in the Council documents have come into sharper relief and been addressed with varying degrees of success, depending on one's viewpoint. At the same time, a number of important steps have been taken to embody the Council's spirit of renewal and to implement its directives. In regard to ecumenism, it could be argued that, in addition to specific documents and actions aimed at implementing the Council, every internal development has exerted an effect on the ecumenical environment and the way in which others regard the Roman Catholic Church. Thus, controversies such as those surrounding the 1968 encyclical on birth control, *Humanae Vitae*, or the 1976 "Declaration on the Admission of Women to the Ministerial Priesthood," as well as more recent disciplinary actions against theologian Charles Curran and Archbishop Raymond Hunthausen of Seattle, have as much bearing on ecumenical relations as do more formal developments such as the theological dialogues between churches or cooperative action in matters of peace and justice.

A number of post-conciliar documents relating to ecumenism nevertheless deserve mention before going on to consider some of the advances and hesitations in the ecumenical arena in the years since the Council.[16] The first substantial statement from the SPCU was the "Directory Concerning Ecumenical Matters: Part One" in May 1967, followed by "Part Two: Ecumenism in Higher Education" in April 1970. The latter document in particular merits more attention than it has received to date; taken seriously, it could transform both Catholic education in general and the formation of priests and other ministers by means of its more expansive view of the Church and the nature of Christian unity. The 1975 statement on "Ecumenical Collaboration at the Regional, National and Local Levels" is also worth noting. A number of instructions and clarifications on the matter of eucharistic sharing reflect not only increasing difficulties with unauthorized experiments but also an increasing desire on the part of Catholics and other Christians to join together in the common celebration of the Eucharist. There is, as well, a considerable body of papal statements bearing on relations with the Anglican and Orthodox churches, which have been a priority concern of both Paul VI and John Paul II. All these documents, along with various implementing activities and public gestures of reconciliation, are embodiments of the Council's concern with renewal and spiritual ecumenism as paths toward unity.

Another fruit of that concern is the process by which churches which were simply observers at Vatican II—breakthrough though that was—have become genuine partners in an on-going ecumenical dialogue. In bilateral dialogues since Vatican II there has been substantial progress in clarifying and in some instances resolving doctrinal differences that have separated the Roman Catholic Church from other churches of the West. Lutheran-Roman Catholic and Anglican-Roman Catholic conversations at both the international and national levels have been particularly fruitful, issuing in agreed statements on such once-divisive topics as justification by faith, Eucharist and ministry, ministry and ordination, authority in the Church, and the role of Peter.[17] Perhaps because there is so little doctrinal distance between the Orthodox and Roman Catholic churches, as well as because of a long history of estrangement and suspicion on both sides, dialogue has proceeded considerably more slowly than with the churches of the West. While there have been significant conversations between Eastern Orthodox and Roman Catholics in the United States since 1965, conversations on the international level only began in 1980.[18] Advances in ecumenical understanding and agreement made by these and other bilaterals owe much to Vatican II's recognition of the ecclesial reality of other Christian churches and to the methodological freedom granted Roman Catholics through the Council's insight into the hierarchy of truths.

In addition to the theological achievements of the bilateral dialogues, the Roman Catholic Church has become involved in the work of the World Council of Churches, without, however, seeking membership in that body as such.[19] From being observers at the Third Assembly in New Delhi in 1961, Catholic interaction with the World Council has increased significantly in the years since Vatican II. The Joint Working Group between the WCC and Rome, established in 1965 to promote ecumenism through common witness, has since 1983 begun to focus on three additional topics as well: ecumenical formation, the way toward unity, and social issues. Roman Catholics are also official members of the Faith and Order Commission of the WCC and Catholic representatives to that body have contributed substantially to its work, particularly its convergence statement on *Baptism, Eucharist, Ministry (BEM)*.[20] For the future, the question of membership does not seem to me to be as important as the way in which Rome will respond to the agenda of Faith and Order as well as to the WCC's stand on a number of social issues.[21]

The process of *reception*, by which convergence statements such as *BEM* or the agreed statements from bilateral dialogues are evaluated, recognized and acted upon by the churches involved, not only is a concern of the WCC within its own membership and in relation to the Roman Catholic Church, but also applies to the various bilateral dialogues. Indeed, reception is one of the crucial issues of ecumenism in this latter part of the twentieth century. How it is resolved will have a profound effect on the direction of future steps toward unity. Ecumenical progress will also depend on the way in which the churches handle difficult social issues such as peace and disarmanent, liberation movements, development, population issues and women's rights, all of which have the potential for becoming either a new locus for church divisions or an effective means toward the unity of the human community.

The direction that Roman Catholic ecumenism will take as the century draws to a close will depend in good measure on the personality and intentions of Pope John Paul II, not only in his ecumenical agenda and priorities, but also in his more general exercise of authority as teacher and pastor.[22] At the same time, however, the future also depends in equal if not surpassing measure on the attitudes, practices and desires of Catholics throughout the Church. For, as Vatican II taught, ecumenism is not simply a papal or clerical responsibility, any more than the church is simply a papal or clerical institution. Rather, the responsibility of actively seeking the unity of the Church of Christ is a gift and a task incumbent on all the people of God who are making their way in this pilgrim Church toward the one promised banquet in the household of God.

NOTES

1. Thomas F. Stransky, C.S.P. recounts the perplexity caused by Pope John's announcement: "The Foundation of the Secretariat for Promoting Christian Unity," in *Vatican II Revisited*, ed. Alberic Stacpoole (Minneapolis: Winston Press, 1986) 64–65. See also Yves Congar, O.P., "A Last Look at the Council," ibid., 337–38. For the meaning of "ecumenical," see John Anastasiou, "What is the Meaning of the Word 'Ecumenical' in Relation to the Councils?" in *Councils and the Ecumenical Movement*, World Council of Churches Studies No. 5 (Geneva: WCC, 1968) 23–33. Henry Chadwick offers an elegant argument in "The Origin of the Title 'Oecumenical Council'," *Journal of Theological Studies*, n.s. 23 (1972) 132–135.

2. In the bull of December 25, 1961, convoking the Council for 1962, John remarked on its initial inspiration; text in *Council Daybook: Vatican II, Sessions 1 and 2*, ed. Floyd Anderson (Washington, DC: Na-

tional Catholic Welfare Conference, 1965) 6–9, quotation p. 8. The opening address is in the *Daybook*, 25–29, quotation p. 26. Both are also in *The Documents of Vatican II*, ed. Walter M. Abbott, S.J. (New York: America Press, 1966), 703–709 and 710–719.

3. References to section numbers of UR will be cited parenthetically; quotations from the translation of Austin Flannery, O.P., *Documents of Vatican II* (Grand Rapids: Eerdmans, 1975) 452–470. This essay will concentrate on UR and aspects of Christian ecumenism; other Council documents such as the Decree on the Relation of the Church to Non-Christian Religions (*Nostra Aetate*) and the Decree on Religious Liberty (*Dignitatis Humanae*) are important for what has been called "the wider ecumenism," but cannot be considered here.

4. *Daybook*, 2.

5. *Daybook*, 7, 8.

6. *Daybook*, 20.

7. *Daybook*, 28.

8. For early Roman Catholic responses to the ecumenical movement, see Oliver Stratford Tomkins, "The Roman Catholic Church and the Ecumenical Movement, 1910–1948," in *A History of the Ecumenical Movement, 1517–1948,* ed. Ruth Rouse and Stephen Neill (Philadelphia: Westminster, 1967) 675–693. Paul Minus evaluates the effect of papal pronouncements on ecumenism in *The Catholic Rediscovery of Protestantism* (New York: Paulist Press, 1976) 74–84, 166–183.

9. Stransky, op. cit., recounts the origins of the conference and its influence on the formative years of the SPCU, 63–64.

10. For a popular account, see Xavier Rynne, *Vatican Council II* (New York: Farrar, Strauss and Giroux, 1968) 98–122. For a more detailed history, see Werner Becker, "Decree on Ecumenism: History of the Decree," in Herbert Vorgrimler, ed., *Commentary on the Decrees of Vatican II,* vol. 2 (New York: Herder and Herder, 1968) 1–56, especially 7–18. Becker comments that "a new understanding of the ecumenical scope of the Council was surprisingly evident in this debate" (14) leading to the rejection of the schema on the Eastern churches, and he asserts that the nearly unanimous vote to combine the three schemata into one document (2068 to 36, with 8 invalid votes) "affirmed the true ecumenical purpose of the Council, and also expressed with surprising unanimity their trust in the Secretariat for Unity, the proposed text of which was in fact still unknown to them" (19). Stransky, "Foundations," 70–71, 80–83 reveals some of the politics behind these decisions.

11. There are numerous commentaries on the decree itself, from the time immediately after the Council as well as on the occasion of its

anniversaries. For very detailed analysis, see Johannes Feiner, "Commentary on the Decree," in *Commentary on the Documents of Vatican II*, ed. Vorgrimler, 57–158. Thomas Stransky's study guide is still useful: *The Decree on Ecumenism of the Second Vatican Council*, transl. SPCU, with commentary by Thomas Stransky, C.S.P. (New York: Paulist, 1965). For essays on the twentieth anniversary of the decree, see W. Macbeath Brown, "Commentary on the Decree on Ecumenism, Unitatis Redintegratio," in *The Church Renewed: The Documents of Vatican II Reconsidered*, ed. George Schner (Lanham: University Press of America, 1986) 37–54, and Agnes Cunningham, S.S.C.M., "Decree on Ecumenism: Unitatis Redintegratio, 21 November 1964," in *Vatican II and Its Documents: An American Reappraisal*, ed. Timothy O'Connell (Wilmington: Michael Glazier, 1986) 62–78. For a brief Protestant assessment two decades after the Council, see Harding Meyer, "The Decree on Ecumenism: A Protestant Viewpoint," in *The Ecumenical Review* 37/3 (1985) 320–25, who argues for a rereading of the decree in light of its subsequent effects.

12.　For an account of the difficulties once caused by the possibility of Catholics and other Christians praying together, see George Tavard, A.A., "Praying Together: *Communicatio in Sacris* in the Decree on Ecumenism," in *Vatican II Revisited*, 202–219.

13.　In a letter to the co-chairs of the Anglican-Roman Catholic International Commission II (ARCIC-II), Cardinal Willebrands suggested that these discussions might lead to a new context in which the present faith of both churches allowed for the overcoming of the Roman Catholic objections to Anglican orders promulgated by Leo XIII in 1896: " . . . if both communions were so clearly at one in their faith concerning the eucharist and the ministry, the context of this discussion would indeed be changed." Text of Willebrands' letter and reply from the co-chairs in *Origins* 15/40 (Mar. 20, 1986) 662–664.

This hopeful development ignores the question of Anglican ordination of women to the priesthood, which Roman Catholics and Orthodox have repeatedly raised as a hindrance to progress in their dialogues with Anglicans. For a sampling of the effects of the issue, see the exchange of letters between Paul VI and Archbishop Donald Coggan, in *Doing the Truth in Charity: Statements of Pope Paul VI, Popes John Paul I, John Paul II, and the Secretariat for Promoting Christian Unity, 1964–1980*, Ecumenical Documents I, ed. Thomas Stransky, C.S.P., and John Sheerin, C.S.P. (New York: Paulist, 1982) 259–262; more recently, letters between John Paul II and Archbishop Robert Runcie, and an exchange between Archbishop Runcie and Cardinal Willebrands, in *Origins* 16/8 (July 17, 1986) 153–160. For Anglican-Orthodox conversations, see the 1978 Athens Statement, sections 5–14, in *Growth in Agreement: Reports and Agreed Statements of Ecumenical Conversations on a World Level,* Ecumenical Documents II, ed. Harding Meyer and Lukas Vischer (New York: Paulist and Geneva: World Council of Churches, 1984) 51–54.

14. Brown, op. cit., 48.

15. For discussion of the ecumenical potential of the hierarchy of truths, see Yves Congar, O.P., "The 'Hierarchy of Truths'," in *Diversity and Communion,* trans. John Bowden (Mystic: Twenty-Third Publications, 1985), 126–133, and Gustave Thils, "Hiérarchie des vérités de la foi et dialogue oecuménique," *Revue théologique de Louvain,* 15 (1984) 147–159. As early as 1973, developments in ecumenical theology and elaboration of the hierarchy of truths concept was producing nervous reactions in Rome, as witnessed by the assertion in the declaration *Mysterium ecclesiae* that "all dogmas, because they are revealed, must be believed with the same divine faith"; text in *Vatican II: More Postconciliar Documents,* ed. Austin Flannery, O.P. (Grand Rapids: Eerdmans, 1982) 428–440, quotation p. 433.

Karl Rahner proposes that, alongside an objective or dogmatic hierarchy of truths, there is an "existential hierarchy" of those truths that constitute the motivating awareness or understanding of particular persons, groups and ages: " 'Hierarchy' of Truths," *Theology Digest* 30/3 (1982) 227–229, and "Is Church Union Dogmatically Possible?" in *Jesus, Man, and the Church,* trans. Margaret Kohl, *Theological Investigations* XVII (New York: Crossroad, 1981) 197–214. The idea of a central or foundational core of Christian faith as the basis for unity is also the premise of the argument presented by Rahner and Heinrich Fries in *The Unity of the Churches: An Actual Possibility,* trans. Ruth Gritsch and Eric Gritsch (Philadelphia: Fortress, 1983), a work that has not been well received by the Sacred Congregation for the Doctrine of the Faith (SCDF) and its prefect, Cardinal Joseph Ratzinger.

16. These documents can be found in Flannery, *Documents of Vatican II,* 471–563, and in *Vatican II: More Postconciliar Documents,* 153–189, where they are arranged chronologically. Most of the same texts are also collected and arranged topically in *Doing the Truth in Charity,* ed. Stransky and Sheerin.

17. Agreed statements from the Anglican-Roman Catholic International Consultation (ARCIC) are presented in *The Final Report* (Cincinnati: Forward Movement Publications, and Washington, DC: National Conference of Catholic Bishops, 1982). Roman Catholic reactions to the report have been disappointingly doctrinaire and seem to have misunderstood the spirit as well as the method of the discus-

188 VATICAN II: THE UNFINISHED AGENDA

sions. See the letter of Cardinal Ratzinger to the Catholic co-chair of the commission, *Origins* 11/44 (April 15, 1982) 703–704, and the formal observations of the SCDF, *Origins* 11/47 (May 6, 1982) 752–756. A second commission (ARCIC-II) was subsequently appointed by the Pope and the Archbishop of Canterbury to examine outstanding doctrinal differences, to study "all that hinders the mutual recognition of the ministries of our communions," and to recommend practical steps when restoration of full communion becomes possible; joint statement in *Origins* 12/4 (June 10, 1982) 49–51.

Lutheran-Roman Catholic dialogue in the United States produced a number of important early reports, including *Eucharist and Ministry*, Lutherans and Roman Catholics in Dialogue IV (New York: USA National Committee for the Lutheran World Federation, and Washington, DC: Bishops' Committee for Ecumenical and Inter-Religious Affairs, 1970) and *Papal Primacy and the Universal Church*, Lutherans and Roman Catholics in Dialogue V (Minneapolis: Augsburg, 1974). More recently, the volume on *Justification by Faith* has been published, Lutherans and Roman Catholics in Dialogue VII (Minneapolis: Augsburg, 1985). For agreed statements from Lutheran-Roman Catholic and other international conversations, see *Growth in Agreement*, ed. Meyer and Vischer.

18. For the U.S. discussions, see Edward Kilmartin, *Toward Reunion: The Orthodox and Roman Catholic Churches* (New York: Paulist, 1979). The international conversation has so far produced only one document, from Munich in 1982, on "The Mystery of the Church and of the Eucharist in the Light of the Mystery of the Holy Trinity," English translation in *Origins* 12/10 (Aug. 12, 1982) 157–160. A second statement is in the final stages of preparation.

19. For a brief survey of Roman Catholic relations with the WCC, see Marlin VanElderen, "The WCC and the Roman Catholic Church," *One World*, Oct. 1986, 11–15. More detailed reflections are offered by W. A. Visser 't Hooft, "WCC-Roman Catholic Relations: Some Personal Reflections," *The Ecumenical Review* 37/3 (1985) 336–344, and Thomas Stransky, C.S.P., "A Basis beyond *the Basis*," *The Ecumenical Review* 37/2 (1985) 213–222.

20. The so-called Lima statement: *Baptism, Eucharist and Ministry*, Faith and Order Paper No. 111 (Geneva: WCC, 1982). See also *Ecumenical Perspectives on Baptism, Eucharist and Ministry*, ed. Max Thurian, Faith and Order Paper No. 116 (Geneva: WCC, 1983).

21. See Thomas Sieger Derr, *Barriers to Ecumenism: The Holy See and the World Council on Social Questions* (Maryknoll: Orbis, 1983).

22. For an intriguing glimpse into the Pope's understanding of

Vatican II and its ecumenical attitude, see his 1972 programmatic exposition of the Council's central documents: Karol Wojtyla, *Sources of Renewal: The Implementation of the Second Vatican Council,* trans. P.S. Falla (San Francisco: Harper & Row, 1979), especially 15–18 and 310–329. The Pope reaffirmed the work of the SPCU in an address to the Roman Curia on June 28, 1985, "The Twenty-Fifth Anniversary of the Secretariat for Promoting Christian Unity," *SPCU Information Service* 59, iii-iv (1985) 1–6. Likewise, the Extraordinary Synod of Bishops, Nov. 25–Dec. 8, 1985, reaffirmed the Council's ecumenical outlook: see sections of the synod's documents pertaining to ecumenism in *SPCU Information Service* 60 i-ii (1986) 19–22. Text of the synod's "Message to the People of God" and its "Final Report" can be found in *Origins* 15/27 (Dec. 19, 1985) 441–453.

Paul J. Roy, S.J.

THE DEVELOPING SENSE OF COMMUNITY (GAUDIUM ET SPES)

The Second Vatican Council was convened at a time and in a world where people were becoming more conscious of the interconnectedness of nations and more concerned about the possibilities of connections between and among individuals on our planet. What emerged from that Council was the promise of community in ways that had not previously been thought possible or even desirable. In many ways, the Council fathers were reflecting a realization that the whole world was moving in a direction that even now in the last half of the 1980s has yet to come to full fruition.

In this chapter, I will look briefly at the call to community that has been issued by Vatican II, especially as this call is articulated in the Pastoral Constitution on the Church in the Modern World (*Gaudium et spes*). I use this document because of all the documents to have come out of Vatican II it is here that the concept of community is most developed and where it is used with the greatest variety of possible implications.

The first paragraph of GS highlights how the Council fathers saw a link between the cares and concerns of the world and the cares and concerns of the Church. In this paragraph, the "followers of Christ" are referred to as a "community composed of humans" and it is asserted that this community cherishes "a feeling of deep solidarity with the human race and its history" (GS 1).

In the next section, reference is made to the whole of humanity. Later, this phrase will be used interchangeably with "the whole human family" and "the human community." And throughout this document we will hear about this human community in a number of its various dimensions: the political community, the economic community, the social community, the national communities, the community of nations.

If we read GS with community in mind, we may read it a bit dif-

190

ferently from the way David Hollenbach or Judith Dwyer have read it in previous chapters of this volume. And reading the document with "the developing sense of community" as a focus might be going beyond what was actually intended by those who wrote it. Rather than taking an historical perspective on the document, I suggest that we take a contextual and a retrospective look at some important parts of it. In other words, it may be time for us to read it from the vantage point of the twenty years that have elapsed since this prophetic document was written.

THE CHURCH AND THE WORLD

The document juxtaposes two communities—the Church and the modern world—and tries to set out ways in which these two communities can interact. Two major considerations for this kind of juxtaposition have to be that the two communities are not mutually exclusive (the Church is part of the modern world), and that interaction means that each is likely to influence the other. The Council fathers seem to admit this, at the same time that they try to suggest that the Church is other-worldly, and that the influence should be more uni-directional than otherwise. Thus the fathers can write:

> . . . the Council, as witness and guide to the faith of the whole people of God, gathered together by Christ, can find no more eloquent expression of its solidarity and respectful affection for the whole human family, to which it belongs, than to enter into dialogue with it about these different problems [namely, problems which arise from the discoveries and power of the modern world, the anxiety about the current trend of the world, the place and role of human beings in the world, etc.]. The Council will clarify these problems in the light of the Gospel and will furnish [humankind] with the saving resources which the Church has received from its founder under the promptings of the Holy Spirit (GS 3).

In its introduction, the document outlines the situation of the modern world. Here is the Church reading the signs of the times and interpreting them in the light of the Gospel. It is a sketch of the world as it passes through a new stage of history—as it experiences a crisis of growth, a transformation that brings with it serious difficulties. The contradictions of the modern world are starkly evident, and these contradictions call for a conversion of the human community.

Never before has the world had so much. Yet a large proportion of the human family is in want. Never have we had so much freedom. And yet never have so many been enslaved socially and psychologically.

> There is on the one hand a lively feeling of unity and of compelling solidarity, of mutual dependence, and on the other a lamentable cleavage of bitterly opposing camps. We have not yet seen the last of bitter political, social and economic hostility, and racial and ideological antagonism, nor are we free from the specter of a war of total destruction (GS 4).

The Council fathers write about the scientific spirit of this age, technology, advances in biology, psychology, and the social sciences— all of which exert considerable influence on the various dimensions of human existence. They write that "the destiny of the human race is viewed as a complete whole, no longer, as it were, in the particular histories of various peoples: now it merges into a complete whole" (GS 5). The result is changes in the social order which have psychological, moral and religious implications and which create serious imbalances and discord in the modern world. Within the individual, these imbalances are between an

> outlook which is practical and modern and a way of thinking which fails to master and synthesize the sum total of its ideas. Another imbalance occurs between concern for practicality and the demands of moral conscience, not to mention that between the claims of group living and the needs of individual reflection and contemplation (GS 8).

Also included in the imbalances of the modern age are those within and between families, between races and between various kinds of social orders; and, finally, "we find them between international bodies set up in the interests of peace and the ambitions of ideological indoctrination along with national or block expansionism" (GS 8).

The document acknowledges that these imbalances co-exist with what we might call holy desires of the human family: progress, participation, interdependence, the elimination of world hunger.

> These claims are but the sign of a deeper and more widespread aspiration. Man as an individual and as a member of

society craves a life that is full, autonomous, and worthy of his nature as a human being; he longs to harness for his own welfare the immense resources of the modern world. Among nations there is a growing movement to set up a worldwide community (GS 9).

What the Council is addressing is really the interaction of faith with practical reason. Is it possible for the Church to speak to the practicalities of human development or the development of the human community? It does not seem to be the case, even in a document like the American bishops' peace pastoral, that it is the Church's place to try to determine practically what will best serve the needs of the world. At least this is debatable.

Tissa Balasuriya, a Catholic theologian from Sri Lanka, speaks to the inadequacy of Vatican II in precisely these terms. In his book *Planetary Theology*[1] he writes:

[Vatican II's] inadequacy was due partly to its lack of an adequate social analysis of what was going on in the world at the time. It had no real sense of the struggles of the poor, the working class, of women, of oppressed racial groups. It did not deal seriously with racism and white supremacy, with sexism and male dominance, with classism and capitalist exploitation. It did not come to terms with the Russian revolution or even consider seriously the Chinese and Cuban revolutions and the Vietnamese struggle. There was no deep dialogue with other religions, cultures, and ideologies as offering alternative analyses and worldviews to the white, Western, capitalist, male mind-set that still dominated Catholicism. Some of the main theologians of the Council—Congar, Rahner, Ratzinger, Küng—rendered valuable service as far as they went, but their experience was European and Church-centered. The Council had no clear vision of the type of world it envisioned as against the present exploitive world system with its assault on nature by the exhaustion of non-renewable resources and environmental pollution. Hence it did not propose relevant practical goals in the real world and strategies for transforming mentalities and structures. Its relationship to the world order and human development remained within the framework of "aid" to the poor by the rich.

We will return to this critique later in this chapter when we consider some of the writings of Harvey Cox and Karl Rahner.

THE DOCUMENT

There are four chapters in the first part of GS. Chapter 1 considers the dignity of the human person: how we, made in the image of God, are sinners; how there is a basic unity in the human person; how the human person seeks truth. This chapter looks at questions of liberty, conscience, the mystery of death, and atheism—all with a view to understanding better how the dignity of the human person can be promoted and protected. This one chapter on the individual human person serves as the foundation for the rest of the document.

Chapters 2, 3 and 4 of Part I, as well as the five chapters of Part II, of GS focus on the communal or societal aspects of human existence. Right away at the beginning of chapter 2, the Council fathers state their intent for this important document:

Some recent pronouncements of the Church's teaching authority have dealt at length with Christian teaching on human society. The Council, therefore, proposes to repeat only a few of the more important truths and outline the basis of these truths in the light of revelation. Later it will deal with some of their implications which have special importance for our day (GS 23).

The three documents referred to in this paragraph are John XXIII's *Mater et Magistra* and *Pacem in Terris,* and Paul VI's *Ecclesiam Suam.* In the Message to Humanity that opened the Council, we read that the Council fathers equated the promotion of human dignity and the development of the human community. "As we undertake our work, therefore, we would emphasize whatever concerns the dignity of man, whatever contributes to a genuine community of peoples."[2]

Chapter 2 looks at the community of humankind, chapter 3 at human activity throughout the world, and chapter 4 at the role of the Church in the modern world. Yves Congar, in an early commentary on this fourth chapter,[3] writes:

What the Council has said about the dignity of the human person, the life of men in society and the significance of their earthly activity, represents the immediate reasons for the relation between Church and world and provides the basis of their mutual dialogue. Because the Church has something to say on these three themes of a comprehensive doctrine of man, it has a function in relation to the world. It is therefore possible throughout the Pastoral Constitution to consider the Church, not in itself (as in *Lumen Gentium*), but in its life and action in the world.

Congar explains that there are two domains of activity for the Church. The first mission of the Church is to convert the world to the Gospel: as a result of this activity, the world becomes Church. A second mission—the other domain of activity for the Church—is the function it exercises in the world and for the world in the world's own structures and activities. It is with this domain of activity that GS is concerned. Very little is said about the relationship of these two domains of activity which form the total mission of the Church but Congar emphasizes that "in the realization of the Church's mission it is impossible to separate work for the welfare of mankind from the preaching of the Gospel" (p. 204).

Another point made by Congar about this document has to do with the activity of the Church as having validity only to the extent that it spiritually transforms human beings. The question is present implicitly, and in chapter 4 the Council more clearly affirms that there is an inseparable link between the spiritual action of the Church and its social action (as will be explicitated in part II of the document):

> The Church, then, believes it can contribute much to humanizing the family of man and its history through each of its members and its community as whole (GS 40).

The second part of the document then goes on to suggest ways in which that might be done. The five chapters of part II deal with marriage and the family, the proper development of culture, socio-economic life, the life of the political community, and the fostering of peace and the promotion of a community of nations.

For our purposes here, I would like to focus on the last of these issues, the fostering of peace and the promotion of a community of nations. Chapter 5 of part II begins with the anxiety-producing observation that "the whole human race faces a moment of supreme crisis in its advance toward maturity" (GS 77). The Council fathers say once again that an indispensable part of the mission of the Church is that of constructing a more human world, and they insist that this can-

not—indeed, it will not—happen unless each person devotes himself/
herself with renewed determination to the reality of peace.

The first part of this chapter addresses the nature of peace and
the avoidance of war. In this are phrases that have become familiar to
many—especially since the American bishops promulgated their peace
pastoral (which was certainly influenced by GS):

> Peace is more than the absence of war . . . it is appropriately
> called "the effect of righteousness" (GS 78).

> . . . peace is also the fruit of love, for love goes beyond what
> justice can ensure (GS 78).

> Every act of war directed to the indiscriminate destruction of
> whole cities or vast areas with their inhabitants is a crime
> against God and man which merits firm and unequivocal con-
> demnation (GS 80).

> Whatever one may think of this form of deterrent, people are
> convinced that the arms race, which quite a few countries
> have entered, is no infallible way of maintaining real peace
> and that the resulting so-called balance of power is no sure
> and genuine path to achieving it. Rather than eliminate the
> causes of war, the arms race serves only to aggravate the po-
> sition (GS 81).

> The arms race is one of greatest curses on the human race
> and the harm it inflicts on the poor is more than can be en-
> dured (GS 81).

> Those engaged in the work of education, especially youth ed-
> ucation, and the people who mold public opinion, should re-
> gard it as their most important task to educate the minds of
> men to renewed sentiments of peace (GS 82).

The second section of this chapter addresses the building up of
the international community. Again the Council fathers recognize the
need for interdependence among nations, the inequalities that exist in
the world—especially the "excessive economic inequalities"—and how
the inequalities and injustices break down the possibility of conscious
and free interdependence and lead to war.

In setting forth norms that seem appropriate for cooperation among nations, the document comes close to reflecting a particularly American stance toward progress—one that in recent years has been most clearly articulated by Ronald Reagan and members of his administration. The first norm is one that calls on the developing nations to keep the total human development of their citizens as their express and unequivocal aim. They are reminded that "progress is based, not only on foreign aid, but on the full exploitation of native resources and on the development of their own talents and traditions" (GS 86). A reading of this norm could leave one with a sense of having been given a "pull yourself up by your bootstraps" kind of exhortation. Do the poor, if they read this document, get a sense of being blamed for being poor because they have not made full use of their own resources?

The second norm reminds advanced nations of their obligations to help developing nations; the third is a call to the international community (as though it existed) to see to the coordination and stimulation of economic growth; the fourth is a warning to all not to let the quest for material advantage work against—or vitiate—the spiritual nature and development of human beings.

It seems to me that the Church, in this instance, is reflecting a mentality (or at least using a language) that sends mixed messages both to the poor (for whom the Church claims to exist) and to the rich of the world. And to the extent that it does this, it continues to fall short of what it set out to do and to be. This is, I think, substantially what the critique by Balasuriya is suggesting.

On a more positive note, the Council does make some very important assertions. At the end of this section on norms (GS 86), the document states: "Every branch of the human race possesses in itself and in its nobler traditions some part of the spiritual treasure which God has entrusted to men, even though many do not know the source of it." The document also urges collaboration by Catholic experts in studies and research; it insists that it is the duty of the whole people of God, following the teaching and example of their bishops, to do their utmost to alleviate the sufferings of the modern age; and it affirms that "the Church ought to be present in the community of peoples" (GS 89).

Obviously, there is much more of a particular nature that could be gleaned from this document. (See *Questions of Special Urgency*, edited by Judith Dwyer,[4] for further, contemporary reflections on the importance and impact of GS). What I have tried to do here is to give a broad overview of the document in light of the question of the development of community. The conclusion I would draw from my reading of the document—and of the needs of the world of our day—is that the major promise of community put forth by GS is not that of the development of the Church as community—nor even the development of the Church community as a priority—but the development of the human community as the fulfillment of the very mission of the Church. With this promise comes the commitment of the Church to be fully in the world, to be a part of the world community, and the willingness to see itself as being in possession of only a part of the truth. Congar writes:

> It is not sufficient to regard the Church and the world as two powers which do not overlap but are merely juxtaposed (or placed one above the other). The "world" is not simply the power of the state, it is mankind at work; it is capable of becoming Church and is called by the Church, if the Church is understood to be what reveals to the world its own ultimate meaning (p. 212).

NEW COMMUNITY IN A NEW WORLD

Let us briefly consider how community might come about in the world of the 1980s, given that it is the whole human community that we are talking about.

In a recent work,[5] Harvey Cox has argued that we are moving into the "post-modern world" and that this movement has three implications for the way we will do theology. The first is that the end of the modern age also points to the end of "modern theology" which tried to interpret Christianity in the face of secularization. Cox argues that a fundamentally new theological approach is needed. The second is that basic elements of this new theology have already made their appearance through what he calls "vigorous anti-modernist religious movements." And the third is that the accomplishments of modern theology must be appreciated and used if we are to assemble the various components of the coming theology. Cox's thesis is that the resources for a post-modern theology will come

> not from the center but from the bottom and from the edge . . . from those sectors of the modern social edifice that for various reasons—usually to do with class or color or gender— have been consigned to its lower stories and excluded from the chance to help formulate its religious vision (p. 21).

The two anti-modernist movements that Cox is referring to are the largely North American fundamentalist, conservative, evangelical movement and the radical, liberation theology movements coming out of the third world. His conclusion is that it is largely through the latter that we will be able to move from modern to post-modern theology.

It is easy to understand how Cox can arrive at his conclusions. What is coming out of the liberation theologies of the third world is largely focused on the development of community as the basis for a new understanding of the world and of the Church within that world. It is a theologizing similar to that which led to GS and which flows out of the spirit of this document.

If we are to take GS seriously in the 1980s and into the 1990s, then we must pay attention to the suggestion of theologians like Cox and Balasuriya that GS was good as far as it went, and that it will continue to be good only to the extent that we are willing to go beyond it. That is the nature of the kind of prophetic document that GS has been and continues to be for the Church and for the world.

Cox describes the modern world as being supported by what he calls the five pillars of modernity. They are: sovereign national states as the legally defined units of the global political system, science-based technology as the modern world's principal source of its images of life and its possibilities, bureaucratic rationalism as the world's major mode of organizing and administering human thought and activity, the quest for profit maximization in both capitalist and allegedly socialist countries as the means of motivating work and distributing goods and services, and the secularization and trivialization of religion and the harnessing of the spiritual for patently profane purposes as its most characteristic attitude toward the holy (p. 183).

When we look at the implications of these five pillars in the world of the 1980s, we can more readily call into question—at least from a Christian, but perhaps also from a humanist, perspective—the effort we put into assuring the continuation of this modern world.

Our North American culture (and politics) promotes isolation and chauvinism. The challenge of community that emerges from the Second Vatican Council, and especially from GS, is a call away from isolation to identification with all peoples. We are part of a global community; the world is one family, one people; and our survival on this planet will be as a world community or not at all. If community is to emerge, then, it will likely flow out of a concerted effort of people to do away with that first pillar of modern society. The legally defined units of the global political system will transcend national boundaries.

Likewise, if we are to be true to the spirit of GS, we will reassess our use of technology and will challenge the unbridled production of new things simply because the technology is available to produce them. We will define new modes of leadership where power and authority are shared and where new institutions provide alternatives to bureaucratic rationalism. The world's political and economic power will be shared more equitably, and the genuine good of the people will prevail over the quest for maximization of profit. And theology will pay attention to the role religion actually plays in society (cf. Cox, pp. 205–215).

COMMUNITIES OF LIBERATION

The contemporary North American Church, twenty years after the Second Vatican Council, must become willing to look to the margins of its own institution if it is to rethink the Gospel in light of GS. What it will find there—at the margins—is a growing number of Christians who seek a kind of community that gets its life from reflection on human experience, that finds its authority in the life of Jesus freely given for the liberation of the poor, that is motivated by a quest for global survival rooted in love for God, for God's people, and for the earth that is God's creation.

It will be a collection of people who are becoming community because they choose relationships characterized by mutuality rather than by dominance of one over the other. It will be authentically Christian because its members will share Jesus' sense of indignation at oppression, his anger at those who would "lord it over" others, his valuing of freedom and truth and justice, his determination to remain faithful to self and God and creation, his willingness to die that the world might live. It will be a community of people who, in Cox's words, "have been excluded from or trampled by the modern world" (p. 208), victims of poverty, racism, and sexism.

CONCLUSION

I have tried in this chapter to raise the question that comes directly out of the pastoral dimension of Vatican II: What is the place of the Church in the development of a world community? And how then does this world community call for us to be a world Church?

Karl Rahner has suggested that Vatican II seems to have been the first act in a history in which the world Church first began to exist as such. In his article on the importance of the Second Vatican Council for our day,[6] he describes it as a Council of the world Church. Balasuriya, however, contests this thesis and maintains that Vatican II was largely a Council of Euro-American bishops, concerned with the agenda of first world prelates who were continuing the theological debates of the 1950s and early 1960s. It was not a Council that reflected the concerns or clearly heard the voices of the peoples of the third world (p. 147).

The creation or development of a world Church requires an interreligious dialogue that must take into consideration the fact of religious pluralism and that must take place within the context of the hard reality of social conflict rather than of the exchange of ideas by scholars or ecclesiastical leaders whose positions make them more attuned to confessional than to class differences. As Cox suggests (p. 239), our theologizing will be different if we enter into the struggle for the liberation of humankind in concert with our sisters and brothers from other cultures, races, and religious beliefs. Our willingness to be a world community in this struggle will disempower the powerful barriers that now divide us.

The Second Vatican Council, through GS, has made a prophetic assessment of the world and issued a prophetic challenge. Now, twenty years later, the challenge takes on a new urgency—for we find ourselves ever closer to the catastrophe of nuclear war, ever more in need of establishing a world community. The challenge of GS is the formation of a human family in which no member will be seen to be expendable or undeserving of a fair share of the goods of our earth. Now, twenty years after the Second Vatican Council, the Church must intensify its efforts to truly live its "worldly mission"—to make real its promise of community, and to contribute significantly to the humanizing of the human family and its history through each of its members and its community as a whole.

NOTES

1. T. Balasuriya, *Planetary Theology* (Maryknoll: Orbis Books, 1984), p. 148.
2. W.M. Abbott, S.J. and J. Gallagher, eds. *The Documents of Vatican II* (Washington, D.C., The America Press, 1966).
3. H. Vorgrimler, *Commentary on the Documents of Vatican II* (NY, Herder and Herder, 1969), part I, chapter IV, p. 203.
4. Judith Dwyer (ed.), *Questions of Special Urgency* (Washington, D.C., Georgetown University Press, 1986).

5. Harvey Cox, *Religion in the Secular City* (New York, Simon and Schuster, 1984).

6. Karl Rahner, "The Abiding Significance of the Second Vatican Council," *Theological Investigations* (New York, Crossroad, 1981), vol. 20, pp. 90–102.

Leo J. O'Donovan, S.J.

DEATH AS THE DEPTH OF LIFE: A REREADING OF ESCHATOLOGY IN GAUDIUM ET SPES*

The prospect of death has long disturbed the dreams of humanity. In the last four decades, however, a new nightmare has been unleashed, haunting more and more of us, especially among the young. From the hidden recesses of matter human ingenuity has managed to release unimaginable realms of energy and with it has fashioned: The Bomb. Through this discovery, as Jonathan Schell has eloquently argued, an entirely unprecedented situation has emerged. Humanity stands face to face not simply with the grievous loss of its individual members but now with its own *extinction*. "The spectre of extinction hovers over our world," Schell writes, "and shapes our lives with its invisible but terrible pressure."[1] The destruction promised by a nuclear holocaust defies all our previous expectations about life and death. It calls into question every logic by which we have estimated life's value and our care for it. If we have indeed the power to destroy our race, as the American bishops have also warned us in their recent pastoral letter,[2] language and thought are bound to falter before death's new face. How can we speak of it? It is "the second death," Schell suggests, the entire loss of our common human world. It means "the death of birth," "the murder of the future." And "with the air so full of death, every death becomes harder to face."[3]

Undoubtedly other generations in the West have regarded their times as doomed and have foreseen the end of the world.[4] But such predictions of the end were always woven together with a traditional Christian eschatology in which God's saving judgment remained cen-

---

*This essay, thoroughly revised, is printed with permission from Elmar Klinger and Klaus Wittstadt, eds., *Glaube im Prozess. Christsein nach dem II. Vatikanum. Für Karl Rahner* (Freiburg: Herder, 1984).

tral. "The end of history which we in the late twentieth century must contemplate, however—an end brought about by nuclear holocaust— is conceived primarily not as God's doing but as ours. Moreover, it is not part of a grand plan bringing about the salvation of humanity; it is, rather, the extinction—the total obliteration of humanity."[5] Indeed, the new situation bears unmistakable religious characteristics in reverse. Robert Jay Lifton has called it nuclearism, "a secular religion, a total ideology in which 'grace' and even 'salvation'—the mastery of death and evil—are achieved through the power of a new technological deity."[6] Nuclear weapons inaugurate the era of a new divine power, capable both of destruction and of creation. They are explained in language remarkably reminiscent of conversion experiences, tracing a movement from profound anxiety through exhilarated rebirth. A new salvific force has entered the world, a new deity provides for our safety. Nuclearism, Lifton summarizes, "involves a search for grace and glory in which technical-scientific transcendence, apocalyptic destruction, national power, personal salvation, and committed individual identity all become psychically bound up with the bomb. The weapon itself comes to dominate pathways to symbolic immortality."[7]

Many other features of our nuclear age deserve consideration, not least the "psychic numbing" which deadens public awareness to the threat of nuclear war and indeed lets it seem inevitable.[8] In this essay, however, I step back from this great, overriding issue and propose something much more modest and restricted. I shall try to recover some of the perspectives on death which the Second Vatican Council offers us and which are significant for Christian doctrine in general as well as for any theology of peace that seeks to counter the threat of nuclear war. The Council, of course, was by no means unaware of the latter issue; it showed itself, in fact, remarkably prescient.[9] But let me concentrate here on one theme from a more traditional eschatology. I hope it may be a not entirely inadequate tribute to the man to whom this volume is dedicated and who himself wrote so many profound essays on the theology of death.

THE MYSTERY OF DEATH

The Second Vatican Council, for all its concern with the Church's relations to secular society, has a strong eschatological perspective as well. Perhaps most memorable is its conception of the Church as a pilgrim people.[10] One might argue that an even more dominant motif is sounded when the Council speaks of Christ as the Second Adam, the "novus homo," or of the new earth that God is preparing. But the most concentrated individual statement on an eschatological question is to be found in the Pastoral Constitution on the Church in the Modern World, Art. 18, "de mysterio mortis." In this document on the Church's dialogue with the world over its most basic joys and hopes, griefs and anxieties, Part One is chiefly doctrinal, while Part Two discusses special problems of contemporary society in view of the doctrine outlined. The Constitution's teaching in Part One addresses in turn four basic themes: personal dignity, human community, the value of secular activity, and the role of the Church.[11] The first of these four chapters, on the transcendent value of the human person, treats the mystery of death in a style quite unlike that of any previous Church document on the subject of eschatology.[12]

One question clearly focuses the entire dialogue initiated in *Gaudium et Spes:* "What is a human being? What is this sense of sorrow, of evil, of death, which continues to exist despite so much progress? What is the purpose of these victories, purchased at so high a cost? What can a human being offer to society, and expect from it? What follows this earthly life?" (GS 10) This *status questionis* is notable in several ways. First, its concern for the meaning of humanity reflects the real urgency of a genuine humanism in the contemporary situation. Second, it gives marked prominence to the issues of death and human destiny, apparently for both apologetic and doctrinal reasons. Third, its mode of stating the question prepares for a gradually developing appreciation of the human condition as mystery. As in the Constitution on the Church, the depth and breadth of the question at hand is indicated by recognizing that it is not merely a problem to be solved but rather a reality inexhaustible for reflection and commitment alike.[13] Further, implicitly in Art. 12 and then explicitly in Art. 13, the question of the human mystery is seen to encompass a dramatic tension between the grandeur and the misery of our condition.[14] In addition, as the chapter progresses, we find an increasingly clear correlation between the mystery of the human and the mystery of Christ. (Indeed, some critics have regretted that the Christological dimension is not prominent even sooner.) Finally, as we shall see in greater detail later, there is a certain ambiguity in the way the question is posed, allowing the first chapter of the Constitution to respond in terms of the individual and the second in terms of community. One may resonably ask what advantages might have accrued if this order of treatment had been reversed.

We may better appreciate the reflection on death in Art. 18 if we recall its immediate context and some of the major points made there.

Art. 12, for example, begins with a fairly restricted view of humanity created in the image of God. A theology of creation dominates here, but with little sense of the eschatology to which a genuinely biblical protology is open. In Art. 13 on human sin as an abuse of liberty, human sinfulness is discussed in a general way; by intention, no reference is made to Genesis' account of Adam and the "fall." (Added to the original drafts of the Constitution, the paragraphs of this article make a realistic statement about the division in the human heart; they also affirm the possibility of healing fulfillment.) Earlier drafts of the text that follows had treated first the dignity of the human body and then the dignity of the human soul and intellect. Revised so as to reduce any suggestion of dualism, the text now emphasizes that human beings are one in body and soul (Art. 14) and that our spiritual dignity is exercised by the mind's search for wisdom (Art. 15), through the rule of conscience (Art. 16), and in our freedom (Art. 17). With regard to the question of death, it is noteworthy that Art. 14, when speaking of the resurrection of the body on the last day (par. 1) and of our possession of an "anima spiritualis et immortalis" (par. 2), offers no interpretation on either of these points. Rather, it is primarily concerned to assert the dignity and destiny of a whole human being who is truly bodily and yet never reducible to mere matter.

We come thus to the Constitution's reflection on death itself, which Cardinal Ratzinger has called "a piece of existential analysis."[15] Ratzinger interprets the text as moving on three planes: existential, ontological, and theological. With equal plausibility, I believe, one may say that the text poses the question of death *in view of* the teaching and experience of revelation—though in a sense I shall try to make more precise later. This is the question that renders the human enigma[16] most acute. Before it, our hearts judge rightly when they refuse to admit that our personal lives will simply be extinguished.[17] An "eternal seed" within us rebels against death, and no technological advance can entirely still the anxiety we experience about our fate. For the desire of a higher life is alive in the depths of human hearts. What, then, can we hope for?

God's word, served by the Church's ministry, responds that we are created for a lasting happiness. That "beatus finis" is beyond every earthly suffering. If we let ourselves be restored for it by the Savior, we will conquer even that bodily death which, apart from sin, could seem a natural passage from time to eternity. "For God has called all human beings and still calls them so that with their entire being they might be joined to God in an endless sharing of a divine life beyond all corruption" (GS 18.2). The liberating death and victorious resurrection of Christ pledge this vocation for us. To any thoughtful person's anxiety about the future, faith can respond with sound reasoning and offer assurance of union in Christ with all those loved ones who, we may hope, have found "true life with God."

The mystery of Christ, emerging fully here for the first time in the Constitution, gives the article's reflection its real depth and specifically Christian tone. Nor is the theme forgotten in the subsequent articles on atheism, in which the enigmatic character of both life and death is restated and humanity is presented as an insoluble question for itself.[18] The theme of the paschal mystery returns in Art. 22 as a recapitulation for the entire chapter, providing a full statement of what true humanism is and how it responds to atheist protest. Here we have the explicit correlation of anthropology and Christology: " . . . only in the mystery of the incarnate Word does the mystery of humanity truly become clear" (22.1). In a remarkably forceful and liberating way, theology may now be seen as anthropology, *provided that* Christ is recognized as fulfilling what it means to be human. For in manifesting the intentions of God's love, the final Adam "fully reveals humanity to itself and makes our supreme calling clear" (ibid.). The revelation, of course, is an historically progressing one. Through incarnation the perfect man unites himself "in some fashion" (*quodammodo*) with every human being (22.2). Through his cross he sanctifies life and death and gives them new meaning (22.3). Through his resurrection he makes available for all the indwelling Spirit of love and renewal (22.4). Through these mysteries in their unity Christian existence is given its new pattern of life, "in the strength which comes from hope" (22.4).

Such a pattern of life in union with the paschal mystery is in fact valid for all human beings of good will, as the Constitution makes bold to say. Christ's death has universally saving significance and his Spirit works in every human heart (22.5). I shall return to this point later, but it it should be noted here how significantly this fifth paragraph of Art. 22 advances beyond the statement in *Lumen Gentium* 16 on God's universal plan of salvation and its relation to the people of God. Not only does GS 22.5 specify the paschal and pneumatological depths of the salvific economy; it also represents with much greater nuance how firmly the initiative of salvation originates and remains with God. This refinement helps the article's concluding paragraph to offer its final artful word on the enigma of death and its new meaning in Christ, who has won such fullness of life for us that as "sons and daughters in the Son, we can cry out in the Spirit: Abba, Father" (22.6). Thus, a chapter that began by asking what it means to be human concludes by directing

us to worship, where we may best be present both to God and to our
own hearts.

THEOLOGICAL DEVELOPMENT

The Christological dimension of Part One, chapter I in *Gaudium
et Spes* is deepened through the three chapters that follow it, especially
in their closing articles. Art. 32 recalls in biblical terms how human solidarity "is developed and consummated in the work of Jesus Christ."
Reflecting on the value of human activity in the world, Art. 38 says that
the risen Christ "arouses not only a desire for the age to come, but, by
that very fact, he animates, purifies and strengthens those noble long-
ings too by which the human family strives to make its life more human
and to render the whole earth submissive to this goal." A careful distinction must be made between earthly progress and the growth of
God's kingdom. Nevertheless, God is vitally concerned with the development of the world's potential, and we rightly hope to discover its
full truth and goodness, transfigured in Christ and his Spirit, when the
kingdom finally comes. "The expectation of a new earth must not
weaken but rather stimulate our concern for cultivating this one. For
here grows the body of a new human family, a body which even now
is able to give some kind of foreshadowing of the new age"(GS 39).[19]
In a mysterious way, that new earth has already begun. When the body
of Christ is whole, the new earth will be fully present. And that is the
Church's "single intention: that the kingdom of God may come and
the salvation of the human race may be accomplished" (GS 45).

Thus, with the hope that all may be renewed in Christ, the Church
journeys toward the consummation of history, striving to remain faithful to its calling as "the universal sacrament of salvation" (GS 45, quot-
ing LG 48). Looking toward Christ as its goal, it confesses him as the
interpreter of all human hearts and their promised joy. While chapter
one had first spoken of humanity as the image of God in a general,
creationist way, the closing lines of Part One now quote Revelation
22:13, letting the Lord himself reinterpret our time for us: "I am the
Alpha and the Omega, the first and the last, the beginning and the
end."

As is clear from these texts, Christology and eschatology, while
distinguishable, are with equal truth inseparable in their relation to the
anthropology outlined by *Gaudium et Spes*. In Karl Rahner's well-
known formula, Christology is the true meaning of anthropology and
eschatology is its fulfillment. The eschatological dimension of the Con-

stitution develops cumulatively in Chapter I, but it is there from the beginning. The very first article sees the Church as a community of disciples "united in Christ . . . led by the Holy Spirit in their journey to the kingdom of their Father," cherishing the news of salvation meant for all women and men.[20] Art. 2 speaks of the world's emancipation by Christ so that it might be fashioned anew for fulfillment ("transformetur et ad consummationem perveniat"). Art. 3 asserts that, despite the remarkable discoveries of human invention, anxious questions still remain, prominent among them the human world's ultimate destiny ("de ultimo rerum hominumque fine"). In its earliest articles the Constitution repeatedly recalls the high vocation offered us.[21] It also speaks of the mutual relations between the present life and the life to come.[22] Thus it prepares the fuller perspective which emerges in later chapters.

This eschatology recalls many of the accents set by *Lumen Gentium*, Chapter VII. There the Council had detailed the pilgrim status of the Church which shares the conditions of this transient world, even though the restoration promised to humanity has already begun in Christ and continues through him in the Church (LG 48). During its journey, the Church looks toward the appearance of the Lord in majesty, when "death will be destroyed and all things will be subject to him" (49). It considers itself united as well with those who have died in Christ and recognizes the still closer union among the saints now in heaven (ibid.). The pilgrim Church prays for its dead, venerates the apostles and martyrs, takes inspiration and guidance from the lives of the saints, and depends on their intercession—all with a view toward celebrating more appropriately the praise of God's majesty (50). Our confidence in the communion of saints should lead us not to multiply external rituals but much rather to intensify our practice of love, deepening the bonds of human solidarity in praise of God and thus "sharing in a foretaste of the liturgy of perfect glory" (51). Of this perfection toward which we strive we have a pre-eminent and altogether singular example in the Blessed Virgin Mary (Chap. VIII, Art. 53).

Granting the consistency between the two documents, one should note as well their difference. For the eschatology of *Gaudium et Spes* has clearly been deepened in its relation to the paschal mystery, broadened in its appeal to the whole of the human race, and given greater density in regard to the range of secular reality its promise includes. Above all, the more developed dialogical method of the Pastoral Constitution influences not only the presentation but also the fundamental perspective of its eschatology. In drafting the document there was a notoriously recurrent difficulty in establishing the starting point for its various chapters and even articles. In the article "de mysterio mortis," for example, our focus in this essay, it may seem that an existential question is first posed in a primarily philosophical way, with a theological answer then provided from revelation, much according to the method of correlation consistently advocated by Paul Tillich and to some extent by Karl Rahner. But today we may be more comfortable in recognizing that no single starting point is likely to recommend itself once and for all. Rather than read the text as elaborating first a question on an ontological plane and then an answer on the historical plane, we do better to see it as an historically expressed conviction about the depth and breadth of the experience of death in a world of paschal grace. This conviction then relates itself reflectively to other human perceptions of death and the language that may be useful in speaking of them. Thus there is an interplay of historical experience and language developed to express it, a dialectic of experience and appropriating interpretation rather than a succession of philosophical question and theological answer.

Every question is evoked, and sometimes provoked, by the intimation that an answer is available.[23] Art. 18 is structured not so much by a division between ontological and historical planes of reality as by the recognition of a radically historical world whose real structures repeatedly require interpretation, analysis, and fresh linguistic expression.[24] To put it in Rahnerian terms, we do not have a philosophical foundation upon which is erected a theological superstructure. Rather, in a world oriented always toward deeper union with God through Christ, we are empowered by their Spirit to probe the wisdom of that world—but then also its cross. Again and again we must seek more adequate expression and practice of the grace that is transforming nature or, better, of God's reign that is gradually encompassing God's creation for us.[25] An historical experience, in short, suggests a reflection on how it came to be and what future it may have. In more current terminology, we may say that there is a fundamentally narrative structure to the expression of our faith and hope. But the narrative structure can be clarified, corroborated, and fully appropriated only with the aid of a critical analysis accompanying it. Basically we tell stories about our world's history, and about the mystery of death that confronts it. But we must also stop repeatedly for reasonable argument about the terms, the relations, and the judgments those stories require.

Now it is clear that the text of *Gaudium et Spes* does not intend to offer us in a complete way just this view of history, experience, and language. Throughout the Council session, great care was taken to overcome an extrinsicist, authoritarian, static view of God's world. More biblical, personalist, and dynamic categories were adopted and placed in a salvation-historical frame of reference.[26] But we cannot expect that a fully coherent theology would have been uniformly present. And yet as we reread the texts, we may legitimately recognize a new vision of human reality and Christian vocation suggested in them. We may recognize, in fact, that the Church's creative fidelity to God's world and Catholic tradition have opened for us the possibility of a new language. With that new way of speaking comes a whole new access to grace and history, a fresh possibility of communication between God and God's world in process of redemption. Thus, we must balance our knowledge of what the authors of the documents intended with an appreciation for the fuller sense of theological reality that they have made available through their method, their selection of topics, and their openness to the "signs of the times." Where positions have been carefully balanced so as not to exclude one another, we may rightly suspect that it is not so much one or the other which will finally prevail; another still more inclusive view is likely to do greater justice to both. An historically oriented Council, in short, should be historically read, its story generating fresh interpretations of the reality to which it has sought to be faithful. In its renovation of our religious language we have the surest test of how profoundly Vatican II has opened us to the expression of God's word and the embrace of God's Spirit.

REREADING ARTICLE 18

How can this perspective on historical and theological development be verified in the Pastoral Constitution's reflection on the mystery of death? How has the Constitution helped us to approach death more truly, by suggesting new ways to speak appropriately of it? We do best to answer this question by first recalling the major significance of recognizing death as a mystery. Speaking of death as mystery reminds us that it is not a mere fact of life, not simply an end before which we are dumb, nor a cipher about which only an esoteric revelation can speak significantly. Historical and literary studies over the past two decades have helped us to see how inexhaustibly various are the ways in which death can be experienced and yet at the same time how ineluctable a part of the fundamental human question it remains.[27] Again and again it is a mirror held up to life, albeit in countless guises. As novel and yet as constant as human history itself, the prospect of death asks us in a privileged way what we take to be the

heart of reality—or its emptiness. Axiologically present at every moment of life, as Karl Rahner so well recognized,[28] at issue in our
thoughts and desires as well as in our deeds and trials, it is a mystery
charged, as few others are, with ultimacy.

Perhaps GS 18 has also helped us, paradoxically enough, to see
death in a more genuinely eschatological way, not simply from the side
of our dying, but also, and much more, from the side of God's kingdom to come.[29] The article does begin, of course, by speaking of the
way human beings recoil from death. But it speaks generally, and does
not warrant our reading into human experience a universal fear of
death as its dominant motif. In fact, as several authors have argued,
seeking to prove a universal fear of death may well be beyond the logic
of the question itself.[30] In this regard, the central point made by the
Pastoral Constitution seems rather to be the full desire for life which
struggles within the human heart with the sure knowledge of death.
In a searching study of the intimate relation between immortality
myths and social structures, John Dunne has summarized the question
this way: "If I must someday die, what can I do to satisfy my desire to
live?"[31] Ultimately the Christian message is grounded in the promise
of a life fuller than any heart had yet imagined, not in an anxious apologetic responding to the threat of death. Fear and courage are com-
panions in human history, one heightening the sense of the other.
Illuminating this permanent tension, the cross of Christ offers a radical revelation of what is at stake in each.[32]

If our text opens us to a more historical and pluralistic view of the
mystery of death, it nonetheless continues to reflect the entire chapter's existential sense for the combined grandeur and misery of the
human condition. This emphasis guides me in interpreting what the
text says about the "sound arguments" which accompany faith, offering a response to human anxiety about the future.[33] Without using
Art. 14's language concerning the "anima spiritualis et immortalis,"
Art. 18 contains an implicit but extremely open argument for the transcendence of death, an argument that may best be characterized as dialectical. On the one hand, it appeals to an "eternal seed" within us and
our desire for a higher life. But on the other hand, it clearly indicates
that God's word alone tells us how this seed may be nurtured and
brought to full fruition, namely, through the paschal mystery. Insis-
tent on real dialogue, the text is ready to discuss the understanding of
its faith; confident at the same time in its hope, it confesses the experience that has brought it to this understanding.

Thus, Art. 18 suggests a way to overcome the sterile debate con-
trasting faith in the resurrection of the body with arguments for the

immortality of the soul.[34] The article obviously does not offer a new correlation of the themes. It does, however, open the possibility of seeing arguments for immortality as intimations of the full promise of life at work in a world which God's grace has encompassed from its beginning and one day means to embrace entirely. Rather than diminishing the radicality of our hope in resurrection, every sense for the transcendence of death, in whatever form it is imagined, can alert us to the care with which God fashions the processes of the world in order to bring them to eternal life. Paul Tillich, for example, simply misreads the relation between religious symbolism and philosophical analysis when he rejects Plato's arguments for immortality in the *Phaedo* in favor of the image of the dying Socrates and his courage.[35] By contrast, a post-critical, realistic theology can discern objective truth in the subjective relations incorporated in symbolism.[36] General structures of transcendence may then be realistically recognized within the historical process which God alone, it is true, can finally bring to eternal life. Likewise, we are now in a better position to see that a sense for the transcendence of death has been expressed in many ways, biblically as well as extra-biblically. Resurrection, however dominant canonically, is by no means the only model for expressing Christ's victory over death. "We must also take into consideration other New Testament languages," writes Claude Geffré, "those of life and exaltation, which have precisely the role of correcting and completing resurrection vocabulary."[37]

The "bodily death" of which Art. 18 speaks may thus be understood as the loss of life and our world of relations which results from rejecting God's promise of life and grace. Wherever human solidarity and interdependence are threatened, death takes on the aspect of sheer disintegration and annihilation. But where human community and relationship are fostered, death becomes once more imaginable as a passage, however mysterious, to eternity. In the former case it points toward material disruption, the sin of Adam whereby our bodily existence is worked out in estrangement and sorrow. But in the second case, death can be an irruption of Spirit, a companionship with Christ in the course of his obedient life, whereby our lowly material world is in process of transformation into the likeness of his glorious body (Phil 3:21).[38] If Socrates could enjoin "the practice of dying" on his followers, the disciples of Christ may still more appropriately seek the practice of resurrection, through lives dedicated to transforming their social world into a realm of justice and peace which the Spirit of God can one day bring to completion. If we understand "sin" in our text as the radical disfigurement of the human community in its relation to

God, then we may also understand "bodily death" as the disintegration of the social as well as individual body which is the consequence of sin. Our text is thus not so far removed as it may seem from the heightened social sense in eschatology that has emerged in various political and liberation theologies since the Council. Art. 21 supports this interpretation, I believe, with its strong, and typical, statement: "This faith needs to prove its fruitfulness by penetrating the entire life of believers, including its worldly dimensions, and by activating them toward justice and love, especially regarding the needy. What does the most to reveal God's presence, finally, is the brotherly charity of the faithful who are united in spirit as they work together for the faith of the Gospel and who prove themselves a sign of unity."[39]

NEW PERSPECTIVES ON DEATH

Current reflection on the mystery of death can reach further insight precisely through this greater sense for eschatology in its social dimension, together with "the practice of resurrection" it demands. For too long we have emphasized that every woman and man dies alone. But this is only part of a dialectical truth. We need to see also how much we are implicated in one another's deaths, what we receive through the death of others, what responsibilities we bear for the inhuman conditions of living and dying to which so many of our fellow men and women are subject.[40] GS 18 opens the way for such reflection through its careful formulation of faith's promise of communication in Christ with loved ones who have died. Arousing "the hope that they have found true life with God," faith directs us beyond every individualistic conception of death and Christian destiny toward realizing the mysterious bonds we share as we move toward death and, still more, as God's kingdom moves toward us.[41] In the reserve of its language, the text also represents an improvement on LG 49, which proposes somewhat too ideally that "the union of the wayfarers with the brethren who have gone to sleep in the peace of Christ is not in the least interrupted."

Theology today may hope to develop in several ways a more social appreciation of death and general eschatology. The Council's strong statement on the doctrine of the communion of saints can be carried still further, especially in view of the communion of living believers with the deceased members of their more immediate communities. If the local church truly represents the Church of Christ, then the communion of saints may likewise, for all its unity in Christ, be radically particular in the Holy Spirit. The sacramental life of the Church should also contribute to our sense of social eschatology. Through the Eucharist in general and the anointing of the sick in particular, we may come to appreciate, in what we celebrate, how radically communal is our hope. With regard to the community's life of worship, we also have much to learn from Orthodox theology, which closely relates eschatology and the doctrine of the sacraments. In ecumenical discussion, furthermore, we can profit significantly from Protestant theology, which has so often in our century emphasized the dialectical relation between historical justice and the love of the kingdom of God.[42] Finally, and perhaps most important of all, as we have seen at the beginning, the nightmare threat of nuclear war must also lead us to a new vision of our interdependent human future—or else to a vision of ultimate disaster.

Further questions for our understanding of death are also raised by recent studies in world religions. Interreligious dialogue is indispensable for a realistic theology of the universally saving significance of the paschal mystery. But it will clearly bear as well on death and eschatology. For Roman Catholics, Vatican II's "Declaration on the Relationship of the Church to Non-Christian Religions" (*Nostra Aetate*) is the charter document in this regard. Its first article takes up again the question of *Gaudium et Spes*, "What is a human being?" The Declaration proceeds to ask, "What is the truth about death, judgment, and retribution beyond the grave?" On such questions we can scarcely ignore the rich symbolism and profound human experiences enshrined in the traditions of the great religions. A recent study on Islamic thought, for example, tells us that "despite certain variations in interpretation among modernists and traditionalists, the basic message to which all contemporary Muslims attest is that God has created humanity for a purpose, for the continuation of life and for ultimate accountability. In the next world injustices will be corrected and God will lead us to a perfected existence."[43] The contribution such studies make to our knowledge of comparative eschatology could be accompanied by greater mutual understanding in the realm of public discourse, which would certainly be a desirable outcome in view of current tensions in the Near East.

The intensification of dialogue between Christians and Jews recommended by *Nostra Aetate* is also affecting our approach to the mystery of death. Of the two central issues in Jewish-Christian dialogue, the holocaust and the state of Israel, the former bears all too immediately on the question of death. Like nuclearism, the holocaust shocks us into wondering whether we have ever really faced the void of communal death. "At Auschwitz," Elie Wiesel has said, "not only man died but the idea of man."[44] Some see this "double dying" as one of the most horrific and disfiguring events in human history. But for others it is utterly unique, a desecrating assault on the chosen people whose God had promised faithfulness. We shall have to keep asking what this experience really was if, indeed, it merits being called experience at all. What are its historical implications and enduring significance? It is even disputed whether literature and art can help us to imagine it, whether it presents us with an untellable tale or perhaps one reserved only to survivors. Here Christians of every church must listen carefully and share their humanity with heart and hand, practicing a new compassion for the stock of Abraham and its covenanting God. As Leander E. Keck has written in another context, "the starting point for a theology of death and of resurrection is moral outrage against the world in which there appears to be no justice on which the weak can count, a world in which sucklings are bombed and rabbis gassed. . . . In the last analysis, the central theological issue in the death of man is the character of God."[45]

The advances of medical technology over the last three decades constitute a third major source for new experiences and new questions about the meaning of death. Accompanying the scientific progress has been the development of a highly sophisticated bioethics. Warren T. Reich, editor-in-chief of the *Encyclopedia of Bioethics,* defines it as "the systematic study of human conduct in the area of the life sciences and health care, insofar as this conduct is examined in the light of moral values and principles."[46] Including but also extending beyond traditional medical ethics, bioethics must attend to the relations emerging among the life sciences, medicine, law and public policy, philosophy and religious culture. Significantly, the *Encyclopedia,* a milestone in its field, devotes eighty-six double-columned pages to aspects of death and dying, presenting a treatise that would be a sizable book if published separately.[47]

Medical technicians, for example, can now maintain the operation of a human being's heart and lungs for long periods of time after partial or even complete destruction of the individual's brain. On the other hand, special conditions have been devised to preserve the integrity of the brain while suspending cardiac and respiratory functioning so as to permit open heart surgery. Thus, individual vital functions that once were intimately linked and mutually dependent can now be at least temporarily dissociated, so that the criteria for pronouncing on a patient's death require renewed consideration. Nevertheless, the debate around these questions suggests that we now have more reason rather than less for maintaining that neither our lives nor our deaths can be adequately explained in purely phenomenalistic, natural terms. As Dallas M. High points out, the concept of the person as a whole has been regaining its central value in our understanding of death. Likewise, a strong distinction is now generally made between definitions or concepts of death and the criteria to be used in certifying it. In High's view, "twentieth-century man has not encountered a new death or a need to update death, popular language to the contrary, but has gained, perhaps, a renewed sensitivity to mortality."[48]

THE DEPTH OF LIFE

Or perhaps, in concluding, we should say that every human approach to death is at once utterly familiar and utterly new. Like the mystery of God in our hearts, this is at the same time what we know best and what we must always continue to learn. Here, with fascination and fear alike, we face the final solution or dissolution of our lives— in the mystery of death for our shared human time as well as for individual lives, in its various aspects expressed by the world's religions, in its permanent question to the accomplishments of science and to ethical reflection. Death is the depth of life in a double sense, the furthest extreme of human suffering and the final test of God's redemptive power. This is the depth to which Jesus of Nazareth has descended before us, in fidelity to his proclamation of God's reign in the world. It is also the depth from which God has raised him, in fidelity to the kingdom already begun in Christ. Only through the Spirit of God, however, can we say with confidence that this mystery of death is a true passover. Above all, only in the Spirit of God can we live it as paschal.

In a singular way, Karl Rahner meditated for us repeatedly on death's dark conjunction of activity and passivity. In death, our existence ends as eternity meets us, emptiness and plenitude coincide, the certainty of destruction stands before the hope of consummation. Some critics consider Rahner's view overly speculative. Yet it continues to throw light on a wide range of human experiences and many doctrinal questions. Probing what is truly personal in the event of death, it suggests how dying is present throughout living, the sense in which it reflects guilt, and why it can be genuinely redemptive both for Christ and for ourselves. In a remarkably powerful way, Rahner's interpretation concretizes once again the interdependence of anthropology, Christology, and eschatology.

Today, in this new moment of nuclear threat,[49] we need to test

Rahner's insight further. As the threat of nuclear holocaust provides us with a new imagery of emptiness, we become all the more dependent on the imagery of fullness that is related to the kingdom of God. The American bishops' pastoral letter is extraordinary in the sobriety with which it holds the two in tension. Indeed, the patience, faithfulness, and courage with which the pastoral letter conducts its analysis are typical signs of the Spirit's fruitfulness. Notably devoid of apocalyptic language and reserved even in its use of prophetic stance, the letter presents its reflections as a carefully reasoned contribution to moral discourse in the Church and in society. With renewed inspiration from the promise of God's kingdom and reinvigorated hope for its coming, the bishops remind us that "peace must be built on the basis of justice in a world where the personal and social consequences of sin are evident."[50] With crucial calm, they rephrase a central theme from *Gaudium et Spes:* "Christians are called to live the tension between the vision of the reign of God and its concrete realization in history."[51]

Perhaps the fearful responsibility of this present moment will also teach us what it is in humanity that can bear the paradox of coinciding emptiness and fullness. Or perhaps, more accurately, we may say that we are learning precisely what we cannot fully bear, namely, *final* responsibility for our shared lives. At this critical juncture of human history we must of course respond immediately and practically to the call for peacemaking. But the experience may also be showing us in a new way how radical in the heart of the human community is its dependence on God, how profoundly we cry out to have our hearts searched and our hands guided in caring for the creation we have been given. If we take the cross of Jesus as our way to God, it is not because we seek or condone the suffering of the world but because the cross teaches us how much love is willing to suffer for the world's hope. If we are guided in our quest for peace by the teaching and example of Jesus, it is not because we are resigned to the world's futility but because we envision its fulfillment. How is it that, communally as well as individually, we can bear this contrast between cross and glory, between futility and fulfillment? I suggest that only the Spirit that poured from the broken body of Jesus, irrupting now in the midst of our struggle truly to be members of Christ, can enable us to endure the test.

The fullness of God's love and the self-emptying of Jesus' life are bound together in the one Spirit who is our special need and gift, *donum Dei,* at this time. As a community of faith, with such different and rich forms of expertise to contribute, we are called to respond now to the challenge of peace. The commitment will undoubtedly be exacting. How can we live out, how can we *become* the suffering love that will be required of us? We shall need a renewed outpouring of the Spirit, holding together our action and our passion, our accomplishments and our sacrifices, the constantly challenged continuity of our spiritual finitude through time and toward eternity. In the Holy Spirit, God's fullness and self-expression are lovingly one. Through that same Spirit, God's world, Christ's body, may be led today to prepare obediently for its full maturity, turning from the annihilation of nuclear war and toward the cultivation of a more peaceful and human earth.

"Let us have the courage to believe in the bright future and in a God who wills it for us—not a perfect world, but a better one. The perfect world, we Christians believe, is beyond the horizon in an endless eternity where God will be all in all. But a better world is here for human hands and hearts and minds to make."[52] Or, to give Karl Rahner the final word: "Humanity is stretched out between anxiety about salvation and hope for it, and this tension is the finally guiding principle of its history."[53]

NOTES

1. *The Fate of the Earth* (New York: Knopf, 1982), p. 169.

2. "The Challenge of Peace: God's Promise and Our Response," *Origins* Vol. 13: No. 1 (May 19, 1983) 1–32. The bishops quote several strong statements from Pope John Paul II. They themselves comment: "Today the destructive potential of the nuclear powers threatens the human person, the civilization we have slowly constructed and even the created order itself" (p. 13). And again: "We are the first generation since Genesis with the power to virtually destroy God's creation" (p. 30).

3. Schell, p. 166.

4. See, for example, Barbara W. Tuchman, *A Distant Mirror: The Calamitous 14th Century* (New York: Knopf, 1978), chap. 5, " 'This is the End of the World': The Black Death."

5. Gordon D. Kaufman, "Nuclear Eschatology and the Study of Religion," *Journal of the American Academy of Religion* S1 (1983) 3–14, at p. 4.

6. *The Broken Connection. On Death and the Continuity of Life* (New York: Simon and Schuster, 1979), p. 369.

7. Ibid., p. 376.

8. See Lifton, passim, and "The Challenge of Peace," pp. 13–14, 30.

9. GS 4 speaks of "the peril of a war which would reduce every-thing to ashes"; the Constitution returns to the question for fuller treatment in Part Two, chap. 5, arts. 77–82. Note: English quotations from Vatican II will be taken principally from Walter M. Abbott, S.J., ed., *The Documents of Vatican II* (New York: America Press, 1966), but reference has also been made to Austin P. Flannery, ed., *Documents of Vatican II* (Grand Rapids: Eerdmans, 1975), and corrections made where necessary, particularly with regard to inclusive language.

10. LG 7. Abbott's translation unfortunately obscures the fact that the Council's very first image of the Church, in SC 2, is that of a pilgrim; here Flannery is more accurate.

11. Cf. Paul VI, "Ecclesiam Suam," III: *AAS* 56 (1964) 637–59.

12. To the relatively few documents usually found in collections of official Church teachings should be added the Congregation for the Doctrine of Faith's "Letter on Certain Questions Concerning Escha-tology" (17 May 1979).

13. While the phrase "mysterium mortis" appears in the title of the article, it is not found in the text; both Abbott and Flannery, how-ever, introduce it into the second paragraph as a translation of the phrase "coram morte." GS 18.1 speaks of the "aenigma condicionis hu-manae." Art. 21.3 also refers to "vitae et mortis, culpae et doloris aenigmata," 21.4. sees every human being as a "quaestio insoluta" for itself, and 22.6 speaks of "hominis mysterium" and "aenigma doloris et mortis." Thus, instead of using the vocabulary of "a problem," the text prefers terms such as mystery, enigma, question.

14. GS 13.3: "sublimis vocatio et profunda miseria".

15. *LThK: Das Zweite Vatikanische Konzil* III (Freiburg: Herder, 1968) 333.

16. While Abbott translates "aenigma" as riddle (acceptably, but not entirely so), Flannery misleadingly renders it "shrouded in doubt."

17. Both English translations translate "judicat" too weakly; cf. Arts. 14.2 and 16 for earlier intimations of a strong "philosophy of the heart."

18. See n. 13 above.

19. One indication of the Christian realism encouraged by texts like this may be found in a question posed in George J. Dyer, ed., *An American Catholic Catechism* (New York: Seabury, 1975). Asking, "Can the promised kingdom be equated with heaven?" the Catechism an-swers: "No. Jesus proclaimed the coming kingdom in terms that tran-scended the split between heaven and earth. . . . God's coming victory over evil will take place within history and yet transcend history. By reducing the kingdom of God to heaven, Christians tended to forget

that the earth and its history are the place where God encounters men and recreates their personal and social life. This led to a certain spiritualization of God's promises made to men" (p. 90).

20. Cf. Avery Dulles, S.J., *A Church To Believe In: Discipleship and the Dynamics of Freedom* (New York: Crossroad, 1982), chap. 1.

21. GS 3.2: "altissima vocatio"; 10.2: "ad superiorem vitam vocatum"; 10.2: "summa vocatio" (a vocation to "vita aeterna", as the *relatio* makes clear); 11.1: "de integra hominis vocatione".

22. 4.1: "vitae praesentis et futurae".

23. Cf. Karl Rahner, *Foundations of Christian Faith* (New York: Crossroad, 1978), pp. 24–25.

24. Cf. Edward Schillebeeckx, *Christ. The Experience of Jesus as Lord* (New York: Crossroad, 1980), Part One.

25. Cf. L. J. O'Donovan, "Orthopraxis and Theological Method in Karl Rahner," *Proceedings of the Catholic Theological Society of America* 35 (1980) 47–65.

26. L. J. O'Donovan, "Was Vatican II Evolutionary? A Note on Conciliar Language," *Theological Studies* 36 (1975) 493–502.

27. See Philippe Ariès, *The Hour of Our Death* (New York: Knopf, 1981), and, more briefly, his *Western Attitudes toward Death: From the Middle Ages to the Present* (Baltimore: Johns Hopkins Univ. Press, 1974); Richard Huntington and Peter Metcalf, *Celebrations of Death: The Anthropology of Mortuary Ritual* (Cambridge: Cambridge Univ. Press, 1979); Robert F. Weir, ed., *Death in Literature* (New York: Columbia Univ. Press, 1980)

28. *On the Theology of Death* (Quaestiones disputatae 2), 2nd ed. (New York: Herder and Herder, 1965). The first edition was seriously deficient. For Rahner's personal reflections on the book, and on his theology of death in general, see *Karl Rahner in Dialogue. Conversations and Interviews* 1965–1982, Paul Imhof and Hubert Biallowons, eds., trans. and ed. by Harvey D. Egan (New York: Crossroad, 1986), pp. 238–247.

29. See Eberhard Jüngel, Death: The Riddle and the Mystery, esp. chap. 6, and Joseph Ratzinger, *Eschatologie—Tod und ewiges Leben* (Regensburg: Pustet, 1977), chap. 1.

30. See Ernest Becker, *The Denial of Death* (New York: Free Press, 1973), chap. 2.

31. *The City of the Gods. A Study in Myth and Mortality* (New York: Macmillan, 1965).

32. Cf. L. J. O'Donovan, "The Pasch of Christ: Our Courage in Time," *Theological Studies* 42 (1981) 353–72.

33. Abbott, rather too strongly, translates: "Hence to every

thoughtful man a solidly established faith provides the answer to his anxiety about what the future holds for him." Flannery has: "Faith, therefore, with its solidly based teaching, provides every thoughtful man with an answer to his anxious queries about his future lot."

34. Cf. Edward Schillebeeckx, *Jesus. An Experiment in Christology* (New York: Crossroad, 1979), Part Three, Sec. Two; J. Ratzinger, *op. cit.*, pp. 91–135; L. J. O'Donovan, "Immortality in Judaeo-Christian Perspective," in William C. Bier, S.J., ed., *Human Life: Problems of Birth, of Living, and of Dying* (New York: Fordham Univ. Press, 1977) 276–95.

35. *The Courage To Be* (New Haven: Yale Univ. Press, 1952), pp. 42, 110, 168–69, 181, 189.

36. See Avery Dulles, S.J., *Models of Revelation* (Garden City: Doubleday, 1983), esp. chap. IX.

37. "Où en est la théologie de la résurrection?", *Lumière et vie* 21 (1972) 17–30, at p. 21.

38. Cf. Karl Rahner, "The Sin of Adam," *Theo. Inv.* XI (New York: Seabury, 1974) pp. 247–263 and "Das Sterben vom Tod her gesehen," *Mysterium Salutis* V (Zürich: Benziger, 1976) 473–92.

39. On the practice of resurrection faith, see also, among other texts, LG 48.1–2 and DV 8.2, 10.1.

40. Cf. Matthew Lamb, *Solidarity with Victims: Toward a Theology of Social Transformation* (New York: Crossroad, 1982).

41. See Richard P. McBrien, *Catholicism. Study Edition* (Minneapolis: Winston, 1981), pp. 1141–50; Gregory Baum, *Religion and Alienation. A Theological Reading of Sociology* (New York: Paulist, 1975), pp. 266–94.

42. In the American context, see esp. Reinhold Niebuhr, *The Nature and Destiny of Man*, Vol. 2 (New York: Scribners, 1943).

43. Jane Idleman Smith and Yvonne Yazbeck Haddad, *The Islamic Understanding of Death and Resurrection* (Albany: State Univ. of New York Press, 1981), p. ix. Interestingly, the authors point out that modern Islam considers a matter of complete reasonableness what the Qur'ān had treated finally as a matter of faith. On Indian thought, see Wendy Doniger O'Flaherty, ed., *Karma and Rebirth in Classical Indian Traditions* (Berkeley: Univ. of California Press, 1980).

44. Alvin H. Rosenfeld, *A Double Dying: Reflections on Holocaust Literature* (Bloomington: Indiana Univ. Press, 1980). The range of reactions evoked by Wiesel's writing can be seen in Alvin H. Rosenfeld and Irving Greenberg, eds., *Confronting the Holocaust: The Impact of Elie Wiesel* (Bloomington: Indiana Univ. Press, 1979), and Michael Ber-

enbaum, *The Vision of the Void: Theological Reflections on the Works of Elie Wiesel* (Middletown, CT: Wesleyan Univ. Press, 1979).

45. "New Testament Views of Death," in Liston Mills, ed., *Perspectives on Death* (Nashville: Abingdon, 1966), pp. 33–98, at pp. 97, 98.

46. *Encyclopedia of Bioethics*, 4 vols. (New York: Free Press, 1978), 1933 pp. For an overview of recent discussion, see Richard A. McCormick, S.J., *How Brave a New World? Dilemmas in Bioethics* (Garden City: Doubleday, 1981).

47. Pp. 221–307. Related information may be found under headings such as infanticide, life-support systems, suicide, etc., adding another fifty pages to the treatment of questions related to death and dying.

48. High, *Encyclopedia of Bioethics*, p. 307.

49. See "The Challenge of Peace," pp. 13–14.

50. Ibid., p. 7. I am not suggesting, of course, that the letter is inspired in any technical sense but simply that one may see the fruitfulness of the Spirit in the way it reads "the signs of the times."

51. Loc. cit.

52. Ibid., p. 30.

53. "Der Tod als Vollendung," in *Karl Rahner im Gespräch*. Bd. 2: 1978–1982, P. Imhof and H. Biallowons, eds: (Munich: Kösel, 1983), at p. 124.